It's
MIDNIGHT
in BERLIN

A True Story of an American Girl
in War Torn Berlin 1946-47

It's
MIDNIGHT
in BERLIN

Pat McMann Gilchrist

PAT MCMANN GILCHRIST

Rev. date: 01/06/2014

To order additional copies of this book, contact:
Xlibris LLC
1-888-795-4274
www.Xlibris.com
Orders@Xlibris.com
139981

Dedication

To my husband Denny who has been my rock

CHAPTER ONE

Three events of importance occurred in 1945: (1) the Germans surrendered in May; (2) I graduated from college in June; and (3) the Japanese surrendered in August.

My four years of college were the four years that the United States participated in World War II (1941-1945). By the time my Junior year came around, most able-bodied college boys had gone off to war. We girls gave blood, rolled bandages, and some of us joined the WAACS, WAVES, or Women Marines. I looked into becoming a WAAC because there were more location choices in that branch of the Service.

I was attending Pitt (University of Pittsburgh), and a distinguished Wing Commander from England came to speak to us. I went up to talk with him afterwards and proudly told him that I was about to become a WAAC. He peered down at me and said, "Young lady, you can do more for your country by finishing your education first." It was a jolt, but I took his advice and then, after I had completed my education, the war was over in Europe and almost over in Japan.

I took a position with The Washington Post as Secretary to the Advertising Promotion Manager for $25 a week. It was my first full time job and my boss was very kind, but I believe I gave him a few gray hairs. He said years later that they were still looking for things that only I would know where they were filed.

It wasn't long before I began seeing pictures in the paper and reading articles about young women who had gone to Germany to work, as civilians, for the Army in the Office of Military Government (OMGUS). The pictures of the girls having fun were riveting. There were girls surrounded by soldiers; there were laughing young women waving from the back of military vehicles; there were soldiers and women lined up outside mess halls; there were some working at desks and typewriters; and there were pictures of the headquarters buildings in Berlin. I had not lost my desire to serve overseas or to go where my country needed me, and there was a shortage of office workers over there. Those pictures offered to me a life of adventure, excitement, travel, and of being paid to see the world and have fun at the same time. I went to get more information about how to apply and to get more details.

I came home from work one day and my mother was crying. "Why didn't you tell me you were joining the Army," she sobbed. Apparently someone had called her and told her to tell me to come and get fitted for a uniform. Things were happening more quickly than I had anticipated.

I explained to her that I had been toying with the idea of going to Germany as a civilian; that they wore uniforms similar to officer's uniforms; and that they had a great need for stenographers. I told my mother that I had only gone to ask questions, but that after getting the information, I really wanted to go. "It will give me an opportunity to see what is going on over there. The pay is good and I could send articles back to The Washington Post," I told her.

My father, who had been a political science professor and was then teaching at the Army Industrial College, in Washington, was all in favor of this new idea. My brother, Stan, was in the Marines at Camp Pendleton on the West Coast so my mother and grandmother, who lived with us, were less enthusiastic about having me go so far away. It was December 1945 and the Army wanted me to leave right away. Since Stan was coming home for Christmas, I told them I could not leave until after the holidays. A date was set for me to go. It would be January 4, 1946.

We were one of the families who had given up our car for the war effort, so it was a neighbor who drove me to Andrews Air Force Base on that morning. I wore Army fatigues and carried a knapsack and a duffel bag, all of which had been issued to me. The majority of my clothes were in a footlocker that was to come later. As it turned out, it came much later. I didn't know a soul as I boarded the troop transport plane, a C-54. It was completely full of girls about my age. I was 22.

About 10:00 p.m. we stopped in Stephensville, New Foundland. It was bitterly cold and we tramped through the snow to a Quonset Hut where a hot meal fixed us right up. We continued on our way and I slept easily to the drumming motors, dreaming of the new experiences that lay ahead. I was awakened to see the sun coming up over the ocean. It was an awesome sight.

We landed at 7:30 a.m. on the Island of Santa Maria in the Azores. The Flight Chief announced that Paris weather was very bad and that we would be delayed for some time. There were three planeloads of girls, and we were immediately taken to the DeGink Hotel (The Casa Video). I understood that all officers' hotels on airbases are dubbed "DeGink Hotels". It was a modern one-story affair made of stucco and had an unusually attractive lounge.

We stayed there for three days and played a lot of ping pong. I shared a room with Lyn (Lyndal) Davis from Austin, Texas and right from the start, we became very close friends. Lyn was tall, slender and had a sophisticated appearance, in spite of the Army slack suit. There was a spirit of fun and excitement about her. She had been wearing her long, brown hair in pigtails and she wore long, golden earrings and a red scarf around her neck. Lyn was definitely unconventional. She was friendly and charming and kept the male members on the flight fascinated throughout the entire trip.

Lyn and I sat on our cots and mused about the future. What did Germany hold in store for us? Whom would we meet? We agreed that it was thrilling and a little frightening and that we would stick together.

After washing our faces and combing our hair, we moseyed out to the lounge where we met Ed Ramsey, a plump, self-satisfied Captain, who was waiting to pounce on Lyn. There was another girl named Casey, and three Lt. Colonels in the room. Col. Kimball was a tall, kindly, red-headed man whose looks gave the impression that he was important. Then there was a short, very young, dark haired fellow, who smoked a horrible cigar. The men had obtained a car that we could use to drive to the front gate of the base. From there, it was only a short walk to Villa de Porte.

I was wearing Army fatigues. As we were walking out the gate, the MP called me back. "I'm sorry, Miss," he said, "but no one is allowed to go into Villa de Porte wearing fatigues." It was my first encounter with an MP and I was surprised to have someone telling me what I couldn't wear. I was disappointed too, as I really wanted to see the little village. Col. Kimball, however, had an immediate solution. He told me to roll up my pants legs and put on the overcoat, which I had been carrying over my arm. I did this as the MP looked on and then strolled past him out the gate.

As we walked, I drank in the beauty of the countryside. The picture before me was fresh and green, with stone walls and many sheep. We saw little burros loaded down with sticks and twigs, and old women with shawls trudging along. I had to hold my breath because it seemed that I was in a motion picture and that these surroundings were not real at all, but merely thrown on a screen before me.

Along a narrow street in the village, we saw little shops and white and pale blue stucco houses with red roofs. Most of the women were barefoot. There were dirty children asking for bubblegum, and here and there were a few gray Portuguese uniforms. We wandered about and I bought some jewelry I just couldn't resist. It was a lovely gold filigree necklace and earring set.

The Bar Central stood on a corner. It was a small, white stucco building with green roof and shutters and American signs all around it. It had a little green picket fence surrounding it and a green lawn, and we thought it looked most inviting. We entered a small room with a bar at one end and small tables scattered about the room. The waiter spoke broken English. I couldn't believe I was here on this island drinking champagne out of a tall, multi-colored goblet. Imagine! Drinking champagne!

As we were leaving, a Sgt. pulled me aside. "Pardon me, Miss, he apologized, "but what size shoe do you wear?" It was such an odd question from a stranger that I was startled, but I could see that whatever the reason, he was not being fresh. "I wear a size 6-B," I replied, then waited for an explanation. The young man wanted to have some shoes made for his wife, who also wore size 6-B, and the local shoemaker had no inkling about American shoe sizes. Paper and pencil appeared and the Sgt. outlined my foot and thanked me profusely

We had dinner at the hotel and it was my first full meal since leaving home. After dinner, the members of our group discussed the various opportunities for a full evening. On Saturdays, the Officers Club was reserved for base personnel so that let that idea out. As the little Col. with the cigar knew the base C.O., he obtained a staff car for us. Col. Kimball, who had been there before, drove us all around the island.

The narrow roads were lined with high stone walls, leaving little room to pass. We did meet a few Army trucks and fortunately, in the right spots. We wound down to the beach and became temporarily stuck in the sand. The houses were scattered at great distances from each other and the people, curious to know what an automobile was doing out after dark, would rush to the windows as we drove by.

Col. Kimball told us that there was an old Portuguese custom that all lovers, for the first six months of the courtship, must come and stand at their sweethearts' window. At the end of the six months, and not before, the lover could be invited inside. Lyn and I were quite interested in this extraordinary and unromantic way of making love and urged the men to return to the village so we could see for ourselves. It was quite late by then, but we did see one lad making eyes at his lady love from a distance of ten feet. I don't think Casey and the cigar man noticed, though, as they were making passionate noises in the back seat during the last part of our drive.

Our second day in the Azores, we arose quite late. As we were getting dressed, Lyn pleaded, "Stick with me, Pat. I don't ever want to be alone with that Ed Ramsey. He's quite a wolf and I don't much care for his idea about himself. He is a 'southern gentleman' as he says, and he had a brilliant Army career. It may be true, but I don't want any of it. No thank you. Come on. Let's go out to the gizmo and meet the others for lunch." Lyn's favorite word, I learned, was 'gizmo', which she substituted for other words frequently.

It was all beginning to seem like a vacation at a mountain resort and I was beginning to like the little island. I hadn't had a chance to feel homesick. We walked to the PX and I bought some more filigree jewelry to send home to my mother and grandmother (everyone called her 'Goggy'). "They do have some lovely filigree gizmos," Lyn agreed with me. We raced back up the hill laughing and out of breath

Lyn lost a gold earring and later I came to know that that was standard operating procedure for her. I never did go once with her anywhere that she didn't lose something, or that something unusual didn't happen. Weird events just seemed to follow her.

The Officers Club was elegant. There was a long dance floor, very comfortable easy chairs, a piano, good records, a ping pong table and card tables. I, being the only athletic member of the group, became ping pong champion. I lost, however, in a big game of Hearts. There were two tables of us having an hilarious time. We danced some. There was a bunch of young officers in one corner who made disparaging remarks about us. There was bitterness, we were told, because there were so few American girls on the island that the men who didn't have dates thought the girls were stuck up. We wondered if there would be this attitude in Germany.

By the third day, we were hoping that the weather would never clear up in Paris. We were having lots of sunshine plus a very good time. The pilot arrived at the hotel to tell us that it was still foggy in Paris and there would be further delay. Lyn, Casey and I went to the plane and returned with our duffel bags. We spent the afternoon washing and ironing our clothes. We had made friends with Casey, who was going to be working in Paris. She was a good sport and was sharing a room with Lyn and me.

I had taken the recruiting office at their word when they told me that I would not need civilian clothes on the trip over. My dresses were in the foot locker, which was supposed to come after our arrival in Berlin (ha!). Casey, however, loaned me a black dress, and Lyn draped a pretty green coat over my shoulders. We looked quite presentable as we walked into the dining hall. Lyn was continually the life of the party. I found that Col. Kimball was a remarkable man. He was always directing the conversation to include everyone. He casually mentioned that he was an attorney at the Nuremberg trials and was bringing a paper directly from President Truman.

The cigar man had no opinions except those on women and liquor and he and his girl did all but kiss in front of us. Ed still played up to Lyn and she still avoided him. He obviously was trying to impress Col. Kimball. He said to him, "I believe you are younger than you look. I would say you are well preserved." I don't think that remark made points with the Colonel.

That evening we joined a group that was singing in the hotel bar. We began to sing enthusiastically and the sound became merrier and merrier. We were having such a marvelous time when a little Portuguese boy appeared with a complaint from the General in the left wing that the noise was too loud. The singing ceased for a moment and then we all decided "to hell with the General" and we began "I've been working on the railroad all the livelong day. I've been working . . . ." This time we were interrupted with a message that the General was giving us just five minutes to clear out of the bar. This threat was enough to make us scatter

A base officer offered us a ride to the mess hall. He had a date with a Red Cross girl and she was quite inebriated. She said she had long gotten over the opinions the fellows had of everything she did. She said she just didn't care anymore. She was doing her job and stopped worrying about such things.

We sat down at the snack bar where a Portuguese boy served us pancakes, jelly and coffee. "How is the food tonight, Manuel?" asked the base officer. The kid grinned and spoke with much accent, "It stinks!" he said and we all laughed. It was obvious he had been coached.

"Plane 9108, I repeat, Plane 9108. Leaving in one hour," came over the loudspeaker. We rushed to our room, packed and returned to the plane. It was 3:00 a.m. There were 15 planes preparing to leave as this was the first time the weather in France had been clear for several days. We climbed back into our comfortable, familiar seats. Our three day stay in the Azores had been an unexpected respite, but now we were ready to see what lay ahead of us. The big engine roared, we fastened our seatbelts, and we taxied across the field. Other planes were taking off and we had to wait our turn. Soon we were speeding and lifting off. I looked down and took a last glance at the Azores.

That night I wrote in my diary, "This has really been a wonderful day and I hope that I will never lose my appreciation for all that I'm seeing and going through."

I awakened around sunrise and felt rather disheveled and dirty. The others were awakening and I got them to sign my Court of King Neptune document, a diploma proving that I had crossed the Atlantic Ocean. Lyn already had made friends with the crew and led me to the cabin to have them sign my document. "I had to get away from Ed", she giggled, "and so I came up here." We glanced back at the captain snoring and stretched out across 2 seats.

The pilot, a big blonde, began teasing Lyn about her pigtails. The whole crew was having a gay time joking and kidding with each other. There were eight other C-54's flying close by and now and then we could catch a glimpse of them through the clouds. A thrilling race ensued with plane 9106, which we easily left behind. As we neared Paris, the radio operator handed me a set of headphones and I heard voices from plane to plane and from plane to airfield. It was such an awesome experience.

The ceiling was extremely low. The pilots were all extremely anxious to land and their deep voices came rapidly and concerned over the air. One pilot was very angry and his words were not repeatable, but the voice from the Tower was not persuaded by his plea. The ceiling was definitely too low and no planes were going to land and that was that. The radio operator laughed and said, "He has a date with a little French gal he's hot for." Our pilot was annoyed too, "Carrying V.I.P. with message from the President . . . . must land." Orly Field held firm. No deal. They would take no responsibility and would give no OK. This was disappointing as I was longing to see Paris and was not sure where we would land next.

After a long time of circling and pleading, all of the planes struck out for Istris Field, which was 35 miles from Marseilles. It was the only field in all of Europe that was open. The trip was rough and one girl became ill, but Lyn and I continued to keep up our high spirits, wondering what new adventure lay ahead. We landed at dusk, along with the other planes and, as we were checking in, a curious G.I. nudged me, "Hey, are you K.A.T.'s?" I wasn't sure if it was an insult, but learned that it is a term given to members of the USO show. I was flattered that someone suspected me of being a show girl.

Istris Field was a huge place with many long, low wooden buildings. We had taken them there quite by surprise. There were not enough accommodations for so many people, but preparations were made for all of us to spend the night. Lyn, Casey and I shared a room in barracks used by prisoners of war. It was a cool, barren room with three cots in it. There were men in prisoners' uniforms all over the place. I had to stare at them. These were the first "Nazis" I had seen and I wasn't sure what to make of them. A clean-cut lad came into our room to fix the kerosene stove. "Do you speak English?" I asked him. "A little,' he replied and that was as far as our conversation went because I was unable to think of what to ask him. I had been curious to know what his reaction would be to my question and was surprised to find him so polite.

Along with some other girls, we went to the mess hall. We were handed trays. It was my first experience with a mess line where potatoes are put on top of meat, green beans on top of potatoes and bread stuck where it lands. I devoured my meal and it tasted good, but some of the others complained about the food and were disturbed about coming to Istris Field and about our rooms. As for me, it was an eye opener and I wouldn't have missed it for the world.

As we ate, a group of EATS pilots came in and apparently couldn't believe their eyes . . . . they were seeing American girls. "When did you get here? Where are you going? Where are you from?" were the questions thrown at us. "I've only seen one other 'white' girl in two years. I had a date with a nurse about five months ago, but I had to share her with five other monkeys," one fellow nearly fell off his chair. Another chimed in, "Seriously, are the girls at home as attractive as you are? I'm not being smart, I've actually forgotten." Still another, "Doggone it, I've even forgotten how to ask a gal for a date, but won't you girls come to the movies with us tonight, I mean, please."

We were awfully tired and needed a bath, but they assured us we looked wonderful to them. Because they seemed so pleased and happy and so far from being fresh, we accepted and all set out for the movies. We walked for about ten minutes through dark and sinister streets until we came to the cinema, a cold looking structure. The movie was "On Stage Everybody", a movie which ordinarily would have put me to sleep, but under the circumstances, was fascinating. We imitated the actors on the way out and across the way we found a dirty, little French bar filled with smoke. I had my first taste of cognac and French beer, which, I was warned, was more like water. The warning proved to be accurate.

The boys listened eagerly to news from the States. They wanted to know how difficult it was to buy a new suit and how high prices had gone. "And what of Germany? Will you like it there?" Another said, "I've never been to Germany, but I understand the black market there is even better there than it is here,". We gasped, "Do you mean that you deal in the black market?" "Everyone does. You'll get used to it. The people have so little, they will sell anything for cigarettes. That is real money. I know that in Berlin people just stand and watch you smoke and then four or five will dive for the butt." It was almost unbelievable to me that people had to live like that and that others could talk about it so lightly. Once outside, we danced and sang in the street. The boys were flying to Paris the next day and promised to look us up there

When Lyn and I pulled back the covers on our cots, it was a shock to see that the sheets were dirty. "We can't possibly sleep on these filthy sheets," Lyn declared.

Then I recalled, "Didn't someone mention that a General is coming in and is to sleep downstairs?" We both had the same devilish idea at the same time, rushed out the door, scuffled down the stairs and into a nicely-lighted room. "Too bad the room is allocated to a General," Lyn pouted as we tore the poor man's bed apart and robbed him of 2 deliciously clean sheets and 2 wonderfully soft pillows. We never did find out what happened when the General discovered his loss, but we slept well that night.

At 9:30 a.m. someone opened the door and shouted at us, "Be ready in fifteen minutes. They are down at the field waiting for you." Brr! It was cold in that room! I had slept in my clothes so that all I had to do was splash cold water on my face, comb my hair and put on lipstick. Lyn, however, in her slow, unruffled manner, held us up so that forty minutes had passed before we left the room. A special truck was waiting for us outside and, as we sped over rough, dirt tracks, I felt as though nothing inside of me would be left in place. I had now ridden in an Army truck and this was really rough riding!

Our pilot was leaning against a wall inside the hangar, his flight hat cocked jauntily over one ear. "Couldn't you have taken a little longer?" he demanded with sarcasm. Feeling like the size of a small peanut, I started towards the plane, but was called back. We were still missing one passenger, a Major, who, like us, had overslept. We learned that Col. Kimball had gone on to Paris by train, afraid to take a chance on having to spend several days in Marseilles. Ed had gone with him, much to Lyn's relief.

The hunger gnawing in my stomach was becoming stronger. We spied a snack counter and rushed over to it. Huge grapefruits and delicious pancakes were set before us and, as we grabbed our forks, we heard, "all passengers board 9108 immediately." We glanced longingly at our full plates and turned towards the plane.

CHAPTER TWO

Two hours later we arrived at Orly Field in Paris. We were bussed to a huge building and, inside, in an enormous hall, were several tables with people busily working and lots of hustle and bustle. I was able to get a cable off to my family to let them know that I had crossed the ocean safely. It had been five days since they had received any word from me and I knew they would be anxious.

I then stood in line to get my money changed. I changed five dollars into francs and learned that I had been very lucky. Two weeks earlier the exchange had been 50 francs for one dollar and this day we received 119 francs for a dollar. A big, lanky American, who stood in line behind me, told me that my five dollars wouldn't go very far and he would be glad to give me 125 francs for a dollar. Little did I know that he could then turn around and make more money. I didn't accept his offer because I didn't understand the financial situation. The figures were swirling around in my head and I was confused.

"Now to find out about transportation to Berlin," Lyn said. We were to find out that it was easier to say than do. ATC Headquarters was in downtown Paris so we hopped a bus, which we assumed would take us to our hotel. I gawked like a tourist on the way. Imagine being in Paris! I noticed that there was very little damage, with the exception of a big museum and I was interested in watching the big hairdos and many bleached heads.

The Majestic Hotel was like its name, large and impressive. The man at the desk told us that it would not be possible for us to stay there. "Who told you to come here?" he asked. We found someone who told us to take a bus to the American Express office. There we stood in line and were given billet slips and sent on our way to the Hotel Edward II. Three very tired girls trudged wearily to our room. It was a nice room, with long drapes and soft beds, but it was cold. Lyn loaned me a purple suit and, within an hour, we were no longer recognizable as the tired travelers of the afternoon.

At 9:00 the pilots we had met the night before arrived to take us to L'Amoriel, an officers club. We walked to the Metro and I was impressed with how efficient the metro system was. As we approached L'Amoriel, we saw throngs of unescorted girls standing along the sidewalks, laughing and talking and looking chic and lively. The guys said that they were there looking for an American officer to take them inside and that most of them were prostitutes looking for a good time.

L'Amoriel was a big place with a loud band and small dance floor. We sat at a small table and the waiter brought a bucketful of ice and a bottle of champagne and it was fun to hear the pop when he opened the bottle. A flower girl came around and the fellows bought us red roses.

We stayed in Paris nearly a week. Lyn had a sore throat. We found a dispensary and I went with her and the doctor wrote us each a note in case anyone should question us about our prolonged stay. My note read, "This is to recommend that Miss Patricia Williams be authorized to stay in quarters for five days. (Nasopharyngitis Acute)

The only catch was that we had to move out of the Hotel Edward II, but some ingenious person had our luggage moved to the Hotel Lafayette, which was, at the time, a billet for men only. We were given a suite of rooms so who were we to complain! There were chambermaids all over the place. The dining hall was full of mirrors and chandeliers and garcons and I found my high school French quite useful. I could really talk to the people. The Lafayette was a Red Cross Hotel It cost nothing to stay there and the meals were free. I was surprised to learn that everyone tipped in cigarettes.

Eight of us went to the Bel Tabarin that night. What a nightclub! Never before had I seen such a floorshow! It was elaborate and not much clothing was worn. One of the girls was embarrassed and wouldn't look. The walls opened up, the floors opened up, and various acts came down out of the ceiling. I couldn't have known then, that eight months later, I would be back here on my honeymoon.

After the Bel Tabarin, we went to a speakeasy in Pigalle. The thing that amazed me was that the men and women both used the same lavatory. The men's booths were on one side of the room and the women's booths were on the other side. This was apparently quite common in Paris.

After several attempts on different days, and after trying to get transportation at two different ATC offices, we were sent to the EATS office and assigned space on a plane that would leave for Berlin in three days.

While in Paris, I had my first taste of escargots (small snails in butter and garlic). We had special little forks to reach in the shells and pull them out. I didn't mind too much until I looked at one and saw its eyes! I had my first Jeep ride in Paris. We drove around and saw the Palace at Versailles, the monument to the Bastille, the famous book stalls along the Seine, and the Latin Quarter. We stopped at the Cathedral of Notre Dame and it is too splendid to describe in words. Inside it was tomb-like and cold, but to stand and look at it from the outside was inspiring. We wanted to go to the opera, but it was on strike.

On Monday morning, January 14, the day we were to leave Paris, we were supposed to catch the 7:00 a.m. bus at the EATS office. Somehow or other, the alarm never rang and when I opened my eyes, it was already 6:30. We hit that floor and were dressed and packed within twenty minutes. The next problem was to get a taxi or a Jeep over to the EATS office, which was about twenty blocks away and our bags weighed around 60 pounds each. We failed miserably to obtain any kind of conveyance and, becoming desperate, started out dragging our duffel bags behind us.

It was about 8:00 as we were passing the American Express office and we saw that they were opening for the day. There we got a Jeep ride to the EATS office in time for the 8:30 bus. It was a long way to the field and the plane was to leave at 8:55. We had heard, though, that EATS planes rarely left on time, and, as though to prove it, the radio operator of that plane spoke with us on the bus, and so we relaxed. We arrived at the terminal in time to watch the plane plummeting down the runway and lifting off. So much for rarely leaving on time.

A major who seemed to be in charge there said that that was the only plane leaving for Berlin that day. He suggested that we go to Orly Field as more planes left from there. How did he suggest we get there, we asked. It took some persuading, but he finally managed to get us a ride.

At Orly, they didn't know much about any planes leaving for Berlin. A captain, however, overheard us talking over our dilemma in very discouraged tones. It just so happened, he said, that he was leaving in fifteen minutes in his B-24 and was taking a couple of other passengers and we would be most welcome to come. What a relief! That was the first time I had hitchhiked a ride on a plane! My heart was really pounding as we rose into the sky and, as I climbed into the tail gunner's compartment, I listened to the captain pointing out the trenches below from the war.

CHAPTER THREE

We stopped in Weisbaden for about five minutes and then on to Berlin. After a four hour trip, we set down at Tempelhof Airport. It was 3:00 p.m. and we were tickled to find that we had beaten the EATS plane.

Being hungry, five of us stopped at the airport snack bar for a hot dog. Casey was no longer with us as she had remained in Paris to work there. Being a mustard enthusiast, I spread it on thickly and put a huge piece of wiener in my mouth. For the next five minutes I saw nothing but black and thought I had swallowed the entire Chicago fire. I had had my first taste of German mustard.

We were taken to the Visitors Center, where we signed in, and thence to the Gossler Hotel, which was the American hotel in Berlin, although the elegance of the Paris hotels was completely missing. There were no rooms available, but the German manager said that he had a "nice" apartment around the corner, where we could stay. That sounded pretty good. Gosh! Our own apartment! We dumped our things in the apartment and asked where the nearest mess hall was. The nearest was Harnack House, the officers club.

We boarded a bus. It was an old, German omnibus, taken over by the Americans. Dark and dirty green in color, it was a two-story affair, with a German driver, and we entered from the rear. There was a German man standing at the rear entrance in a heavy, dark, blue coat. We asked him to let us off at Harnack House and he then pulled back the heavy curtain at the doorway and we went inside and sat down.

Harnack House was a large, red brick building with a short, curved driveway in front of it. The entrance was very grand and the hall thickly carpeted. We went downstairs and checked our coats. There was a large crowd there and the air buzzed with conversation. As we made our way to the dining room, we were stopped short by the mess sergeant, who, in a stern manner, said, "You can't eat here." We gave a half-hearted laugh, "Why not?" "No one is allowed to enter the dining room in slacks. That is why not.".

We explained, very carefully, that we had just arrived in Berlin; that we had not had time to unpack; and that as it was very late, we had come straight here before the dining hall closed. That was too bad, he said, but we couldn't eat there. "What alternative do we have?" "You might try Headquarters Command. They are a little less strict there."

I came very near to sitting down and crying on the spot, but Lyn was very incensed and the diatribe she gave the mess sergeant is likely one he still remembers. It did no good, however, so I meekly asked where Headquarters Command was, and, as we dejectedly turned to leave, he broke down and said we could have a bite to eat, but we were NEVER to return there in slacks.

It was 9:30 when we got back to our apartment and, boy, it was freezing cold in there! To top the day off, all of the gas knobs on the stove had been turned on and we were sure that someone was planning to kill us. We didn't know if it would be safe to go to sleep. I finally managed to build a fire in the tiny, iron stove and we both climbed under the covers on the couch. It seemed like a week since we had left the Hotel Lafayette that morning.

We meant to get up at 7:00, but it was 11:15 when we arose. We were supposed to be in the Chief of Staff's office at 9:00, but decided it would be OK to go there the next day. There didn't appear to be an organized plan of what we were supposed to do and when. We went to the Billeting Office and, by the end of the day, we had secured a permanent apartment for ourselves. This was most amazing to us as we had expected that we would be living in barracks. It was Apartment No. 6 on 9 Herrfurthstrasse. It had 5 rooms: living room, dining room, two bedrooms, kitchen and bath. It was long and spread out, rather dark and old-fashioned. It wasn't exactly swanky, but we thought it was pretty neat. We were amused to find that there was a bell in each room, including the bathroom, for maid service. Unfortunately, there was not glass in all of the windows and cardboard was tacked up where the glass was missing. We couldn't get sheets right away and the beds felt something like a dining room table, but it was all OK with us.

The big surprise came when we discovered that a maid came with the apartment for six and one half days a week and that a fireman kept the fires going constantly in the tile furnace in each room. All of this was for $13.50 a month! The maid was a woman in her fifties, did not appear too bright, and spoke only German. She was pleasant and eager to please. We were delighted with our new home.

At lunch time the next day, we still had not turned our dollars into American marks. A major bought our lunch and invited us to his office. There he proceeded to tell us that he was returning to the States and would be glad to buy our dollars at a higher rate than the finance office. I wasn't sure that this was proper and declined.

In the late afternoon, after filling out many WD forms, we started to go home. We weren't just sure how to get there. A Jeep driver in a khaki jacket said he would take us there and we hopped in. We weren't sure whether he was American, but he knew a lot about the United States. We drove for what seemed like a long time and I asked him, "Where are you from?" "Cincinnati", he replied. "What State is that in?" He refused to answer my question and, by that time, we were on a large boulevard where there were very few houses. We were being kidnapped, I thought and Lyn was getting nervous too, so we insisted that he let us off. He did so and drove off.

The sky was dark gray; no cars were coming by, and we were really lost. I don't know how long we stood there, but, finally, a Jeep came along and we rushed into the street jerking our thumbs madly. The Jeep slowed down and stopped. There were three people inside: a German driver and two Frenchmen in U.S. uniforms. They turned out to be radio technicians working as civilians for the U.S. Government. They spoke little English and, with my broken French, we told them where we lived and conversed fairly well

As we came back to familiar territory, a German in a white coat covered with blood rushed out waving his arms frantically and crying. He was screaming that a Russian had just shot and killed his best friend. Lyn and I wanted to stop and help, but the driver kept on going. Then, as we pulled up in front of our apartment, an MP Jeep came alongside and questioned the Frenchmen. We were never sure what had happened back there, but we later learned that the MP's took the Frenchmen with them because they had not stopped.

One of the French fellows was Andre Mercier and his family was well known in France as owning the company that produced Mercier Champagne. He told us about the wine-making process that he had grown up with. I had several dates with Andre in January and February and he spoke only English and I tried to speak only French to him. It was awkward at times and sometimes hilarious. He was a dear, sweet, young man, but it was not a romantic relationship. The experience of dating a man with that beautiful French accent was something I never dreamed I would be doing.

That had been our second day in Berlin and so much had happened already. Would there always be this much excitement and unexpected happenings? Did the Russians still go around killing Germans?

The following day we started out for the Chief of Staff's office to find out where we would be assigned to work. On the bus, we met the Editor of The Grooper, which was the American newspaper put out for the civilians and army personnel working in Berlin. He invited us to come to his office and we went. After talking with us for awhile, he said he would like to have us both on his staff of reporters. This seemed like a marvelous opportunity to meet people, to learn the latest about the situation in Berlin and we could even travel about Germany on special occasions. We accepted his offer.

We were required to turn in our papers at headquarters and we would let them know of our decision. Once there, however, we were told that we had a lot of nerve and were strictly out of channels. The personnel officer was not happy with us. Lots of phone calls. I had come over as a CAF3 stenographer and there was a big shortage of stenos. We found a kind soul and she said she would see what she could do.

We returned next day and nothing had been decided about our jobs. More phone calls. We went for lunch at Headquarters Command mess hall. They had a ping pong table there and we started to play. We had no sooner begun, when in came two second lieutenants who were annoyed to find the table occupied. Someone suggested that we play doubles and my partner was a fellow named Bob McMann. Lyn played with his roommate, Paul Ruth. Bob was the Adjutant of Headquarters Command and Paul was his assistant. Bob and I easily won the match and then they had to go. Hmmn! He wasn't bad looking, I thought. He was six feet tall, dark, sandy colored hair, an attractive smile and, gee, he really was handsome!

After they left, we called the Personnel Office again. They had decided that since Lyn did not take dictation, she was released to go to work for The Grooper, but I would have to go where they wished to send me. The Grooper later became The Observer, a paper for all of the American occupying forces and she traveled all over Europe covering some exciting and most interesting occurrences. I was pretty disappointed, but realized that we had been pretty brazen to expect such a thing and, after all, I had come over to help my country any way that I could.

We were telling the mess officer about it and he said that he had a lot of friends and we could call them to see if they had any good jobs open for a steno. More phone calls. We got someone who wanted us to come to his house for a drink, but we declined that invitation. Then, as we were walking towards our apartment, a captain came rushing out of a house, grabbed us and escorted us into his house for a drink. It was Hank Rommele, the fellow we had talked to on the phone. We stayed for awhile and then went home.

That night Lyn had a date with an MP major. I tagged along with a friend of his. We went to a German club in the British Sector of Berlin, The Club Royale. It was on the sixth floor of a tall, bombed-out looking building and was lit by candlelight. A frau (very slinky) ran the club and she came to our table to talk to us.

The major told her that I was interested in writing and asked if there was anyone in the club who could help me in my writing. She took me to another table to meet Herr Ullstein, who was with his wife, a play director. Herr Ullstein, I learned, was the publisher of a paper called "Zie", which had just published its 7th edition. He was Jewish and, before the war, had been head of the Ullstein Publishing House, which published seven newspapers. He told me where his office was and invited me to come there and he would show me around and introduce me to various people. He seemed very friendly and nice. Looking back I can see that I missed a great opportunity by not folloing through. The fact that the only German I knew was counting to ten made me feel intimidated and not experienced enough to take advantage of this invitation.

I reported to go to work on January 19th. Lyn and I went to the Chief of Staff's office.

We had heard that the colonel was very strict and we were afraid he would bawl us out for delaying our journey. We walked meekly into his office, expecting stern words, but the colonel smiled and welcomed us to OMGUS. As we left, his words were "danke, bitte, bitte danke" (thank you, please, please). The Germans were extremely polite and used their "Bittes" and "dankes" profusely. Colonel Marcus became known as "Bitte Bitte Danke". Col. Marcus, who was well liked by everyone was later killed in Palestine.

Lyn and I had more papers to fill out, an orientation to attend, and for lunch we went to Headquarters Command mess hall. There were four mess halls in

Berlin and we were assigned to that one, although everyone ate at Harnack House whenever they wanted to.

   Who should sit across from us but Bob McMann and another of his housemates, Don Ryan. I was out of cigarettes and Bob went to his office and brought me a pack. This was quite a sacrifice, considering what the value of cigarettes was in those days. I did think he was pretty nice.

CHAPTER FOUR

I need to explain here that at that time Germany was divided into four zones: American, British, French, and Russian. Berlin, which was situated in the middle of the Russian Zone, was also divided into four sectors. The Office of Military Government for Germany (US) had its headquarters in the U.S. Sector. This was always referred to as OMGUS, pronounced as spelled, and its offices were in the building compound that had been used by the Luftwaffe (German Air Force). OMGUS was divided into eight divisions, the largest being Economics Division.

The Coal Section was one of the sections in the Economics Division and it was this section that I was assigned to. Briefly, it was the function of this section to implement within the U.S. Zone of Germany, on a Four Power basis, the established policies with respect to the production of coal and non-ferrous metals and control of all mining materials. Here records were kept of coal production; methods of improving production were discussed and implemented; and decisions were made as to who, in the U.S. Zone should get the coal and how much would be allocated.

In the mornings, I walked to the Coal Section office, checked in, and then took a bus to the Allied Control Authority (ACA) Building. It was here that the quadripartite meetings on all levels were held. These were the four Power meetings. Field Marshall Zhukov, General McNarney, General Montgomery, and General Koenig met here three times a month. Later it was General Lucius Clay who headed up the American Zone.

There was a Four Power Fuel Committee that met and I was to be the U.S. stenographer on the Technical Staff of that committee and take the minutes of the meetings. Here they discussed the coal produced in each zone and how much should be allocated to the other zones.

Hank Rommele invited me to a party the night before I started to work. The party was a surpise party for a colonel who was the Commandant of Headquarters Command., which was responsible for servicing OMGUS functions and for the administration of personnel. It was comprised of the Headquarters Regiment and attached service units of a specialized nature. It was responsible for providing all OMGUS personnel with quarters, messes, administration and recreational facilities and transportation. Utilities and construction were under their charge. It also hired, screened, paid and administered all German civilians employed by OMGUS and all troops assigned to OMGUS came under this command.

We walked several blocks to the party and it was alive and well when we got there. Hank began drinking heavily and I joined a small group in the dining room, on the floor, surrounding a small pair of dice. Having never shot dice, I decided it was time to learn. Someone loaned me 50 marks and I got down on my hands and knees with General Edmunds, two captains and two lieutenants, one of whom was my ping pong partner, Bob McMann. I waited my turn and began. The game went on for awhile and I kept winning and winning. I couldn't get rid of the dice. I cleaned out the general and Bob McMann, having accumulated a pile of marks. I returned the borrowed marks and the game broke.

I went into the kichen and chatted with the German housefrau for awhile. A colonel came into the room and in our conversation, he said that he owned a stable full of horses that he had captured when 100,000 Germans surrendered to him. He said he was going to call me and we would go riding one day.

Bob McMann joined us and after awhile we were the only two in the kitchen and the only sober ones at the party. We became so engrossed in our conversation that the whole evening slid by and we learned that we had a great deal in common. He was from the small, lovely town of Norwich, New York and his mother, who he loved very much had died recently and, we discovered that we had attended some of the same parties in Washingto, D.C. He had been staying at my brother's fraternity house at George Washington University while waiting to go into the service. He was a paratrooper and had been a jump master before coming to Europe. He told me about his ride across Germany and France with 30 other officers on a box car and about all of the frantic people he had seen begging to get train rides.

The station in Erlangen was crowded with displaced persons trying to get out of Germany to their homelands. Old women and children had packs on their backs that a large man would have difficulty carrying. Some had been waiting three days to get to Frankfurt and then couldn't get on a train because there was no room. There was no place for them to get food or even get in out of the freezing cold wind. Trains were pulling out with flatcars full of people of every description. It began snowing about 7:00 p.m. One woman carried her legless husband on her back and there were numerous people without legs or hands. Mothers were trying to keep babies warm.

When Bob's train left, there was a mad scramble to get on. People were biting, punching and scratching to stand on the outside of the cars or in between them. Mothers would shove their children through windows of trains only to have them thrown back onto the ground. In the midst of this, both men and women were relieving themselves in full view of everyone, not daring to leave the proximity of the train, nor caring. They were desperate people and the scene would forever be on his mind. Bob's group had a box car that was filthy. The toughest thing he ever had to do was to make a woman and her three children leave the car. They had been waiting for three days. There was no room for them in the car.

On the way to Berlin, all the bridges were destroyed. Most had been bombed in the middle and both ends were sticking up into the air, a very sobering sight. Everywhere there was almost nothing but piled up bricks and masonry.

These were the thirty officers who had been given the top military posts in Headquarters Command: postmaster, motor pool, mess officers, billeting, agriculture, etc. In Berlin they asked him if he had ever been an adjutant or had similar duties and he replied "no sir". And so he became The Adjutant, fondly called "The Adj".

When it was time to leave the party, Bob said he would walk me home as Hank was not in good shape. We walked down the dark, quiet streets and suddenly heard footsteps racing towards us. It was scary and we stood there trying to see what was happening. There wasn't a soul around. It was Hank, who had discovered that I was gone and so the three of us continued on to my apartment door where I said goodnight to them both.

Next day, I reported to the Coal Section , which is where I reported every day therafter, and then boarded a bus to the ACA Building (Allied Control Authority), where the Four Power meetings were held. At first, I was put in a room with 3 British enlisted men, three German girls, and Dotty, a British WAAC, and Simone, a French civilian. They were friendly and welcomed me and I noticed that the British had a variety of accents, which intrigued me, plus they had a lively sense of humor. I noticed that there were very odd signs on all the doors. They were written in English, French, and Russian and, when translated, meant "Please Close The Goddam Door".

The ACA Building was a very large stone building. There was an enormous lawn and a circular driveway in front. Four flags flew over the entrance. This was the former German Hall of Justice and it was here that many Americans had been tried. There was an entrance for the British and the French and one for the Americans and British. I entered the wrong one that first day and the confused guard didn't know what to do with me until, after a few phone calls, informed me that I could enter.

After I had worked there for a while, I was moved into the American office, where there were two officers and a civilian. Next door, was a comparable British office; the Russian office was next to them, and the French office was across the hall.

The first day, I ate lunch in the mess hall on the floor above our office. I had to stare at the Russians as they were the first I had seen and they were so impressive with their broad epaulets. One particular handsome blonde officer sat ramrod straight at his table. When his soup arrived, he grabbed the catsup bottle, emptying nearly half of it into his soup, then leaned down with his mouth level to the bowl and slurped it all in. I had been told that the Russians were crazy about two American products: catsup and coca cola, I believed it after that exhibition.

Lyn and I attended a birthday party we had been invited to. It was held in three rooms in the Harnack House (an officers' club where we usually ate dinner). They had delicious food and just about anything you wanted to drink. It was a swinging party, but I spent most of the evening just listening to the superb music of the three piece orchestra. There was a pianist, a cellist, and a violinist and they played all of the lovely music that touch one's heart: Blue Danube Waltz, Dvorak's Largo, and my favorite Rachmaninoff's Prelude in C Sharp Minor. They also played dance music and this was the first chance I had to sit quietly and think about home. The haunting music brought tears to my eyes as I thought about my family.

The next Sunday was a grand day. The colonel who promised to take me horseback riding came and picked me up. He was an aide to a general and first we went to the general's home, where the colonel also lived. The house was on Swann Island, where all of the higher-ups lived. Lake Wannsee, the largest lake in Berlin, is in the U.S. Sector and is probably twenty miles across. Swann Island is a small island connected to the main land by a bridge, and there were about 50 homes on it. We saw General Eisenhower's home, which was a large, white marble mansion.

The particular home we went to was probably the nicest home on the island. It was very large, but had a thatched roof, which gave it the appearance of an overgrown German cottage. We were served sandwiches before a huge, gorgeous fireplace, and we looked out at the lake and woods through a window that went the length of the spacious room.

After our lunch, we drove to the stables. We picked out a gigantic, black fellow by the name of Schwarz for me to ride. He had been a German military horse, so that when you wanted to say "stop", you instead said, "halt". Schwarz was difficult to handle and every time we saw a Jeep, he panicked. We rode for an hour and a half through the woods. The ground was thick with snow and the barren, black branches against the snow made a perfect study in black and white. When my new acquaintance took me home, he told me that if I called him, I could ride whenever I liked.

Soon after I began working, my boss, Don Wilson, asked me to go with him to Onkel Tom's. I was curious. It turned out to be a covered U-Bahn station (the German subway) There was a commissary, a PX, theater, jeweler, tailor, gift shop, clothing store, photographer, barber, beauty shop, and a picturesque little church. It was fun to be able to buy French perfume there. I got my first PX ration, which consisted of eight candy bars, twelve packs of cigarettes, soap, and certain clothing rations.

When I went to change my dollars into marks, I had an awful time trying to understand what a currency control book was. The whole currency situation was quite a problem. Each of the Four Powers put out its own marks and they were good anywhere in Germany. The U.S. marks were ten for a dollar and were, of course, backed by our currency. There was a funny story going around about the Four Power Finance meetings. At every meeting, the U.S., British, and French would give an account of how many marks they had printed. Then the U.S. member would turn to the Russians and ask, "How many marks have the Russians printed?" To which the reply would always be the same, "We're expecting to hear from Moscow any day now."

The Russians went mad with the printing presses and printed marks whenever they felt like it. These marks were not backed by any currency, which made the situation so difficult, and was one of the reasons that held Germany back economically and kept the mark at such a low value. On the black market, dollars brought s many as 60 marks, and a pack of cigarettes cost as high as 200 marks. Pall Malls brought more than other cigarettes.

The currency control books were a record of how much we, as individuals, should have legally. Every time we were paid, it was marked in our books. Every time we made a purchase over a certain limit, it was marked in our books. Every time we sent a money order home, it was deducted. This was to prevent people from selling cigarettes for marks and using those marks to send money home in huge amounts made from this black market activity.

I was shocked to learn of the large-scale black marketeering that went on. Before November 1, 1945, GI's could send any amount of money home and men became fantastically rich. Some fellows sold cheap watches to the Russians for $1,000. Men sent home as much as $60,000 in money orders. When the new currency came into effect on November 1st, soldiers were showing up at the port of embarkation with $30 to 40,000 worth of marks, which they could not convert. They lit cigarettes with the stuff or gave away cigar boxes full because they weren't able to use the money.

CHAPTER FIVE

I liked the people in my office. The work was very serious, but we had a good time too. I never seemed to make it to the mess hall for breakfast, but every morning about 10:00, we went upstairs in the ACA Building for coffee and they served delicious sandwiches and pastries. One noon, the British enlisted men and women (EM—Enlisted Men) invited me to lunch with them at the Sergeants' Mess. We piled into a British truck and what an odd feeling it was to be sitting on the left of the driver! I could never tire of listening to the British talk and so was surprised when Dotty said that she loved to hear me speak! They thought I was most amusing.

What impressed me about the British is that I never heard them misuse the English language. They do have a lot of Limey expressions, but never poor grammar. It was funny to hear them get "browned off" about something. I had been wanting to drive a British truck and was raring to go when they let me give it a try. What confusion having to double clutch and shift gears with my left hand! It was such fun until we ran out of petrol. They were allowed two hours for lunch, but we were "rescued" so they just barely made it back in time.

The dinners at Headquarters Command were enjoyable and classical music was played by a string ensemble. After dinner, large groups would collect at the bar and we were beginning to know a lot of people. We would sit around and sing when a newcomer would arrive, and the favorite question was, "How are things back in the States?" The American girls were swamped with dates and occasionally had to tell everyone that they had another date that night so they could go home and take a bath, wash their hair, do their nails, and write home.

I had my first date with Lieutenant McMann on Friday, January 25th. It was Lyn's birthday and she and I decided that she should have a "surprise" birthday party. She had been dating Captain Ross Stanley so he and I got together to work out the details. He was unaware that she was behind the idea. The party was to be at his house and he told me that Bob McMann had been trying to get in touch with me for a date. I suggested that he have Bob pick me up at my apartment before the party.

It was very late when he arrived at my door. He had a sad tale, of course. He had started walking and asked a German where Herrfurthstrasse was. The man told him and Bob walked on. Later, he asked someone else where it was and, again, he was told and walked on. This happened several times and he was going in circles. Finally, a German said, "Ach! So you mean 'Herrfurthstrasse'" "And I thought that was what I'd been asking all along,' he laughed.

The party was fun and Lyn was "surprised". They had a scrumptious cake, sandwiches, drinks and an orchestra. Afterwards, we walked home and I made some powdered coffee and we sat with our stockinged feet up against the tile furnace. We talked about so many things and found that we liked the same music, sports, books and movies. Suddenly, on the radio, a disc jockey's voice came on loud and clear, "It's Midnight in Berlin" and then followed the big band music of Glenn Miller, Tommy Dorsey, Benny Goodman, and all of our favorites.

The following Sunday we had another date. We went dancing at Harnack House with a gang of other people. The small, string orchestra didn't lend itself to dancing very well, but no one seemed to notice. One of the other couples was Dick Breeland, another of Bob's housemates, and Marge Ashley. They were a good-looking pair and we were to have many good times with them later. That night, The Grooper photographer was there and a picture of Bob and me dancing together appeared on the front page of the next issue. It just showed the tops of our heads, but we cut it out and had a good laugh over it.

That was one of the coldest Januarys Berlin had ever seen. The wind whistled through our cardboard windows. Lyn and I slept under six army blankets and heated water for two hot water bottles every night. We had settled in for about three weeks when we came home to find that we had a third apartment mate. She was a cute, red-head from Scranton, Pennsylvania and her name was Mim Lydon. She was dating the Billeting Officer, Captain Ray O'Neal and he was unhappy with the apartment and the girls she had been living with. Mim took the front bedroom and Lyn and I moved into the back room. Mim was fun and bouncy and the three of us got along well. At first, we weren't sure we were going to like her when she fired our maid and hired another one. We soon overlooked that and loved to borrow her blue dress. My foot locker still hadn't come. It was to be another month before it did, so we took turns wearing the three dresses that we owned among us.

Bob told me that his buddy, Mac McGilton, was the mess officer at the ACA Building and he suggested that I drop by his office to meet him. I did and we chatted and the phone rang. I heard Mac saying, "Have him eat the whole thing right there." A guard had caught a German employee stealing a loaf of bread. I sat there with my mouth open. The punishment seemed a little harsh to me

Mac had been a paratrooper like Bob and had broken his back when jumping from the practice tower. I was told that there were frequent accidents at these towers and jumping from one was much more dangerous than jumping out of a plane, I was also told that each trooper packed his own parachute. That way they were sure it was going to open. Much later, Mac had copies made of the dishes used in the ACA Mess Hall. They were white porcelain with all four flags on them. I have one of these sets, which may have some value, because Mac had not gotten permission to sell anything with the American flag on it and, therefore, only sold a limited amount of sets.

The German children gathered around on the streets begging for candy and gum and, just as I had been told, they would follow us and dive for any cigarette butts we threw away. It made me sad to see the serious little faces. I saw one boy become very animated over the pictures of food in a magazine. The Americans who had been there for awhile seemed hardened to it, but I wondered if I would ever get used to it.

The Russians were allowed to carry guns, but the other Three Powers were not. At first, the Russians shot any Germans who even looked at them the wrong way, but in later months, they became more careful who they shot. They could come and go into our zones as they pleased, but we had to get special permission to enter their zone. Being in the Russian Zone, as Berlin was, it was not too difficult to leave the city, provided we left by train, plane, or traveled on the Berlin-Helmstadt Autobahn. We could go into the Russian Sector of the city without a pass, but, if caught taking pictures, could be thrown in jail.

Some of the first tales I heard about the Russians were that they were the wildest, dirtiest bunch on earth. Many of them had never seen watches and couldn't tell time. They all wanted watches and the loudest ticking ones brought forth the best prices ($500 to $1,000). In many instances, owning a watch was considered a real mark of distinction. There were very few consumer goods in Russia. A Russian would take his watch back home and promptly would be raised to a higher level of society. Possibly, he would trade it for land. A watch could pay for an acre of land.

Many of them had never seen toilets or sinks. When they saw a toilet, they were fascinated with the white porcelain and, from then on, would use anything made of white porcelain as a toilet, such as sinks, bathtubs, etc. The best story was the one about the Russian who took a big alarm clock to a jeweler, banged it down on the counter and said, "Here. Make two wristwatches out of this."

A lieutenant told of moving into a house that had been occupied by Russians just after Berlin had fallen. The filth was unbelievable. After they had cleaned it out, it still smelled just awful. A look in the back yard solved the mystery. There was a wrecked German plane there with bodies still in the wreckage

I don't want to give a wrong picture as there were many highly-educated, cultured, lovely Russian people. The average "Ivan", however, was crude and uneducated and appalled by the advanced ways of living that the Germans had developed. So that they would not go home and tell about the higher standard of living in Germany, they had to sign a statement before they returned that they would tell nothing of the things they had seen.

Before I came to Europe, my father asked me to try to get my assignment changed to Frankfurt. It was in the American Zone and he thought I would be safer there. I did try, but it was too late to change details. Bob told me that he and his buddies had tried to be assigned in Nuremberg, but fate must have stepped in to bring us both to Berlin.

He lived in a very nice house with five other officers. Three of these I have already mentioned: Paul Ruth, Dick Breeland and Don Ryan. /He told a humorous story about Don Ryan. Don had been the first to move into their house and he picked the room he thought was the best in the house. He then went searching for interesting articles he could confiscate. Bob moved in and had to take the only vacant bedroom left. It was a large room and had a sun porch leading off it. He did a lot of fixing and re-arranging and ordered some nice furniture from his friend in charge of furniture. He then looked out in the garage and found an old German pistol and a motorcycle. When he was settled in, Don approached him with a large sum of marks he wished to exchange for the room and the treasures Bob had found. Bob thanked him, but said that he liked the room and, thanks anyhow.

The nicest houses in the vicinity of headquarters had been requisitioned for the use of Americans. The Germans had been given a few short hours to clean out and to take just what they could carry on their backs. Later, a German billeting office was set up to help them find lodgings, but, at first, it was pretty rough on them. Most of the furniture was taken to a central location and allocated according to needs.

The people who Bob and I did most things with were his housemate, Dick Breeland and Marge Ashley, who was beautiful. She reminded me of an adult, brunette Shirley Temple. Another couple was Don Ryan and a lovely Belgian girl, Regina Van der Vloet. She had grown up in the part of Belgium where Flemish is spoken, but she also spoke English, French and German. She had come to Germany when the Germans entered Belgium and, when we knew her, she was considered a Displaced Person. She had worked for the Bayer Aspirin Company during the bombing of Berlin She told us that the American planes came over during the day and the British planes came at night.

One day she did not feel well and stayed home. When she went to work the next day, she discovered that the bomb shelter she would have used had been completely destroyed during the raid. During the final days of the war, when Berliners weren't sure whether the Americans or Russians would be the first to enter the city, she and another girl hid and slept in the basement of a very large house. They slept with razor blades beside their beds and, in case the Russian soldiers found them, they planned to slit their wrists.

A large Fancy Dress Ball was being planned in the British Sector and the fellows across the hall from me invited me to get a date and come. They arranged for us to go to the opera house and, backstage, we could pick out any costumes we wanted. There were rows and rows of fanciful dress-ups. I chose a gypsy outfit for myself. The top was heavy black lace, and the skirt was several layers of black cotton with a gold design on it. I learned that the dress would be worn three days later in the ballet. For Bob, who could not come down that day, I picked out an 18th century British uniform, in other words, he became a redcoat. Fortunately, it fit him.

We all met at the Sergeant's Mess Hall and, from there, a special bus took us to the dance hall. There was a huge dance floor and that night we danced to "Rolf and His Band". I must say that Rolf was good and the music was wonderful to dance to. We saw every kind of costume imaginable from pirates to William Tell and his Apple. There was a photographer there and we had our pictures taken in our get-ups. The pictures turned out pretty well. Our picture was in color and it was transparent. Bob was holding me and had a saucy look on his face, and I was looking up at him. They put the picture in a nice frame and you could only see it if a light was placed in back of it. Bob kept it in his room with a candle behind it. It was a BYOL party and everyone wanted to taste American whiskey. The ball was "wizard" and we all had a "smashing" good time.

In the first part of February, we took a tour of Berlin in a Jeep. Among other things, we saw the Olympic Stadium, Under der Linden. American Embassy (which had been flattened), the Reichstag, the Chancellery, and Hitler's balcony, which we had seen in newsreels with him ranting and raving at the crowds. The Brandenburg Gate stood solidly separating the American Sector from the Russian Sector.

The most amazing sight was the Tiergarten, which is a huge park near the center of the city. There, daily, hundreds of people were milling around, carrying on black market business in spite of frequent raids by agents of several nations. The Germans had their old hunting knives, cameras, radios, silver, etc. to trade for cigarettes, food and stockings. We saw the monument on which was mounted the first Russian tank to enter Berlin. There was a tall German monument for victories over France and, over it, proudly waved the French flag.

There were many beautiful residential sections of the city. There were piles of rubble everywhere and, yet, it was easy to see that Berlin had once been very lovely. Mile after mile of downtown seemed dead. Every building looked as if giant hands had scooped out the insides and thrown them in the streets and courtyards. The streets had been cleaned up and the U-Bahn was running, but much of the scenery resembled Pompeii.

On another Saturday afternoon, several of us went to a German movie. We were delighted to discover that it was "Baron Munchausen" in Technicolor. Technicolor was very new in the States. The Baron had a gun with a scope sight that could see any object on earth and shoot it. There was a fellow who was the fastest runner in the world. He ran from Persia to St Petersburg, Russia and back in an hour! Quite a guy!

Bob's friend, John Christenberry, was a lieutenant in the MPs. He and Bob had gone through paratrooper training and OCS together. A hot tip had come in that some Russians were trying to buy an American Jeep. John, his buddies following close behind, pulled up to the spot where the transaction was to take place. They put up a roadblock and stopped a Russian car. After forcing the Russians onto the road and subjecting them to a thorough frisking, it was discovered that one was a major general (John had thought him to be a private). Not only was he a major general, but his name was Sokolovsky and he was then the Deputy Commandant and the 2nd ranking Russian in Germany. Poor John got hell for that and General Lucius Clay had to apologize personally.

Every Monday, Lyn and I left our dirty clothes for the housefrau to launder. We had been giving her candy and cigarettes, soap and little things that she seemed to need. One Monday I returned home and the laundry had not been done and she had gone and I found a note pinned to my bed. "I can't make so quick all the baggage ready. The workman are in the building and that make much more work. Have you please a little bit indulgence." She had been trying in poor English to tell us her troubles and we had not understood, so we tried "to make a little more indulgence".

Reggie and I had become very good friends and she sometimes spent the night at my apartment. She and Don were an interesting pair. Don was a big, nice-looking fellow, had quite a temper, and Reggie had a will of her own. They were always thinking of something to quarrel about and then making up.

On a Sunday morning in February, she and I got up early and went to 15 Lanstrasse. We began making snowballs until we had 100 of them. Then we rang the bell and kept ringing it until the boys got up. When they came out the front door, we bombarded them. They quickly recovered and returned fire. We got a little wet in the fracas and everyone had an opportunity to wash each other's faces with snow. Then we enthusiastically began making a snowman. The snow was stubborn when it came to rolling snowballs larger than 4 inches in diameter and so we had to be satisfied with a short, skinny snowman and one we couldn't brag about, but we laughed a lot and thought he was terrific.

Marge Ashley and Dick Breeland made a striking couple. She had long, dark hair and she wore it many ways. She could look sophisticated one day with an upsweep hairdo and like a little girl the next with her hair parted in the middle. When Margie made an entrance, everyone looked up and I believe that almost everyone in Berlin knew who she was. Her husband had been killed in the war. Dick, who was 6'4", was a southern gentleman. He was a year older than the others in the house and they all looked up to him. He was a poet by nature and he had an unusual, pleasing way of describing things. Once, when the six of us were eating at 15 Lanstrasse, Dick, a wine connoisseur, brought out a very special wine and said, "This wine is of rare vintage, you know. It was the year 1913, one of the best years for wine-making the world has ever known." We liked to hear him talk and always learned something when he did.

Dick took us to Lake Wannsee to look at "his" boat. It was a magnificent sailboat, about 45 feet long, and Dick claimed it was the fastest one in its class in Germany. It had belonged to Germany's champion yachtsman and had won the European championship four times before the war. He promised to take us sailing in the summertime. He was so excited about it that he was trying to work it out so that when the time came, he could sail home across the Atlantic. It's a funny thing, ownership in Germany at that time, because later, a mean old Government official came along and said that Dick didn't own the sailboat at all.

Lyn and I discovered that we could draw a piano from the furniture warehouse. It came a few days after we ordered it, a baby grand, and we put it in our living room. I play a little bit and Lyn had a lovely voice. She was taking voice lessons at the time, so we got a lot of enjoyment out of our new acquisition. We also managed to get a nice radio and a pretty set of dishes. Our apartment was beginning to shape up.

My hair was beginning to get straight and I needed a permanent badly. I complained about my hair at work and that was all the British boys needed! They made an appointment for me in the British Sector, sent me over in their truck, paid for the permanent, and had a special jeep bring me back afterwards. I was really pleased with my curls and the fellows said, "That's what Allies are for."

I got homesick every once in awhile. Mother worried about the area in which I lived and was sure I was going to catch pneumonia in the harsh, cold weather we were having. She worried about all the things that mothers worry about and you love them for it. Goggy had enjoyed the jewelry I sent her from the Azores. I had sent a pin and earrings and they both claimed the pin was for them. I sent them more to make them happy. Dad read every letter I sent over and over again. He carried them around with him, "just in case someone spouts off about his children, I can tell him about mine." I had such a dear, sweet, loving family!

I was beginning to like some of the Germans and wanted to know what they were thinking about. An American officer and I were discussing it and he said, "You must remember, the Germans are friendly, but we've got to realize that they are being that way because it pays them to put on that act. They know that 'you can catch more flies with honey than with vinegar'. The surly, arrogant Germans get themselves nowhere. I find it quite easy to get rough with these people because I looked down their rifle barrels for nearly a year, the wrong end pointed my way. You must always keep in mind the terrible things the people have done. None of them will admit to having been a member of the Nazi party."

That was true. You just couldn't find anyone who had been a Nazi. I understood his hostile feelings. It had been a brutal war. The Germans had done more terrible things than any other civilized nation in modern time had ever done. They had deliberately killed six million of the eight million Jews in their country, an indescribable atrocity. But were they all alike? Were they all guilty of cruelties? I was confused about how I should feel and act towards them.

Any Germans I met were pleasant and friendly, and, except for the harsh circumstances they were living under, seemed to be like people I knew back home. I thought about the dark periods of American history, particularly about slavery and lynchings, and the way the Indians had been treated, and I knew that the cruelties were committed by a minority of people. Most Americans in Berlin at that time were unforgiving, but they mellowed with time. I developed a belief that the average Germans had not wanted war and had wanted to live their lives peacefully and without stress.

Gradually, I began seeing Bob every night after work. We usually met Margie and Dick, Don and John, among others, and had dinner at the Harnack house. There was always the same string ensemble playing before and during dinner and, one night, Bob tipped them a package of cigarettes. From that time on, when he and I walked into the dining room, they would smile and begin playing "Der Kuss

Serenade" (The Kiss Serenade). It has a haunting, romantic melody to it and we became known as an item.

There were dances on Saturday and Wednesday nights and we always stayed and danced. Once, someone offered Bob and Don a bottle of cognac if they would get up at the mike and sing "Sentimental Journey". They did and we enjoyed the cognac. It was THE drink at the time and many people used coca cola with it. "Cognac and Coke" was the biggest order. Sounds awful now.

Dick had to go back to his office one night and Bob and Margie and I tagged along. As we waited in the hall for him, we noted that it was filled with potted plants. "It's a shame," said Margie, "that this hall is so over-crowded with plants and one of them would look so nice in your billet, Bob". My eye spotted a beauty of a plant, large and green, and just right for Bob's living room. When Dick came out into the hall, I picked it up (and it was heavy!) and carried it over to 15 Lanstrasse. When I put it down, it brightened up the room and everyone was pleased with the new scenery. I noticed a small sign on the plant that read "potocaupus", so that became a code word in our entourage. The fellows had gotten huge boxes full of K-rations, so we sat around and celebrated the new "potocaupus". It was fun to have late night snacks again.

Paul Ruth had not been well for some time and late in February, we visited him in the hospital. Paul was a tall, lanky fellow, being 6'4", and he was one of the best-natured men I've ever known. He was so proud of his wife and little boy and was always showing us pictures of them. Paul had gone back to the hospital for the third time with some sort of stomach ailment. He was pretty depressed and we didn't know what was wrong with him. He stayed there for six long weeks and, finally, the trouble, whatever it was, cleared up. We never did find out what it was.

My mother had a right to worry. There was an article in the Stars and Stripes entitled "Human Meat Sale Probed in Berlin." Gerda Fischbock, a German civilian typist employed in the Supply Office told her superior that a few days earlier, a girlfriend of hers was stopped on the street by a German civilian man who asked her to deliver a letter for him to a certain address, giving a fairly plausible reason for his own inability to deliver it.

The girl accepted the letter, agreeing to deliver it to the address specified. A German woman, however, who had been standing nearby and who had heard the conversation, approached the girl after the man had gone and advised the girl not to deliver the letter, or, at least not to deliver it without knowing what she was delivering.

The two of them, the girl and the woman, opened the letter and its contents were merely, "Herewith I deliver more fresh meat", or words to that effect.

They went immediately to the police, which was believed to be the basis for the Stars and Stripes article.

The Supply Officer sent a memorandum to his commanding officer, advising that the matter be brought to the attention of all Americans in Berlin, and he emphasized the last paragraph of the news article, which stated that the victims "are lured to destruction by men posing as blind or crippled war veterans who ask to be helped home or have messages delivered to a certain apartment." He went on to say that American personnel should be warned again about the rule "safety in numbers". The article spoke of the victims as having been women, but the Supply Officer felt that it was conceivable that a soldier seen in a lonely spot might be looked upon with favor by the trapper as a substitute for the usual victim, especially if the trapper had not had any luck up to that time.

I had actually felt pretty safe up to that time, but it hit home that I was in a war-torn area that was just recovering from great trauma and I promised myself to be alert and careful.

CHAPTER SIX

Berlin was saturated with ruins. The city seemed completely destroyed, except for some outlying sections. I was told it was one-fourth shattered, but it was largely the central areas that were almost totally devastated.

Driving over to the Russian Sector, we went to see where Hitler lived and the shelter where he took refuge through the bombings. The great hall through which we walked to his office, and the office in which he worked, were all in varying degrees of destruction. The vivid impression was of a fiend who needed so much grandeur to build up his sense of importance. I recalled scenes of him on his balcony with crowds going wild listening to him with adulation. Here was where Hitler beamed with pride as he drew up his insidious plans that were his downfall. Now the walls were littered with graffiti.

I shall never forget the night we went to the Club Femina. It was once a world famous nightclub, perhaps second only to Paris' Bel Tabarin. Seven of us decided to go: Don, Margie, Dick, Mim and Ted (whom Mim later married when they returned to the States), and Bob and me. We took the U-Bahn. I cringed at the way the Germans stared at us with desperate looks, which made the ride creepy and eerie. Every second car was a "Raucher" and, the others were "Nicht Rauchen", which meant "Smoker" and "No Smoking". I never smoked on the train because I hated the looks on people's faces waiting for the butt.

Once downtown, we had to transfer to an S-Bahn (streetcar). The Femina was in a deserted section of the British Sector. We had to walk along some dark, weird streets and, with the moon shining on the ruins, and the silence, we were on edge. Although we were not allowed to carry guns, the boys did take a couple of them along.

The Femina had not been bombed, but it looked dilapidated from the outside. Once inside, there was pure elegance. There were wine-colored velvet drapes on the walls and thick, soft carpets that made you bounce when you walked on them, and there were mirrors everywhere. There were several dance floors and, before the war, there had been lunch rooms and dining rooms and private party rooms. It had been famous for the telephones on each table. Every table also had a large number on it and, if a man saw an attractive woman at another table, he would dial her number and ask her to dance, or he could write a note and have the waiter deliver it to her.

There no longer were any numbers on the tables and only one dance floor was in use. As we stepped into the room, the band was playing "There'll Be A Hot Time

In The Town Of Berlin When The Yanks Come Marching In" We couldn't believe our ears. We looked around and were probably the only "Yanks" in the room. We didn't know if that was for our benefit or not. We had German wine and danced and suddenly it was hard to believe that there had been a war and it was over and the Yanks had come marching in such a short time ago.

In March, a New York Times reporter wrote that we would be at war with Russia by April. This, naturally, caused some concern and hubbub. We didn't believe it, yet we had been having trouble with the Russians on all scores. All of a sudden they were more obnoxious. At the office, I was keeping track of the coal being shipped into the American Zone via rail and water from the Saar (French Zone), Ruhr (British Zone) and the USSR Zone. At least, I was trying to keep track. The Russians weren't delivering the coal to our Zone that they had agreed to and, always, it was a fight to get them to give us reasons and figures. As for the U.S. Zone, we didn't have much coal, certainly not enough for our needs. It was being said that the French got the castles, the British got the industry, the Russians got the agriculture, and the U.S. got the scenery.

We were pretty good to Russia at that time. We were giving her factories and most of the products they requested. In return, we got promises, most of which were not fulfilled. One of the best cartoons I saw was a picture of a cow. Uncle Sam was feeding it and the front of the cow was marked "U.S. Zone". The back half was marked: "Russian Zone" and Uncle Joe Stalin was milking it.

I enjoyed the first Four Power meetings I attended. Everyone acted as though they were about to slit each other's throats and I loved hearing everything translated into the other two languages. Much of the time was wasted with petty disagreements about the use of words and their meanings. Then, when lunch time came, everyone was friendly and slapping each other on the back and, always, the Russians would propose a toast in vodka. I must admit that I was staying up late most nights listening to "It's Midnight In Berlin", so there were times, when I was taking shorthand for the minutes, that I dozed off and the pen would squiggle down the page.

With March, the snow and zero weather left, but it was still plenty windy and cold. We would spend Saturdays looking in the shops along Kurfurstendam with Don and Reggie. This was the main commercial thoroughfare. At one end was a famous church that had been badly damaged. One good idea the storekeepers had had before the war was that in front of each store, near the edge of the road, was a glass showcase that displayed items sold inside. Now the cases were empty.

We decided to take advantage of the free tickets that Special Services had offered the Americans and we went to see "Rigoletto." It was superb! Erna Berger, who was said to be the greatest soprano in Germany (some said all of Europe) played Gilda. She was a petite blonde, with a powerful voice and we were to see more of her. My mother, who sang in some New York operas, used to sing "Caranome" and I always loved to hear it. Miss Berger did great honors to that song that day, but my mother had a softer, sweeter voice in my opinion.

The following day, the British took us to the Staats Opera to hear the Berlin Philharmonic Orchestra. They played from Dvorak's New World Symphony. They also played the Overture to "Alceste" and Beethovan's Concerto in E Flat. The conductor, a tall man with a long, black mane, was Sergei Celibidache, who was very well known. It rekindled my love of classical music. The British boys drove us in their truck to Bob's house and we played some ping pong. Robbie, a quiet, little Scotsman, said, "It's a short 'tyble', isn't it".

We were beginning to feel so cultured that we made plans to take in "La Comedie Francaise" in the French Sector. I had received an invitation that read, "Le Commandant en Chef Francais a Berlin et le Service Social du Troupes Francaises d'Occupation en Allemagne prient Mademoiselle Williams de bien vouloir honorer de sa presence la representation que La Comedie Francaise". The French were very proud of this presentation. It was a troupe of French actors and actresses that moved around in France and had come to Germany for this special show. Tickets were hard to come by because it was so humorous.

We met at OMGUS Headquarters, piled into Army trucks and went to the Staat Deutsche Opera. The costumes were gorgeous, but that is as far as I can go. I thought I knew some French, but they spoke so rapidly I couldn't catch a single word. There was no action on stage. Once in awhile we would hear a "oui" or "non" and the audience would giggle or tee-hee or roar with laughter. It must have been hilarious, but I don't think I've ever spent a more boring three hours. Don fell sound asleep and the rest of us took turns yawning. To top the evening off, we sat through several curtain calls and then had to stand through four national anthems. On the way home, it struck us as quite comical and we laughed and made great sport of it.

Reggie spoke fluent German and acted as our interpreter. We wanted to learn the language because we were ashamed that we were living there and couldn't understand what people were saying. We got hold of a set of records that taught German in forty-two simple lessons. It seemed like a painless method and fun doing it together as a group. It was a riot to see us sitting around and repeating after the announcer. We didn't pick it up quickly, I'm afraid, but we did learn a word or too. "Dumkopf" was one we used on each other frequently. It was a perfect downer.

Early in March, a system was installed whereby we could call any place in the United States for twelve dollars for three minutes. As my dad's birthday, March 23rd, was nearing, I made an appointment to call him on that day at 9:00 p.m. (3:00 p.m. his time). All week I thought about the things I was going to say. In fact, the office gang made up a list of items for me to talk about (and they all wanted their names mentioned). We made these calls from Titania Palast, a large club center. A call would be made the day before my call to make certain that the person on the other end would be there at the arranged time. When I arrived at Titania Palast, it only took them fifteen minutes to put the call through.

Their voices were music to my ears—Dad's, Mother's, Goggy's. I never got around to the list and I even forgot to wish Dad a Happy Birthday. When I got in the booth, my mind went blank. When I came out, Bob asked me what they had said and I could scarcely remember a single word. It took me the whole evening to piece the conversation together. So much had happened since I left home and I felt so fortunate to have such a super family. The experience made me realize that when a witness is on the stand and changes or adds to his testimony later, it could be the same time lapse in remembering events.

At 5:00 p.m., just before I left my office one afternoon, the Chief of the Coal Section came to each of us in the office and told us that we were to be in our billets promptly at 8:00 p.m. and anyone caught out after that time would be incarcerated. There was consternation and bewilderment about this startling and frightening prospect. Bob walked me home after supper and then went on to his billet. Mim, Lyn and I took turns washing our hair and wondering what was going to happen. Mim had brought home a gorgeous metal plate with our three names on it and we put that up outside our door. Nothing happened that night and we went to bed still wondering.

At work next day the mystery was cleared up. The idea had been to pick up any suspicious looking individuals, such as Germans posing as Americans; spies; soldiers who were AWOL, etc. We weren't informed about how many threatening individuals were taken into custody, but we assumed that we were all a bit safer.

Near the end of March, Reggie, Bob and I started out to go horseback riding. Bob was able to get an open C&R, a vehicle that is not enclosed. We rode to the French Zone one night in one and, coming back late at night, I thought I surely had gotten frostbite as it was an hour's ride each way. Anyhow, we set out at 7:00 a.m. for the stables. About halfway there, the old vehicle conked out, but a Jeep came along and we were able to continue. Very few Americans in the American Sector were ever stranded as the only vehicles were American military ones and the drivers were always willing to go out of their way.

I rode Schwarz again and he hadn't had much exercise lately! We rode mostly in the indoor ring, but when we went outside, the black devil took off like a bat out of hell. I was behind Bob when he started to run, quickly passed Bob and he said he heard "BOB, BAWB, Bob, Bob, Bob . . ." And my voice faded away as I disappeared into the woods. As Bob tried to dash to my rescue, the horse he was on decided to go sideways and he never did catch up to me. I was half out of the saddle when I finally got him stopped. I found that, by pulling on one rein with all my might, I could pull his head around so that he couldn't see where he was going. Oh what a rough ride that was! Next day the office gang presented me with a cane—and I used it!

The British major on the Technical Staff was a Major Greene. He was slight of build and had a huge mustache and, to him, everything was "sort of large" "or "sort of extraordinary". He loved his dignity, but he also loved his liquor. I called him "Greenie", which he detested. Nevertheless, he "sort of" appeared at my desk and asked me to have lunch with him at the Embassy Club, which was THE Club in the British Sector. It was so ritzy that I just stood for a few minutes when we walked inside. The red velvet furnishings and cut glass chandeliers and gold fixtures everywhere made me think of a palace. A favorite drink with the British was gin and lime, so I joined the major with one out on the terrace. It was the first warm day of Spring and we ate our lunch outside.

The lunch was very fancy and I couldn't help but think of the story that one of the WAACs told me. She had come here to a big party and wanted to be a huge success. But, as she walked in the door, the elastic on her half-slip broke and she found it down around her ankles. Rising above the situation, she stepped out of the slip and stuffed it in her purse and went on as though nothing had happened.

I spoke with the maid and the fireman often. They thought Truman and Churchill were all right, but they despised Stalin. The German typists in our office were very nice and I began to find out how meager their rations were. They did get a good lunch when they worked for the Allies. One girl in the office had lost a three-year old son with pneumonia; her parents had been killed in a bombing raid; and her husband was a Russian prisoner and she had not heard from him in months. She was cheerful most of the time, but life for her outside the office was quite drab. I gave one girl an apple for her little boy and she was as happy as though I had given her an expensive gift.

I was beginning to believe that it was the younger boys (16 to 25 years) whom we should be careful with. They didn't look like our boys, but were hard and their eyes were cold. Once, on the streets, a sixteen-year old boy passed me and said, "Heil Hitler". I was too stunned to say anything.

I learned that there were three classes of Food Cards for the Germans.

I.   For very heavy workers
II. Heavy workers, or employed by Americans
III. Office workers

Under Category II, a 10-day ration consisted of:

200 grams of fat (butter, margarine, lard, or whatever happened to be in stock).
250 grams of sugar
5,000 grams of bread
450 grams of meat; if no meat, then fish, if no fish, then sausage
400 grams (per day) of potatoes
250 grams of cereal or noodles
200 grams (per month) of coffee (actually ersatz).

A child under 6 got white bread or white flour. No fruit juice, although fruit was sometimes available. Angie (just 4 years old) got fresh fruit 3 times while we were there. A child under 2 received fresh milk; from ages 2 to 6, a child got thick, powdered milk. Salt was not rationed.

Vegetable rations were announced in the paper, as they did not always have vegetables. Ration was according to supply and was sometimes more than other times. There were very few vegetables in winter. There was no vinegar, or anything to can with. There was no cod liver oil for children. Once they gave out cookies instead of sugar.

The ration cost about 30 marks per month per person, but it was impossible to live on this ration and black market prices were unbelievable. Bread was 40 marks a loaf. A small bottle of vinegar was 30 marks. A pound of sugar was 85 marks. A pound of onions was 10 marks.

To show the relationship between wages and the cost of food, the average laborer made 140 to 200 marks per month. Office workers and business employees made between 275 and 300 marks per month.

Every month, each person got a piece of soap the size of a small cigarette lighter, and of very inferior quality. For laundry, they got a powder, which loosened dirt, but had no soap in it.

As for clothing, the only way a lady could get a dress was if she had absolutely nothing at all. If she wanted shoes, she had to go to the government. Someone then came to her house and made certain that she had no shoes that could possibly be repaired. Each person was allowed only one pair of shoes at a time. If socks were needed, a person first had to go to a store and get a slip saying that they had socks to sell. Then the person went to the government and got a slip saying he could buy the socks, then that person had to go back to the store to see if there was still a supply. In order to get a pair of shoes repaired, it was the practice to give the shoemaker a cigarette, or some sugar, or something of value.

We had an unusual situation at the ACA Building. We had plenty of toilet paper around OMGUS Headquarters and plenty of it was issued to us in our billets. However, where I worked, there was none, so that when someone had to go to the Little Girl's Room, or Little Boys Room, they had to take along a supply of typing paper. Naturally, everyone knew where you were going. At first it was embarrassing and a lot of wisecracks sprang up, but soon no one paid any attention.

We were issued uniforms and were supposed to wear them all of the time. An officer gave me some olive green material that officers' uniforms were made of and I had one made for myself. The jacket was Eton and it was quite spiffy. Civilians wore green stripes on their epaulets and I felt safe wearing my uniform during the day. Also, it was a big help in hitch-hiking. It was good for me not to have to worry about clothes, since my footlocker had not arrived, although Lyn and Mim were good about sharing their few dresses with me, and we had never been scolded for dressing up in the evenings. Then, lo and behold! In mid-March, my possessions arrived and I heard a couple of "hurrahs" from my housemates. It came about the time it became legal to wear street clothes at night.

The atmosphere at our coal meetings was becoming even more bitter. The Russians were only sending us 49% of the coal they had promised and were not sending any at all to the French. They were sending the British 105% of their allocation. They needed the British because they were getting hard coal from their Zone and the Russian Zone coal was soft coal. Sometimes the air was blue with angry words.

Bob had a very nice driver at work whom everybody called "Pop". Pop wasn't supposed to, but he came early in the mornings and took Bob to work. On Pop's birthday, Bob gave him a pack of cigarettes and he was tickled to pieces. A couple of days later, he reciprocated by giving Bob a Nazi flag taken from a German submarine. Some time later, he gave him a hand made communist flag, sewn by a German family when the Russians first entered Berlin.

Bob received word that his Dad was going to marry Bob's aunt on March 27th. Bob said that his mother's sister was very much like his mother. This would make his cousin, Marian, his step sister. She was the same age as he was and they had spent a lot of time together when they were growing up. He laughed when he told me that, in his senior year of high school, his mother had called her sister and invited Marian to go to Bob's Senior Prom with him. As much as he liked her, he had thought about inviting another girl, but he couldn't get out of it

Bob decided that the day of the wedding would be an excellent time for him to call his family as they would all be gathered for the big event. He put in a call for 8:00 p.m. (2:00 p.m. there). The call must have invigorated him because afterwards he came to my apartment and he was beaming. "Let's go for a walk" he coaxed.

We walked down the dark streets and it was chilly, although the air still smelled of Spring. We walked along with our hands in the pockets of our Army overcoats not saying much, but it didn't seem to matter. We stopped to read some German signs on an advertising post. They had huge, round posts where they put up their posters and advertisements. We walked to a U-Bahn station and went down the steps. As I looked up at the broken windows of the station and then at Bob, it hit me. Here I was in Berlin, walking through the streets at night with a handsome American lieutenant. It was so unreal! It was as though I was looking at us as strangers from afar and that it was not really me in the picture.

We went back to my apartment and Bob helped me wash my hair. It was then that I knew that he liked me a little bit because he told me, "You're the only girl I've seen who looks good after she has washed her hair." I knew that I didn't look that good. It was proof that love was blind.

I bet him 80 marks that he couldn't give up smoking until Easter and I put 80 marks in a box on top of the tile furnace. I promised to put one mark in the kitty every time I smoked over 10 cigarettes in one day. Bob eventually won the pot, but it seemed strange to have a joint financial plan when we weren't sure how long our friendship would last.

Dick announced one day that his name had been put on a list for a Class B Mess. This meant that he could buy food at the commissary up to $30 worth a month. There were five people on a Class B Mess and one of them was responsible for all of them so that Dick would be the one to pay the bill. Lyn also became a member of one, meaning that we could have dinner parties at our apartment too.

Mail was so important to us. Those letters and packages were always welcome. I requested some things and they arrived: a bathing suit, music, and Mother (a typical mom) had added some vitamin pills to the batch. She also sent me a Brownie Kodak camera, one of those square boxes. Was I delighted! I began right away taking pictures at the same time as others with Leicas, German Kodaks, etc. and the neat part was that my pictures usually turned out the best. I sent home some pictures of Bob and Mother wrote, "Your friend, Bob, is certainly a fine looking chap. Where is his home and how long does he have to stay in the service?" His sister wrote after seeing several snapshots of me, "We think Pat is most attractive, but she looks different in every picture." Margie had been helping me try different hair styles and it must have confused his family.

Two of the boys in Bob's crowd had birthdays on the same day late in March and they threw a big dinner party, just for males, at the ACA Building. It must have been something, judging from the pictures and stories told afterwards. One of the fellows admitted that it was his first birthday party. I remember it, especially as Bob brought me two orchids. I was so astonished and pleased that I gave one to Mim.

Saturday morning, March 30th, a most unusual thing happened. I awakened to find the man who tended our room furnaces standing beside my bed, and, suddenly, there was a small puppy in bed with me. It was a homely, elongated little thing with long, black and brown hair. When I saw it, I said, "Oh no! Oh no! It can't be!" and that is what all my friends said when they saw it. "Is it a dog?" they would ask cruelly. Their taunts only made me love her more. The fireman wanted a carton of cigarettes for it. We settled for five packs because I really loved it right away and, yet, I was doing him a favor by even taking it.

Bob named it Quadripartite and we called it "Quaddie". I never did get Quaddie housebroken. She didn't seem to have much 'upstairs', but we were pals right from the start. Bob's housemates made an awful fuss when I brought her over there and would run and roll up the rugs. They would try to get her drunk and she would run around in circles. Everyone was mean to her except Reggie and Lyn. She had a cute, dumb face and I felt that I had to be her protector.

None of the other dogs we encountered would play with her. Quaddie would see a dog, get all excited and run up to sniff. The other dog would take one look and run away quickly. I took Quaddie to the vet for a distemper shot and some worm medicine. He exclaimed, "Mein Gott! This is not a man, not a woman! For 27 years I have been a doctor and only once have I seen a dog like this. Bob was with me so the story got around and I never did live it down. From all I could tell, she looked like a female dog to me.

The afternoon that I "bought" Quaddie was the day of the Grand Council meeting so we stood around to watch the parade. I was disappointed in Marshal Zhukov. He was short and pudgy and not at all what you would expect a Russian general to look like. Mac took us upstairs to see the "spread" the Russians had ordered and it was spectacular! There was table after table with hors d'oevres, cakes, salads, fancy sandwiches, etc. Mac got us some black caviar and my reaction was "salty, isn't it?" I never could appreciate the big "to do" over caviar!

Paul Ruth was a camera bug. He had more equipment than most people—more junk that I couldn't begin to describe. He was always trying to get people to pose and was setting up lights and tripods. He sold Bob a very fine still projector, a movie projector, and a movie camera, and we began taking moving pictures then. There was such a wealth of scenery and interesting people. You could tell the Americans. They were always taking pictures.

That same Saturday of the Grand Council meeting the French members of the TSFC entertained the British and American members at their officers club, Le Pavillon. I was excited about going to the French Sector. There were 22 of us who had been invited. Dotty, Simone and I were the only females. I tried to rattle off my best French, which often caused looks of surprise, or peals of laughter. We had cherry wine before, during, and after the meal, and some other queer drinks I didn't much care for. The menu was:

Potage St. Germain
Hos d'oevres
Rote de Boef
Pommes Mousseline
Fromage
Dessert

The meal went on and on 'til midnight and there was dancing in between courses. I spent a lot of time trying the various yummy French pastries.

One of our group got tickets for "Hansel and Grettal" and handed them out to anyone of us who considered ourselves "cultured Americans". The scenery was very well-produced and we were mesmerized by the beautiful voices. Erna Berger was Grettal. It became my favorite of all of the operas we saw. Some of the songs were simple enough to get the gist of them and the music was so catchy that I could hum along with it.

One of the nice things to happen early in April was an order that came out giving each of us a flower ration and we began keeping our apartment full of flowers. The arrangements in the flower shop were gorgeous. Once I got a brown basket with moss in it and lilies of the valley, azaleas and cyclamen. It looked and, oh, it smelled so good! Another time, I got tulips in a variety of colors that brightened up our living room. The lilac bush in front of our apartment building was beginning to bloom. Berlin was beginning to look good. Foliage was bursting forth at a great rate. Something I noticed about the Germans was that all of them loved flowers. There was always a crowd around anyone selling flowers or plants on the street and even the poorest homes had a little bit of plant life in them. Their lives were so drab at that time that colorful flowers brought a little cheer into their lives. I wished I could have seen Berlin before the war. The trees were all old and enormous and almost every house was surrounded by shrubbery.

It was beginning to get so warm that a gang of us were brave enough to go swimming. We swam in a pool where the former SS Barracks had been. Someone said that it was the largest indoor pool in the world. I believed it. It was humongous. The Americans were calling it 'Madison Square Garden'. The water was nice and warm, but the building was not heated, so we did not remain heroic for very long. We went on to play some tennis. There weren't many tennis balls at Special Services and we had to wait our turn to get balls. I used to play a fair game, but I was rusty. Bob had played on his high school tennis team and he was a very good player. We played a lot after that day, both singles and doubles.

Bob was Duty Officer at Harnack House on a Saturday night. He had to stand in the lobby and check civilians for identification. Americans frequently tried to bring German girls into the club. We could always tell when an American girl's footlocker had arrived by the new creations she was wearing. Bob phoned me when he got home to give me a report. "It was a very eventful evening," he claimed. "You know that fifth step that has a piece missing?" "Yes". "Well, I counted 17 people trip over it."

CHAPTER SEVEN

In Bob's April letter to his Dad, he wrote: "Another angle is Pat. Unless I'm quite mistaken, she is the gal I'd like to marry some day, believe it or not. That may complicate things a little, but I don't think so. Won't do anything rash, so don't get excited will you Pop?"

Then, on May 12th, he wrote a letter to his father in New Jersey, "I have finally found a girl who really has me on the ropes. The other night I asked Pat to marry me and she accepted. She is the sweetest girl I have ever known and I'm extremely lucky that she'll have me. We have been together constantly since we met each other and we get along wonderfully with never a fight or argument. The gal is smart as a whip and always manages to charm everyone in her presence. We have talked things over and we have no doubt as to whether we're doing the right thing. I couldn't hope to do better and I'm lucky enough to realize it. We have tentatively set Pat's birthday, June 16th, to announce our engagement to the world."

Don obtained two bicycles from somewhere and they were kept in the garage at 15 Lanstrasse. We all took turns riding them. Bob and I rode a lot and it was hard to realize that we were riding through the streets where enemy armies had marched and where conquering armies had victoriously paraded.

They had a system there that we should have here in the U.S. All of the major thoroughfares had a bicycle lane on each side, which made it safe for cyclists.

We had a late dinner one night and sat around talking until quite late. One of the guys told a humorous story with the lights out and using a candle to make hideous faces. He tried blowing out the candle by screwing his mouth around in all directions except the right way to do it. He had us all in stitches. Suddenly, we realized it was terribly late—too late for Reggie to go all the way home to the British Sector. As there was no motor vehicle and only two bikes, Reggie and I started out for my apartment alone, although the others had misgivings. Being on bikes, it would only take a few minutes and we promised to call as soon as we reached our destination.

I had been to the PX that day and had all of my rations so I took the bike with the basket in front. There wasn't a moon or a star in the sky, but we set out bravely. About half way home, I got panicky, hit a huge bump in the road, and down I went, rations and all. I was all for getting back on the bike and high-tailing it, leaving rations behind. But Reggie, who knew the importance of the valuable rations better than I, made me stay until they were all picked up. The situation was so bizarre that we got the giggles and had to stand up and hold our sides

I had a pal at the office, Joe Liammari. He had joined our staff recently and he owned a small Volkswagon and I began riding to and from work with him. I loved those little arms on his car that popped out when you were turning right or left. Joe had a sense of humor and made our days at work fun and time went quickly. He and I made up a silly song about our office designation (TSFC). It was entitled "The Fighting Victory Song of The Technical Staff of The Fuel Committee". The words, which actually rhymed, were to the effect that "we work hard to keep you warm . . . . when you are cold, think of us slaving away", etc. We sang it every morning on the way to work at the top of our lungs.

"As for Bob", I wrote home on April 2nd before Bob asked me to marry him "it is nothing very serious, but we both like to do exactly the same things and I can honestly say that you would all like him very much. In fact, he reminds me of you, Dad—a sharp character. He even plays the piano the way you do—one finger."

We had never said a word about our future, or how we felt about each other, yet we saw each other every day and had become close friends. We went into a store, just browsing, and I saw a lovely set of Hungarian dessert dishes and he saw a set of cut glass crystal punch cups and he paid for both. Another time we bought a pewter tea set and a condiment dish that spun around and had sections in it. In a small art shop, Bob found a painting of two fig leaves hanging by clothespins on a clothesline. It was entitled "Adam and Eve". We had to have it. We bought a lot of things jointly, but hadn't discussed what we were going to do with them.

There was a chill wind blowing on the Sunday when Don, Reggie, Bob and I took a picnic lunch to a beach on Lake Wannsee, where the elite of Europe used to play. This was by far the prettiest part of Berlin. The silver birch trees and the sailboats on the water were a picturesque sight. We hiked around the lake, played touch football, and lounged on the spacious beach. Bob took some movies. We had our picnic in a large bomb crater and could look out onto the next hill and see where all the foxholes were. Bob said he doubted that there would be any swimming in the lake this summer because the water was so impure. We stopped at a German terrace café and ordered a soft drink. What was in it was hard to tell. One sip was enough. It was colored with a brilliant red powder and the color alone was not enticing. Later, we went to a movie at Onkel Tom's theater. I let Reggie wear my G.I. overcoat and I showed my pass as we went in (only those not in uniform had to show a pass),

Bob was given the assignment of naming a new mess hall that would be dedicated on Army Day. It was a tougher assignment than it first appeared to be. He began by trying to find out if any of the Berlin troops had died in glory. He discovered that there were only three American soldiers in the occupying forces of Berlin who had died. One had died of pneumonia, one had died while AWOL, and the third (Andrew Crump) had died while on his way home to the States.

Crump had left Berlin by train and, while the train stopped at a station, he decided to get off and look around. Unfortunately, the train went on without him. He hitch-hiked a ride in a truck, trying to catch up with the train. The truck had an accident and poor Crump was killed. It was thus that Bob came to name the enlisted men's new mess hall, and, on Army Day, the Commandant of Headquarters Command gave the dedication speech (written by Bob) for "Andrew Crump Mess Hall."

There was a British EM, a friend of the boys in my office, who used to come in and try to sell me stockings, which were otherwise very hard to obtain. He invited Bob and me to go with him one evening to the Marlboro Club. It was a British club where officers could not go alone without enlisted personnel and vice versa. He and Bob together qualified for entrance to the club.

The fellow was a member of the British Field Security Section (like our Counter-Intelligence Corps) and, before we went to dinner, he took us to their headquarters. He took us downstairs and showed us the cells where they kept the prisoners. He said that they would bring in Germans who knew something and, if they wouldn't talk, they would put them in a cell where the floor was covered with three inches of water down there. Families would come in and ask the whereabouts of relatives, little knowing they were down below. I couldn't help but think of the awful things that man does to man and how harsh people are in certain situations. It was depressing.

Dick Breeland brought a friend for dinner one night. Sandy was a little red-headed lieutenant and after that would tag along with our crowd often and added to our good times. He was quite a jitterbug and he and I worked out a new step we called "The Snizzle". It must not have been very good because no one took to it. Bob did try to 'one up' by saying that he was a whiz with the One Step.

Sandy had been to Switzerland and told us about the musical toilet rolls he had seen there. This made us all plan on Switzerland as our first trip out of the Russian Zone. Alas, Sandy was one of the first to leave for home and we were sorry to see him go.

In April, the TSFC moved out of the basement of the ACA Building to the first floor and we had much nicer offices. My boss and I had an office to ourselves. He could equal anyone when it came to swearing, but I liked him anyhow. At the next TSFC meeting, the committee took three hours just trying to interpret some instructions that had been passed down to it. They finally had to give up because the argument was mainly about the amount of coal certain industries were using and a feeling that some of it was being sold on the black market.

The male members of our crowd made arrangements to have a stag party at their house and that same night my office entertained the British members of the TSFC at Harnack House. I had a good time at our party and everyone was fun-loving and cordial. Even the old British colonel puffed his way out onto the dance floor and danced with me.

Apparently Bob's party was a huge success. It didn't break up until the wee hours of the morning. And one of the wives kept calling and a fraulein kept answering the phone. That husband was in the doghouse! One of the fellows who had planned the party had arranged to have dancing girls. The girls arrived, but the trouble was that all they would do was dance. A couple of wilder characters in the group, after many drinks, took a Jeep, drove downtown and picked up a whole bunch of frauleins. From reports, the girls were a ratty-looking bunch; and Bob was picked on by a tremendous giant, who got him cornered. Trying to make conversation, he asked her what she did for a living. She confidently told him that she worked in a sideshow and could hold three men on her shoulders. I guess she looked the part, as they called her "Muscles" and Bob was kidded about her for a long time.

Shortly before that, there was much excitement in the air as we learned that the first shipload of wives was about to arrive. Much preparations were in the making; some husbands had to stop seeing girls they had fallen in love with; and most of us were curious to see what certain wives were going to look like. I came home from a date and, as I entered our building, Lyn and Ross Stanley were sitting on the steps and both of them were crying. They had been dating steadily ever since her birthday party and she had been given the reporting assignment of going to Bremerhaven to interview wives as they were coming off the ship. She was going to see Ross' wife before he did. They knew their affair was over and both of them were miserable.

I had noticed one unhappy looking couple dancing at Harnack House recently, both with sad, serious faces. Later I heard that his wife was coming; his girlfriend was pregnant; and, later, she committed suicide. Another pair, who had been having fun together, had the wife join them and the three of them were seen everywhere together. I saw Ross' wife once. She was rather plain-looking and not at all like Lyn. She and Ross were watching a floor show at Harnack House. I noticed that she never clapped at all when others were enthusiastically appreciating the show. I wondered how much she knew about the affair.

Lyn didn't slow down much. She dated a variety of men. The rank meant nothing to her. One night, it was a buck private who was a boxer. One night, it was a Czechoslovakian general. I saw the love letters he wrote her and they were blistering!

Lent came and Mim gave up smoking. She was a Catholic and said she was allowed to smoke on Fridays, although I thought giving something up for Lent meant every day for six weeks. Fridays would come and she would puff like a steam engine. I gave her an unusual pink apron for a bet I lost to her and then said, "Oh my gosh, redheads don't usually wear pink, do they?" She said, "They certainly do! It's my favorite color!"

Easter was the most wonderful Easter I had ever had. A group of us went to Easter Sunrise Service held in the park across from Onkel Tom's. It was chilly and damp that morning, but with the sun coming up over the trees, it was very impressive. The

Easter breakfast at 15 Lanstrasse was lavish. Frau Schneider had made cookies for each of us with our names on them, and, in the center of the table, was an enormous cake with the words "Merry Easter" on it. You can bet we all raved about it and no one mentioned the error.

The house was full of flowers, the prize being a large, wicker duck filled with lovely pink blossoms. After breakfast, we went to the 11:00 service and Chaplain Weaver's sermon impressed us very much.

While we were at church, Reggie hid Easter eggs all around the back yard and we were like a bunch of little kids hunting for them. Margie, Reggie and I had had a swell time shopping for gifts the week before. Bob gave me a gorgeous, black suede evening bag with a gold design on it. I gave him champagne glasses monogrammed with an "M" in gold. Bob and Dick gave Margie and me corsages, but it hadn't occurred to Don to get flowers or a gift for Reggie. I knew she was hurt, especially since she had done such a splendid job of making it all so festive. We played poker in the afternoon, discovering that Reggie was quite a poker player. She had an intuition about cards and in all the various card games we played from time to time, she usually won.

We had Easter supper at Harnack House. The Sunday night suppers were really something because they were buffet style and you could go back as many times as you wanted to. They had cheeses and cold cuts and sumptuous salads. Bob gave me his paratrooper wings that night. It wasn't exactly romantic. We were standing in line to pay to get into the dining room. He slipped them to me and mentioned something about having an extra pair. I put them on immediately and neither of us said much. I guessed that we were "going steady". After supper we went to a play to see Lyn in "Heaven Can Wait". The play is very funny anyway, but, with Lyn in it, it was a riot! There was no end to her talents!

As Adjutant, Bob was in charge of liquor runs to Weisbaden to pick up the monthly supply of liquor for the Berlin clubs. His friends were always asking him to give them a run so they could get out of town for awhile and see the sights. It meant heading up a convoy of trucks and being gone for several days. Finally, he decided it would be a good idea for him to go himself.

The night before he left, he asked me to marry him. He said it had been in his thoughts for quite awhile; he loved me; and he knew we could be happy together. When we returned to the States, he would have to complete his unfinished college career, but we would have saved a good bit of money by then and the GI Bill would help to sustain us for that year and a half. I had wondered what I would do if he asked me but, even so, I suddenly froze up. Two girls I knew back home had gotten divorces and they had been messy and unpleasant. I couldn't envision that Bob and I would become unhappy with each other, but I needed a little time. I told him I would have an answer for him when he got back from his trip and that I knew I loved him, but I was skittish. It was April 25th and I wrote in my diary, "Bob and I have gone together for three months today. He wants me to marry him and I love him so much. What should I do?" Bob was 25 and I was 22.

While he was gone, an amusing thing happened. I took Quaddie to work with me and, at lunch time, left her in the courtyard. It was a small courtyard near my office that was never used. When Don Wilson (my boss) and I returned from lunch, Quaddie was nowhere to be seen, but there, in the same spot where I had left her, was a cat. Don threw back his head and laughed and, boy did that story get around!

I was very worried and called all of the MPs in the building to be on the lookout for her. At 5:00, time to go home, she still hadn't shown up. As we were waiting for the bus, Quaddie, after an afternoon of tearing around the ACA Building, grandly pranced down the main stairway and out the main entrance, where the MP promptly caught her and handed her over to me.

Margie and Don Ryan both had to go to Frankfurt and Dick went into the hospital with an infected throat. Reggie and I felt deserted. Paul Ruth had picked up a Scotty dog and called her Suzy. She was a mean, old thing and wouldn't let anyone but Reggie go near her. Reggie and I put the two dogs on leashes, took the two bikes and went for a long ride. When we brought the bikes back, we thought it would be a good idea to take a sun bath on the sun porch off Bob's bedroom. No one was home, so Reggie boosted me up to the first floor window and I broke in. She took a picture of me that Bob later said was excellent of me. It was a picture of the bottom of my feet as I was sliding in. We cooked dinner there that night, talked about Bob and Don and our deep feelings for them, but we weren't sure we were ready for marriage. After dinner, we went our separate ways.

Dick soon got out of the hospital. Bob, Margie and Don were due home in a couple of days so Dick, Reggie and I hustled around to make their homecoming a pleasant one. We moved a table out onto the sun porch and covered it with a white tablecloth. Dick had gotten hold of a fine wine, and we set the table with wine glasses. The sky was filled with glistening stars and, as we sat there, Dick told us all the stories he knew about the stars and about our missing friends. He was a spellbinding storyteller. We brought the table inside, Dick called for an open C&R for us and Reggie came home with me

Next evening, Dick and I had dinner together at Harnack House and afterwards sat and listened to the music. We talked about our futures and he said he thought Bob and I were perfect for each other. Around 9:00, he called home and Bob had just arrived a few minutes before. We dashed over there.

Bob came to the door and said, "hi". At first, it seemed as though we were strangers, or, at least, friends who had not seen each other for several years. But soon he was telling me about the trip and a great deal had happened to him. That night, neither of us brought up the subject of my promise to give him an answer to his marriage proposal.

In Frankfurt he had run into some old buddies and they had shown him around. They spent an evening at Kronberg Castle, which had become an American club. When he went to visit the wine cellar where he was to buy the champagne, he drove by the place several times before he realized there was any civilization there. There was a pile of rubble where a building once stood. As he got closer, he noticed a door going directly into the ground. The wine dealer had neither cases nor excelsior to use for packing the champagne bottles, but he told Bob that none of the bottles would break if they were laid on their sides and placed one on top of the other. Glass on glass will not break, the dealer explained to him. Bob was incredulous, but an officer, who was also in the place, said that he had done exactly that and none of his bottles had broken.

Before leaving Frankfurt, an officer offered Bob a deal whereby he could take a large number of cartons of PX cigarettes to Berlin, where they sold for the highest price, and he would split the profit with Bob. If Bob had accepted the offer (which he did not) he would have made more than $10,000. Deals like that were being made all of the time.

Near Kassel, in a deserted spot, one of the trucks broke down early in the evening. While the Jeep drove on to get help, a Yugoslav guard arrived on the scene and wanted to buy some champagne. He was persistent and would not take "no" for an answer. Bob sat up all night with a rifle on his lap guarding the truck. The road between Kassel and Berlin was known for being one of the bumpiest and torn up. Bridges were blown out and detours were made that went for as long as forty miles out of the way over rocks and piles of dirt. Yet the first champagne bottle to be broken was done so when the trucks were unloaded.

May 8th was VE Day and we spent it on the beach with Don, Reggie, Dick and Margie. We had a delicious picnic, fixed for us by Frau Schneider, and spent a lazy time just soaking in the sun. I was envious of the others as they all developed golden tans, while I remained as pale as before. Bob and I walked for a long way up and down the beach, not saying much. That night we went to Harnack House. I had been thinking a lot about what I was going to say and, walking back to his house, looking at him in the moonlight, I knew that no two people could possibly be happier than we were and were going to continue to be. I said, "Bob, I really want to marry you and live happily ever after." We stopped and it was a beautiful moment. We kissed and he said he loved me and I had made him the happiest man alive.

It was close to my birthday (June 16th) and we thought we could announce our engagement at the birthday party. I did tell Margie and she said that she and Dick were going to be married too. I felt sorry for her a couple of days later when she told me she has been premature in telling me as Dick wasn't sure.

May 12th was Mother's Day and I cabled my mother and Bob called his new mother. We had discussed waiting until we returned to the States before we married. Then it looked like Bob was going to be discharged from the service in September and he was offered the opportunity of a job paying $5,000 a year if we stayed. That would mean staying for another year. It seemed too good to pass up. With both of us working, we could save most of his salary and live on mine and, when we returned, we wouldn't be so pinched while he finished college. We didn't want to wait that long and, if we went home, there was no easy way to return to Germany.

Something I had always looked forward to was the day my Dad would give me away and my mother and Goggy would have such fun helping me with my plans. I knew what a bitter disappointment it would be to them if we went ahead. I was wracked with guilt. It seemed selfish to rob our parents of their participation in our wedding. I was the only daughter and my mother would never have that activity to tell her friends about.

13 or 14 months, however, was so far away! If we married in Berlin, we would have such a good start financially. We would have our own house and housefrau to cook and clean. Also, by staying there were so many sights and places to travel and we wanted to see them all together. We could have a large wedding with all the trimmings for much, much less than the cost in the States, and a honeymoon in a romantic place would cost hardly anything. There was no way our families could travel to Germany at that time, so that was out.

We talked about it with others and most of them thought it was so natural for Bob and me to be together that it seemed wrong to wait. My father was happy about it and told us to go ahead. He had a cousin who had never married, always lived alone, and became odd in later years and he was afraid that would happen to me (such confidence!) My mother and Goggy told us to do what we thought best and they would do everything they could from the other side.

There were two German girls in my office I particularly liked to talk to. One of them, Alice, was the one whose baby son had died and her parents killed. She told me that both brothers, soldiers, had been killed too. She was short and chubby, not very pretty, but had soft, springy dark curls. It was hard to believe that she could be so cheerful. She had grown up on a farm and she recalled to me lying in bed with her hands over her ears every time she heard the squealing when they butchered a pig. At Easter she gave me a handkerchief and some flowers. She was living with a family who had a six-yearold boy who was not well. I sent him some candy once and her mother immediately sent me some fragrant, lavender lilacs. I sent things to him several times and Alice said that he wanted to give me one of his toys. When Alice told him I was a big girl, he wanted to go shopping and he picked out a set of tiny, glass ducks. I have always kept those ducks on my whatnot shelf—right out in front.

Ingrid was the draftswoman. She was a big girl with red hair and a pleasing manner. Before it started turning warm, she invited me to come to her home and I was pleased to accept. I stayed about two hours and enjoyed myself very much. Her uncle, grandmother, and two sisters were there. We talked, although Ingrid was the only one who spoke English; listened to records; and drank tea with crackers. Their apartment was nice, but we had to sit there with our coats on. The Germans were only given two lumps of coal to burn each day. Ingrid told me that her father had been in a concentration camp and, at present, was in Belgium, but it was impossible for them to visit each other.

We were continually getting a kick out of some of Don's shenanigans. At a Sunday meal at their billet, we were all gorging ourselves when Bob asked Don if he would like to have some more meat. "No thanks. I've never cared much for pork," he answered. "Don, this is not pork, it's beef," we all chimed in. "Oh, actually I did think it tasted pretty good. Thanks. I'll have another helping." We rolled our eyes.

Another time we were all fixing ourselves sandwiches and Don asked Reggie to fix him one. "Don", she said, "Everyone is making his own. All of the ingredients are right there. Help yourself to a plate and you can put everything on it if you want." No, Don wanted her to make him one. She had already made hers and was seated in the other room, but she got up in a huff and hurriedly made one and handed it to him. "There!" He sat there looking at it. "Aren't you going to eat it?" we all sat there breathlessly. "No." "Why?" "Because it wasn't made with love!" That line was used often by all of us anytime it would fit in.

Reggie went home after our supper and Don and I went with Bob to his room for an afterdinner drink. Don was carefully examining the pistol that Bob had found when suddenly there was a loud bang. The gun had gone off and the bullet went through the open door to the sun porch. We were so startled, we froze for a full minute and then Don rushed out into the street to see if he had hit anyone or done any damage. He didn't find any harm and came in feeling dejected and downhearted. He had examined the barrel and saw no bullet in it.

This was the second gun incident since my arrival Bob and I had gone to a house party and were told to go upstairs to leave our coats. On the bedside table was a pistol. Bob picked it up, looked to see if it was loaded, and must have touched the trigger because there was a horrible explosion with a resulting hole in the wall, surrounded by fallen plaster. It was a boisterous party and no one heard the noise of the shot. We went downstairs and told the host and he shrugged it off. We were living in properties that had some kind of damage and it was no big deal, except to Bob, who felt very sheepish. He and Don had had rifle training in the Army, of course, with medals to prove it. It gave me my first belief that even though people feel safe with guns, they are better off without them.

Russia was certainly doing everything it could to make communists out of the Germans. On May Day (their Communist Party Day), they made every German working for them march in a parade. If they refused, they didn't get their pay. An amusing incident concerning a Russian, though, occurred at a wedding we attended. An American colonel on one of the higher echelon committees was the groom and that meant that his Russian counterpart could attend and bring other Russian members. When the champagne was poured, the Russian colonel stood up, raised his glass and proposed a toast. When it was translated, it was, "Death to all bachelors!"

We girls decided that our apartment could stand a little interior decorating. We called the engineers and they sent out some workmen. They started by painting Lyn's and my room a pale blue, which we liked. Quaddie had a big time. She loved to get in the plaster and then jump all over us! Mim's room was painted with green and white stripes. The first morning she got up, she thought she was in jail and she had them come back immediately and change the color.

My housemates were thrilled with my news. All along they had been telling me that they thought Bob was pretty sharp (as if I needed anyone to tell me!) Bob had gotten a new housemate a month earlier. There was a front bedroom that was very nice, but the occupant had to go through Bob's room to get to it. The new man walked up to Bob, but instead of introducing himself to Bob, he said, "Do you mind if I have frauleins in my room?" His name was Dave Chachavadze and he was a Russian prince, but was working for the Americans as a civilian. He was a character, but a lovable one and we came to like him very much. Before Bob asked me to marry him, Dave told me "Bob is a very foolish fellow if he does not ask you to marry him." No wonder I always thought highly of Dave.

CHAPTER EIGHT

On May 27th, Bob and I spent a quiet evening at 15 Lanstrasse writing our first letters to each other's families. I wondered what I could say that would be appropriate and that would make me seem closer to them. I had heard a lot about Bob's family. He had a half-brother and half-sister, 14 and 11 years older than he and three nieces. I closed my letter by saying, "I just wanted you to know how happy I am and, from all Bob has told me, I know I am going to love you all as I do my own family." Bob wrote, "Pat and I have been inseparable since the day we met back in January. Every evening and every weekend we spend together, whether it is a dance or an evening at home writing letters. We get along wonderfully together and neither of us would think of going anywhere or doing anything without the other."

The next week we received cables from both families saying that they were very pleased and very happy for us. I got a letter from my kid brother, still in the Marines at Camp Pendleton. He wrote, "Hi beautiful! How does it feel to be engaged? Yesterday was really a big day for the Williams clan. It's not every day we get some sucker to give the smallest member of the family a ring. I hope the poor guy knows what he is getting into. Gee, kid, I certainly wish you all the happiness in the world."

Bob had been looking for a job in which he could civilianize when the time came. He found one, which he could transfer to soon. He accepted. It would be with the Prisoner of War and Displaced Persons Division and he would be the assistant to the head of the division. It was the function of this office to supervise the repatriation of United Nations prisoners of war, as well as the disposition and return of displaced persons and refugees. It was also concerned with the tracing of United Nations missing persons. Every place we went, we saw people in black uniforms, the displaced persons who had been brought from other countries to work for the Nazis. The task before this division was overwhelming. By the time Bob became a civilian, the job would be paying a sum that seemed large to us and we figured we could save a bundle in a years time. If only we had known then that there was a law in Virginia that taxed both your income and your money in the bank. When we, in our innocence, returned to live in Virginia, we were double-taxed!

Later, when he was discharged, we got a chuckle about a document typed up by a German typist. Instead of "The civilianization of Lieutenant Robert C. McMann", it read "The civilization of Lieutenant Robert C. McMann"!

John had been dating the cutest, prettiest, petite French girl. She had lovely dark hair in one of those big French hairdos and she wore the uniform of French

Social Services. He met her when the Jeep she was riding in had a flat tire. The MPs were called. John arrived on the scene and took it from there.

Josette had a little round face, enormous brown eyes, and her hair was done with a pompadour in front. She had the smile of a cherub and wore a most innocent expression on her face at all times. She really and truly was doll-like. She would look up at John, wrinkle her nose and say, "Johnny" and coo in her French accent and John was a goner.

Dick was getting ready to return to the States, but he promised to take us sailing before he left. On a lovely, elegant, warm Sunday in late May he requisitioned a sailboat. He no longer had the use of the one he had thought he owned. Ten of us were going: Mim and Ted, Dick and Margie, John and Josette, Bob and I, and Major Keyes and his wife. The latter was head of the Commissary and he brought along some big sandwiches, pickles, fruit and other things that make up a delicious picnic. We were going to eat on the boat. I had never sailed before, but Dick was a seasoned sailor so there was nothing to worry about. We arrived at the Anchor Club and I had my faithful Brownie and got some good shots of the group before we set sail.

There was a goodly breeze blowing out on Lake Wannsee and we agreed that it would make for an eventful ride as we climbed onto the boat. We had bathing suits on under our slacks and the temperature was just right for a suntan. As we started towards the middle of the lake, it seemed like a perfect day. The breeze got stronger as we went along and the old boat rocked and rolled from one side way over to the other and back again. It was hard to relax and I began to wonder if the whole afternoon was going to be like this.

There were several Germans swimming that day and we noticed one about 200 yards from us with his arm up in the air. Then suddenly we thought we heard him yelling "Help! Help!" He appeared to be in trouble and Dick started to turn the boat around to go to him. As he did so, I felt a swish and then cold water all around me. The boat had gone completely over on its side. I had been sitting on the edge of the boat and was right under the sail. I swam under water until I thought I was clear and came up several feet away.

As I came up, there was a frantic counting of noses. Bob had been standing next to the sail and had had a struggle getting free from the ropes. Eight of us had been spilled into the water, but Mim and Josette did not know how to swim and had stayed with the boat. They were half in and half out of the water. They were as frightened as they will ever hope to be.

The door to the cabin had been open and Bob dived down and rescued some of our belongings from there. It wasn't long before help arrived to pick us up, but it was two hours before they pulled the boat to shore. We stood around waiting for it and the sun went behind clouds and it was beginning to get cold. All we had on then were our wet bathing suits as we huddled together shivering. We were thinking of those beautiful sandwiches and pickles floating around out in the middle of the lake. My Brownie was completely ruined. My purse was water-soaked, but the first thing I looked for was my watch, which had been a graduation present from my parents. It was a plain old Bulova, but it continued to run and keep proper time for several years. I opened my wallet to look at my identification papers and the only one that I would have to replace was my PX card. We never found out what happened to the German who had been shouting and the result of that afternoon was that I never cared much for sailing.

We had a party for Dick Breeland on May 30th and, on May 31st, he departed for the States. We were sorry to see him go, but he promised to return soon. He was to be discharged from the service and then would return to OMGUS as a civilian. He parted with the words, "I call our group 'The Beautiful People' so you know I shall return. Don't you dare have the wedding without me as I want to be a part of it." I gave him my family's address in Arlington and he said he would look them up. He did and they were impressed with him and eager to hear recent news first-hand.

Dick never returned and we lost contact with him for awhile. Years later, we did see him and learned some things about him we had not known. He was raised by his grandmother and his parents lived across the street. They were so in love with each other that they hadn't much time for their little boy. He used to cross the street at night and sit on their porch and listen to his father read to his mother. When he heard, "Nell . . . . Nell . . . . Are you asleep?", he would silently slip off the porch and go home. Then, when his father died, Nell became very attached and possessive of Dick. She had talked him out of going back and marrying Margie. He never did marry. He did become a state senator in South Carolina and people called him a "Nigger lover" because he backed civil rights legislation. He would say, "I don't love 'em, but I don't hate 'em.", which was a courageous stance back in those days.

We only saw him once or twice in Washington. His mother was coming to visit him and I invited him to bring his mother for dinner. He said, "Oh no. When Mother and I get together, we talk way into the night." I could see his need for his mother's approval and attention and now he definitely had it. Sadly, Dick in later years became blind and he and his little dog that he loved so much died in a house fire.

Right after Dick left, I came home from work to find the housefrau crying and Lyn was getting her some tea to drink. The fireman was there and they all had long looks on their faces. Lyn explained that the housefrau had been walking Quaddie when the puppy suddenly pulled loose from her and dashed away—leash and all. She had hunted all afternoon, but still no Quaddie.

I immediately called John and asked him to have the MPs on the lookout for her. For days I went around everywhere looking, but she never showed up. About that time a lot of dog meat was being sold to the Germans and some believed she had been caught by such people, but there wasn't enough meat on her to fill a thimble. Most everyone, except Lyn and Reggie, were tickled to death and let me know I was better off. They all wondered who could want it.

I suspected the maid and fireman of a deliberate conspiracy to lose her. I couldn't see that Quaddie had the strength to pull away and, even if she had, I doubted she would run away. I had no grounds to go on but she did seem genuinely sad about it. Maybe they sold her. I could see that it had been a nuisance for her to walk the dog and to bring scraps from the mess hall every day. I was devastated, though, as she was always so glad to see me when I came home each day, and I loved that funny little face and yip she had when she saw me.

One thing I had to say about the Germans was that they were very polite and thoughtful. Every time I turned around, I saw some shaking hands. The little boys tipped their caps and the little girls curtseyed. Birthdays, Easter, and other special days, meant a great deal to them. There were two little boys always playing on Herrfurthstrasse when I came home. They used to bring me roses. They would come up to my apartment and bang around on the piano and I would give them candy and cookies and sometimes food to take home. They were Francisca and Gerhardt Muller.

Mim and I awakened one morning to discover that Lyn had not come home at all. We weren't too alarmed because, transportation being what it was, she had occasionally stayed with a friend on the other side of town. We went to work and didn't think too much about it. She didn't come home the second night, though, and Mim and I worried about it over a piece of toast and a cup of Nescafe. I said I would call her at her office, which I did. They had not received any word of her. I called everyone we knew mutually, including the friend she often stayed with and there was no trace.

Lyn had not been too well lately and I was beginning to get scared. We checked hospitals to no avail. The last I had seen of her had been the morning before she disappeared. It had been a Sunday and she said she was going to go to a party that night. She left with a bottle of liquor and some food for the party but I couldn't remember who was giving it. Finally, someone was able to tell me whose party it was. I didn't know the people, but I called and Lyn had never arrived at the house.

That night, Mim, Bob and I were reluctant to call the CID (Central Intelligence Division) because we didn't want to get her in trouble, but we agreed that since she hadn't phoned us something must be wrong. No American girls had been harmed in Berlin, but we were fearful. A CID man arrived and went through all of her things. We found a picture of a guy I'd never seen and a love note signed "Arthur". We had to sit down and each of us write a report. Mim and I became so scared that she came in my room and we slept with the light on.

Lyn came in the next day looking not too well. She said she had fainted on the U-Bahn and a German man revived her and helped her off. They were near the home of a girl Lyn knew and the German helped her to the house. Lyn said she had been too sick to call and the girl had tried, but had been unable to reach us. She was angry at first that we had called the CID, but then realized it had been our only course. We were pretty relieved to have her back.

Lyn, in her charming way, soon was dating the CID man and I don't think a report ever went on her official record. She did have a way with men. I never saw anyone with such a variety of admirers, and she was completely uninhibited. Once she came home with a colonel after they had been to a movie. Ted and Mim were in the living room and the four of us sat and chatted for a few minutes. Lyn disappeared and returned in her pajamas and robe, yawning. "Please excuse me, but I suddenly got very sleepy. Goodnight." Exit! It didn't slow down their friendship, as he kept coming back. Lyn had a heart of gold and kept our lives interesting.

Many years later, Mim and I got together. She said, "Remember that time Lyn mysteriously disappeared? I know what actually happened to her." "I know", I said, "she fainted on the U-Bahn and was too ill to call us." "Wrong! Lyn had an abortion." I was stunned. That had never occurred to me.

CHAPTER NINE

My birthday, June 16'" was approaching and Bob was planning a big party at his house to include all of our friends. We would announce our engagement at the party. I received a most welcome birthday box from home. I opened it at the office and a bunch of people gathered around and were as excited about it as I was. There was a cute doll to hang on the wall, cookies, several cans of canned milk (a big treat, which disappeared rapidly as milk was scarce), lovely black, dressy gloves, pretty underwear, and a pink jersey blouse and black skirt. I wore that outfit to my party,

My birthday really began on Saturday, June 15th, when the TSFC gave me a luncheon at the ACA Building. All of the French, British and Americans were there, as well as some of the Russians. They seldom came to any kind of a social event unless their commanding officer was there. Bob and Don Ryan had also been invited. We had cocktails beforehand and the Russians insisted on a Moscow cocktail. We were all aware that when the Russians entertained, a drink glass never remained empty and. although they were not the hosts today, they did a good job of refilling our glasses.

After the delightful luncheon, there was an elaborate birthday cake. I remember clearly the little Russian, Malcumov, who looked like a monkey and whom I had never seen smile, saying, "We must allocate the cake evenly." As we had been having such difficulty with coal allocations, this humorous remark coming from him made us all smile.

My boss, Don Wilson, gave me an enormous box of Whitman's Chocolates; two German girls gave me roses and another one gave me daisies. My housefrau and Bob' s housefrau, Frau Schneider, gave me roses.

I was inundated with flowers and I loved it! One note read, "Congratulations and all good for your engagement." I was deeply touched.

Bob outdid himself with party plans. We had a string quartet, food, drinks, flowers everywhere. and a big sign, "Bob and Pat Are Going To Be Married". Twenty people attended and we told them what they already knew. They pretended to be surprised, but, actually, they had known we would become betrothed before we did.

Bob had given me my ring that afternoon and I was as proud as a peacock. I kept looking at it until my friends said. "It's going to put your eye out". It had a Tiffany setting, except that the gold pan of the ring came up high on either side of the diamond. There was a lot of fire in it and a design in the ring part. He had gotten it on the black market and there was a teensy, flaw in the stone. To my eyes, I had never seen such a valuable jewel! He said I could get a better one later, but that idea never entered my mind. I wore it until years later when I was washing our dog and it slipped off my finger without my knowledge into a bucket of soapy water. Although I searched and searched for it after I emptied the pail. It was never found.

When he gave me the ring, we both said our love would be forever. We jokingly rigged up and signed a fake document that committed us to seventy-five years of marriage, after which we were entitled to go our separate ways! This agreement came in handy when, after an argument, we would say, "only sixty-five more years to go (or whatever year it was) and then we would have to laugh

The party began at 6:00 and at 8:00 we had a regular feast: beef, carrots, lima beans, noodle ring, plus several other appetizing dishes, and topped off with ice cream. We were so full that we couldn't eat any of the birthday cake, which had "Happy Birthday Par' and pink rosebuds decorating the white icing. Frau Schneider had made me another cake with two rings intertwined on top of it.

I received numerous gifts. Bob gave me a set of dishes, service for twelve. The plates were white china, with tiny blue and pink forget-me-nets as the design. Some of the pieces were odd. There was a soup tureen; egg cups; and tiny, individual butter dishes. All of the vegetable bowls were covered and, there were a few tiny gravy boats for sauces and condiments. He also gave me a set of water glasses, a set of alpaca tableware (service for eight), and a darling little clock that hangs on the wall.

Other gifts I received were: cut glass liqueur glasses and jug, silver pin and bracelet, gold bracelet, wristwatch, and cute ashtrays. I got a compact, two Rosenthal vases, perfume, silver coffee service, cigarette box, coaster set with little birds on them, and, almost best of all, a pair of nylons! I was so overwhelmed that I was literally speechless. How did I deserve all of this and to be so happy! I have a picture of me surrounded by friends showing off my ring and, in the background, is the wallpaper with the big flower designs that was in all of the finer homes.

The Saturday after my party, we went to a wedding at the Ernst Moritz Arndt Church at Onkel Tom' s, the church where we would be married. The couple was Gus and Olga Guston. Gus had come overseas with Bob, had been a paratrooper, and Olga was an American civilian with OMGUS. She worked for the Payroll Office and her boss had told her that she had to be married right after a pay period so she would be back in time for the next one. They were planning on a Swiss honeymoon.

Years later, Gus was called back in service for the Korean War. A letter I wrote to him over there came back marked "Deceased". He had been killed in action and Olga was a widow with two little boys. Gus was the first person I knew to be killed at war as my relatives and acquaintances had all survived WWII. I was overcome with sadness because I had liked both of them so much and it was so unfair.

We had been very surprised when, on my birthday, John told us that he and Josette were planning marriage also. They had only known each other a little over a month then and they thought August would be a great month. Josette was learning English, but when she spoke, the words came out so rapidly that it was difficult to understand her. As we began associating with them, we could learn from her facial expressions what she meant. They were both young, though and impulsive. John often tried to do the same things that Bob did and Bob had gotten him out of trouble a few times before. We were very happy for them anyhow, and no wonder! Their faces just beamed!

They approached us at the end of June and thought it would be a lark if we had a double wedding in August. It seemed like a tremendous idea. We were already talking about an August wedding and were in the process of collecting information on how to proceed.

There wasn't anyone to tell us how wording should be on a double wedding invitation. They would have to be in French, as well as in English. Together, we chose Chaplain Captain Arthur Weaver to marry us. He was a smiling, kindly, fatherly man and we admired him. He counseled us and the best piece of advice he gave us was, "In an argument, the person who knows he or she is right should be the one to make up". He told us that, in a double wedding, the brides were each other' s maids of'honor. I chose Lyn for my attendant and Josette picked Reggie. Don was to be Bob's groomsman and John's MP pal, Ruick Rolland, would be his.

Chaplain Weaver served us tea and sandwiches and told us that the most important things to be in complete agreement on were finance, our attitudes concerning each other's families, the planning of our family to come, and religion. We felt very good when we left his home as all of the thing s he stressed, we had already discussed and had agreed on.

Bob gave me 15 yards of parachute material. Reggie knew a dressmaker named Minnie and she, Lyn and I visited her. She made me a beautiful wedding dress from that material, unlike any I have seen before or since. For the two bridesmaids, we obtained some aqua material. I think it had rayon in it, but it draped nicely and they, with their enviable figures, looked great in them. It was a bit shocking for the time, but the front of those dresses were open to the waist and clasped together mid-way with a large brooch. I asked Mother to send me some white slippers as there was nowhere to get anything like that. Minnie was such a whiz; she made me several dresses after that. All I had to do was bring some material and a picture.

We set a date for August 25" and made arrangements for the church at Onkel Tom' s and for a reception at Harnack House. The latter was John's present to us. The florist shop promised the flowers we wanted and I had asked for white roses. Bob and I settled on Paris and the French Riviera for our honeymoon. He would be discharging from the Army when we returned, but would still be in the Anny for our honeymoon so our train rides would be free and hotel rooms and meals at the rate for service personnel. At that time, service people could ride trains for free throughout most of Europe.

For much of that summer, there were phone calls and problems that arose and more phone calls. Josette learned that the "Alien Marriage Law" called for a long wait before Americans could marry someone from another country. We held our breath, but it worked out so that we could proceed. We attended a meeting to learn the procedure and paperwork. for exiting Berlin through the Russian Zone. There was a large audience and ever since that meeting. I've been reluctant to ask questions in a large group for fear of sounding foolish as one girl did when she asked, "What if you don't want to leave Berlin on your time off?"

At this time, we were all very excited for Reggie. She had applied to work for UNRRA (United Nations Relief and Rehabilitation) and passed their examination. This would mean that she could work in the same kind of uniform that American civilians wore, with a different colored epaulet, and she could have PX and mess privileges. She would be able to go to the movies with us and to the officers clubs. This would be perfectly wonderful to have her included in our group everywhere we went. Just as her hopes were at the very highest, she found out that she would have to go back to Belgium on the quota in August. We were all terribly disappointed about this; however, she was able to delay her departure date until after our wedding.

On a windy Sunday, we went to a German fair in the British Sector. Reggie told us that the newspaper accounts were excellent, so she and Bob and I decided to go. Paul Ruth came along, too, because he wanted to take pictures. The fair consisted of a two hour show of tight-wire artists. Imagine a girl riding a motorcycle up a 250 yard cable to a tower 100 ft. high! Another girl walked up it, taking 15 minutes to do so. She had a long, balancing pole that must have been 12 ft. long and weighed about 20 lbs. She would walk a few feet and then kneel on one knee and rest for a minute before going on. It was quite a feat.

One of the most astonishing acts was a seven-man pyramid on a wire 40 yards above ground. There was no net underneath them! I still can't believe what I saw. There were throwing games with little pieces of paper for prizes. I didn't play, so I don't know what was on them. The only refreshment was German beer and, as the man said, the beer tasted like tap water. We didn't know what time it was so I asked two German cops. Paul caught my picture with them and entitled it "Fraternization".

Bob's new job started on Monday, June 24th with the Prisoner of War and Displaced Persons Division. He would work there as an Army officer until his discharge in September and then start at his higher pay as a civilian. Right away he had to visit camps throughout the American Zone and it sickened him to see how emaciated the German prisoners returning from Russia were. The top man in the division was Col Harry Messer and Bob was his assistant. Harry's secretary was a beautiful redhead, Mary Tate. Harry invited us for dinner at his house one night. When no one answered the door, we walked in and found them kissing in front of the fireplace. It wasn't long after that that we attended their wedding. When we later returned to the States, we became friends with Mary's brother and his wife.

I had a letter from a British boy who had been in my office and gone back to England. He was apparently enjoying himself in London as a "civvy" for the first time in eight years. He wrote that he wanted to ask me a "wee favor". He had a girlfriend who was in need of" something very important to a young lady, namely nylon stockings ", he said. She was soon to make a trip to Ireland and thought that, in exchange, I might like some Irish linen or lace.

This seemed like a wonderful exchange. Ladies stockings were hard to come by. My rations at the PX were for rayon stockings and I sometimes wore them with runs in them until it was time for my next allotment. Those of us who were lucky to have someone at home got an occasional pair of nylons from them, but they had trouble finding any and had to stand in line when they did. I gave up a pair of nylons I was saving and mailed them to the British boy, but, alas, I never saw the linen or lace.

The OMGUS swimming pool opened and we spent a good deal of time there. It was a very small pool in back of Harnack House, but it was a good place to cool off, then lie in the sun, only to get hot all over again. Reggie found a place where we could get bathing suits. She bought an attractive one and I found a print in a latex material that suited me fine. When I put it on, it fit perfectly. Everyone said it looked like it was made for me.

I made my debut in it at the OMGUS pool and felt proud to be seen in a suit that fit me so well. It was especially hot that day and I was anxious to get in the water. I beat the others to the side and dove in. The instant I hit the water, I felt a terrific pull. My gorgeous suit bagged down to my knees and the top was stretched to my waist. I was horrified! It was a few seconds before I came up. gasping and clutching and holding myself together. I looked like one deflated balloon. It was most embarrassing! Later, I did realize what an amusing sight I must have been and, after I was through feeling like crying, I had to laugh with the others who were holding their sides and guffawing. It never pays to be vain!

There was an unforgettable night at the pool. It was one of those nights that made you feel tired and dragged out. Not a breath of air stirred anywhere and, although it was getting dark. it still seemed that the sun's rays were directly on us. We gathered at the Marine Room. It was a brand new addition to Harnack House and was extremely modem. All around the room were huge tanks with brightly-colored fish in them. It made us feel like we were in a ritzy New York nightclub. Margie was there and Paul Ruth and Ruick Rolland, John's MP buddy, joined us later.

Even in the Marine Room, we drooped over highballs, until someone got the bright idea of going swimming in the OMGUS pool. We paid our bill, dashed out and loaded into Ruick's MP Jeep. We drove around to our various pads and got our suits, picked up Don and Reggie and headed for the pool. By the time we arrived, it was midnight and was beginning to get cool. We lined up at the edge, gently dipping our big toes in the water. Brr! Cold water! After a long discussion, Paul leaped in and we had no obvious alternative but to do the same thing. Wow! It was cold! In a few minutes we warmed up and were having the time of our lives.

All good things must come to an end. Before too long, a couple of MP Jeeps drove up and flashlights were flashing out onto the water. Guess who it was! One of them was John and, boy, was John mad! A call had come in that a noisy group of people were swimming in the nude in the pool. The caller said they were all drunk and had been swimming there every night without suits. That shows you how stories grow.

Margie, Reggie and I huddled together in the back of John's Jeep while the guys gave a "logical" explanation. John took us home and, afterwards, we decided that he was mad because he hadn't been in on the fun.

I answered the phone at work one day and Bob asked me, "How would you like to be a bride tomorrow?" I said, "I think you just asked me to be a bride tomorrow? What is this all about?" He went on to explain that Mac was to be married the next day. Mac had gone with a cute little gal named Ginny for a long time before he had come overseas. Now they wanted to be married, but the trouble was that she was in California and he was in Berlin and he wasn't ready to be discharged for a while. He couldn't get her to Germany because they weren't married. They had concluded that the only solution was to be married by proxy. Two weeks earlier Ginny had stood up before a Justice of the Peace and had signed her marriage papers. Now it was Mac's turn to do the same in Berlin and he needed a proxy bride.

We stood in the bar lounge of the ACA Building. Glasses were clicking all around us. We got Ginny on the phone (in Los Angeles) and Colonel Gerhardt married them. We signed papers and it was a done deal. They were legally married.

CHAPTER TEN

My Aunt Rena sent me an expensive pearl necklace as an engagement present. I was so wrapped up in all the activities that I didn't write her right away. My mother, in her letter, rebuked me, "You are looking at the world through rose-colored glasses. Stop and do what you should to show your appreciation to someone who has done something nice for you." I was ashamed and my mother was right to make me think beyond my own plans. I sat right down and told Aunt Rena how lucky I was to have such a thoughtful aunt and that I would always cherish the necklace.

I had always thought golf to be a rather foolish sport for older people. I enjoyed almost all sports, but set golf aside for the previous generation. Bob played a good game and he attempted to get me interested. There was a very good course in the American Sector. I believe it was the only course in operation in all of the city, but only Americans could play there, so it was never crowded. It covered a lot of territory, was hilly, had a great many sand traps, and there were several wooded valleys to shoot over. In other words, it was difficult.

Bob took me out there on a fine, early morning and, after a short practice, we went around the first nine. Needless to say, I did badly. My feet hurt and I was dragging. Back we went the next week. I could see already the improvement I was making and I really enjoyed going around that time. From then on, I was a "golfer". I loved the game and we played as often as we could with whomever wanted to play.

The original clubhouse had been bombed out and a small building served as a locker room. We could rent clubs and balls there. The following year they put up a larger, temporary building, in which there was a snack bar, and we would sit down to a delicious sundae after playing a round. An interesting thing about those links was that on the fourth hole, there was an additional obstruction. It was an American tank. Once Don lost a ball under there and I wondered how many other balls had rolled beneath it before. I also wondered what had become of the soldiers who had been in that tank.

There was always a group of young German boys hanging around the clubhouse. These were the caddies and they carried your clubs for a few marks, cigarettes, or whatever you wished to give them. Most of them were cute, dirty, little fellows, so eager to help and I felt sorry for them. At that, they were better off than most of the German youth because they had plenty of sunshine and probably enough to eat.

Bob and Don played on a softball team. Bob played third base and Don was in left field. The games started early in the evenings. Reggie and I would do something together and then have dinner ready for the boys when they came home around 8:30. We used to kid them a lot and tell them, "Don't come home unless you win." We felt like 15 Lanstrasse belonged to us as well as to them, although we always went back to our own pads no matter how late. They would come in and either their faces would be beaming, or they would say, "We had a good time anyhow."

Sometimes we would go to the games and they were really hot! Margie came once and she and I umpired that game as none of the umps had shown up. Margie was base umpire and I called the balls and strikes. I got a little confused when a guy on the other team accused our pitcher of a "balk". I had no idea what a balk was, but a short conference settled the matter. We were very strict with our calls so it was no thanks to us that our boys won by a big margin, although the other guys grumbled about us being prejudiced.

The Fourth of July was undoubtedly the hottest day of the year. There had been very few uncomfortable days, but this one was unbearable. Bob and I went swimming in the morning and, after lunch, met John and Josette. We drove around in John's jeep, taking pictures and looking in quaint little shops. Then we drove to the French Sector to Lake Tegelsee. We had a snack there on a terrace overlooking the lake. There were little tables with red-checked tablecloths and it was a picturesque scene.

Josette got two little kayaks and fishing poles and we set out to try our luck. They got four five-inchers, but Bob and I did not have the proper technique. Our score was zero, but it was cool out on the lake and fun to just loaf around.

Josette took us to her mess hall. It was an amazing and delicious meal. In keeping with French customs, we had two kinds of wine and champagne. First, we had thick vegetable soup and next came tiny fish with sauce. The third course was crayfish and, gosh, what a time I had! Josette just picked them up and ate them. Bob, John and I had them all over ourselves, and the table, and the floor. I must say that the small amount we were able to put in our mouths was scrumptious. Next came steak and fresh peas. What a pig I made of myself! They were the first peas I had had in Berlin and, being my favorite vegetable, I had four helpings. Then came cherries, gooseberries, and figs; and, after that, coffee and brandy. We weren't able to move for some time afterwards, but finally found our way to the Council de Guerre Club. It was high on a hill, with a tiny path winding around up to it and lanterns lighting the way. It was a wonderful ending to a wonderful Fourth of July.

The strange thing about the summer nights in Berlin, was that it stayed light much longer than it did back home. I didn't think of Berlin being that far north, but it didn't get dark until 11:00 p.m. I remember reading outside at 10:45. That second summer, when we had double daylight saving time, it was light until almost midnight. The change was put into effect to conserve electricity.

Bob was pretty busy these days. Between trying to push his Army discharge, getting our home fixed up, learning a new job, planning for the wedding and subsequent honeymoon, investigating a reserve commission, starting a new bank account, changing insurance beneficiaries, and converting his to civilian insurance, he began to feel as though he didn't have enough time to get it all done. Don and John weren't much help and John was coming to him with more problems. I was pretty busy, too, because of Josette's language barrier; most wedding plans were left up to me.

Along about this time, I received word from home that my little dog, Bruce, had died. Bruce was a short, black and white mongrel, very loyal, very faithful, and he had been mine for 13 years. He had been suffering from asthma and had been taking digitalis pills for his heart for a couple of years. His coughing had become so bad that Goggy had had to take him to the vet and she held him when he was put to sleep. It was very hard for her when he looked up at her with that pitiful look at the end. I felt pretty miserable for a while. I had suspected when I left home that I might never see him again because of his age, but I kept hoping he would make it until I returned. My lovable, little Bruce was gone!

Other news from home was that my brother, Stan, was home from the Marines and planning to go to George Washington University in the fall. Dad had written a book on "American Diplomacy" and it had been accepted by the publisher, and Mother was busy shopping for wedding items. She sent me some veiling material and some blue satin and pink crepe for dresses for my trousseau. I was getting swell letters from Bob's family, too, and I was anxious to meet them.

The 14th of July was Bastille Day, so away we went to celebrate in the French Sector. The celebration was at Lake Tegelsee and they had a Ferris wheel and all sorts of games to play. John and Josette were always late and this evening was no exception. It was 8:30 by the time we arrived, and, by the time we got our meal tickets, it was 9:00. We were hungry enough to eat grass. We stood in line, plates in hand, drooling for our supper. When we reached the window, we discovered that the food was almost all gone. They handed us one slice of dried bread, a bread stick, and a tablespoon of dried meat. We took our plates down to lakeside and were so hungry that we just looked at our plates and laughed until we cried.

There were huge floats out on the water with costumes and unusual portrayals that were magnificent. There was dancing on the terrace and a stage show. Then, at midnight, they had fireworks. What a splendid way to spend Bastille Day!

Don came home from Frankfurt on a Saturday with a jeep. It was an exciting day, as he was one of the first Americans in Berlin to own a jeep. It was an open jeep and was in fairly good condition. We all wanted to ride in it. Our first ride was to Lake Wannsee to a picnic that 8 of us had planned. Berlin ruling permitted only 4 people in a jeep at a time, so Don had to make 2 trips.

Bob had been one of the instigators in the plan to allow Americans to buy jeeps. Earlier, he had been ready to go to Paris to make the arrangements for a jeep lottery. Those plans fell through, but another plan was set up whereby we put our names on a list and, as a name came up, that person would go to Frankfurt to get his jeep.

We listened to the radio on July 24th to the underwater explosion of the atomic bomb test. It was not very clear, but we gathered that it was a success, and that the Salt Lake City was the only ship left afloat.

To show you how the Russian propaganda worked, we read a bulletin stating: "In the Russian Zone at a celebration over the failure of the atomic bomb, it was announced that the U.S. Military Government will leave Germany by fall".

"Look at what I have," Lyn yelled as I came in the door. She was on the floor with two six-week old wire-haired terrier pups. Were they ever adorable! They were lively little fellows, so cute together, and they developed a habit of chewing our hair when we picked them up.

Their names were "Brother" and "Sister". Poor Brother met with an early fate when a workman dropped a heavy tool on him and he died instantly. Lyn kept "Sissy" for about a year. Sissy, though, had rickets and her poor, little legs were terribly bowed. She became somewhat cranky later on, but she adored Lyn and when she died a year later, Lyn was very sad.

We turned in our application for marriage, letters of acquiescence, and an affidavit, several copies of them. Lyn's newspaper agreed to do our invitations in English and in French. They were done on very low-grade paper, but we thought they were perfect. They read:

> The honor of your presence is requested at the marriage of
> Patricia Gwynne Williams
> to
> Robert Case McMann
> 2nd Lt., United States Army
> Sunday, the twenty-fifth of August
> At four o'clock
> Ernst Moritz Arndt Church
> Onkel Tom Strasse and Wilkistrasse
> Berlin

A most unusual experience happened to Reggie and me. It was one that we have laughed a lot about since, but one that made us angry at the time. Don had become a civilian and was working for the Road Branch of Transportation Division. His new job took him out of town a good bit and he would leave his jeep in Bob's trust. Bob's birthday, August 8th, was approaching and, when Reggie and I suggested that we do some shopping for his birthday and couldn't we use the jeep, he found it difficult to refuse. I phoned the U.S. Traffic Officer and told him I didn't have an army license yet, but that I had my stateside one. He said it would be all right to do a little driving, but to hurry up and get a Military Government license.

Reggie and I set out and, during the course of the afternoon, we wandered over into the British Sector. We bought a lot of things and were enjoying ourselves immensely. My favorite purchase was a large oil painting of a ship at sea. Reggie bought a figurine of the three monkeys, "see no evil, speak no evil, hear no evil". It was so adorable, I was sorry I hadn't seen it first. We had completed our shopping and were on our way home when a British MP jeep pulled alongside and beckoned us to stop. They said they had never seen a civilian woman driving a jeep and wanted to see our trip ticket. A trip ticket is the acknowledgment given out by the Motor Pool when you use one of their vehicles.

I explained that the jeep was a privately-owned one and I produced the ownership papers, along with my picture on my identification as an American civilian. This meant nothing to them because they had not heard that Americans were purchasing and owning jeeps. We just couldn't make them understand. Then, since Regina had an accent, they conceived that we were German and, making themselves out to be great detectives, concluded that we were two German girls who had stolen a jeep.

They told us to follow them to their station. You have heard of bull-headed people, well, these Limeys certainly were. They called us "damn Germans" and wouldn't let me call Bob because, "you'll change your story". After two hours, at my suggestion, they called the American MPs. Two jeeps showed up with laughing and smiling guys who wanted to get a look at us and they escorted us back to our sector. I'm sorry I never reported those jerks because they were anything but nice to us and apparently couldn't read.

Margie began dating Chris Christiansen, a former major in the airborne. He was a crazy guy, with cropped, blonde hair, and an exuberant manner. We loved doing things with him because the unusual always happened, and he was always "on". He was good for Margie because Dick's rejection had been very hurtful to her. Chris came to Bob and wanted him to join him as a volunteer to jump into the Italian Alps to find a plane that had crashed there and to see if anyone was alive. Bob was interested, but couldn't get away. Chris went and they found the plane, but there were no survivors. He said he came upon a ghastly scene and it bothered him for some time.

As I said, I was never comfortable on a sailboat again, but we did a lot of sailing that summer, as Chris was an expert. Usually, after sailing, Don and Reggie would go with us to the golf course. On a particularly hot afternoon, after we had finished 9 holes, Reggie and I were ready to quit, but Bob and Don wouldn't give up and went on to attempt the last nine. She and I were pretty annoyed as there was nothing to do while waiting, and we decided to set out by ourselves. At the parking lot was a hospital truck, just ready to leave. It was full of doctors, who had just finished playing, and they were going right by 15 Lanstrasse. We smirked all the way, wishing we could see the looks on their faces when they discovered we had gone.

We were calmly sitting on the porch, sipping cool drinks when the fellows returned (about 15 minutes after we did). They had gotten tired around the 12th hole and had stopped there. They had been quite startled when they got back to the clubhouse, but were too tired to argue with us about it. They looked so pooped that we fixed them a cool drink too and we all sat there looking frazzled.

I was living in a dream world, but there was misery all around me and it gave me pangs of guilt because I wanted everyone to be as happy as I was. I kept my mind busy with all of the preparations I had to make, but the situation of the Germans was very depressing. People were starving, children were skinny, and many of them wore rags on their feet for shoes. I rounded up shoes for several children and gave out food often.

The papers were full of the trials against the Nazis taking place in Nuremberg. People were afraid to testify against them for fear of disappearing. We began to understand the fear they had under Hitler in talking about their political beliefs. It could mean torture or the incarceration of loved ones and people didn't discuss what they thought in front of their children for fear the children might slip and innocently repeat what they had heard.

Hitler had surrounded himself with a small clique of fanatical, ruthless henchmen, a violent group, who rose to power in the Third Reich and established political and economic institutions of legitimized terror. These masterminds of death were found to be psychologically normal. They had standing in their communities, were husbands who loved their wives and read bedtime stories to their children. But atrocities, brutalities, tortures, cruelties and murders were every day occurrences.

Heinrich Himmler was one of the worst. He was behind the master plan for the elimination of the Jews as the head of Hitler's SS organization. He was seen by many as the "personification of evil". After the German surrender on May 7, 1945, he disguised himself as a German Gestapo Agent, wearing a mustache and eye patch, but the allies were on the lookout for him and he was captured. He had a vial of cyanide in his mouth, which he bit into. Doctors tried to remove the poison by inducing him to vomit, but he died a long, 12 minute, agonizing death, There were no mourners.

CHAPTER ELEVEN

Twelve of the top Nazis were condemned to death by hanging. Martin Bormann, successor to Hess as Hitler's deputy, and behind the scenes organizer of the Brown Shirts, had disappeared, never to be found, but there were sightings of him over the years in Brazil. The remaining eleven men were: Herman Goering, Joachim von Ribbentrop, Wilhelm Keitel, Ernst Kaltenbrunner, Alfred Rosenberg, Hans Frank, Julius Streicher, Fritz Saukel, Alfred Jodl, Arthur Seyss-Inquart, and Martin Goebbels. Walther Funk, Rudolf Hess, and Erich Raeder received life imprisonment; Albert Speer and Baldur von Schirach got 20 years; and Karl Doenitz 10 years.

An appeal was made to change the method of death by hanging to shooting, however it was turned down. Col. Alfred Jodl's wife sent an urgent appeal to General Eisenhower, to no avail. Three men were acquitted. The Russians were enraged. Of the three men, Austria demanded that Franz von Papen and Hjalmar Schacht be turned over to it. The former had to do with the assassination of the late Chancellor Engelbert Dolfuss, and the latter was to be charged with "destruction of the City of Vienna in April 1945 before the Russians liberated the city".

Field Marshal Wilhelm Keitel was reported to be in the depths of depression, but told his lawyer he was determined to "die like a soldier". He said that if he was hanged, "this would be yet another blot upon my name." Fritz Sauckel, who brought five million unwilling foreign workers to Germany, was reported to be convinced that he could still do something to persuade the world he was innocent. He prepared a statement for the Allied Control Council, in which he swore he was only an "honest workman". Julius Streicher, the Jew baiter, reportedly said, "I'll be glad if I'm sentenced to death, because it will mean I can sleep at last. These American guards are always waking me up."

In a 250,000 word summing up, Chief United States Prosecutor, Robert H. Jackson, declared, "It was these men, among millions of others, and it was these men leading millions of others, who built up Adolf Hitler and vested in his psychopathic personality, not only in innumerable lesser decisions, but the supreme issue of war. They intoxicated him with power and adulation. They fed his hates and aroused his fears. They put a loaded gun in his eager hands . . . . His guilt is the guilt of the whole dock and of every man in it . . . Let it be said, plainly now, that these defendants are charged also as common murderers."

In October, when the men were hanged, Hermann Goering had managed to commit suicide beforehand. An article in the newspaper said, "The Allied Control Authority today gave a three-man board the job of finding out how a small vial of potassium cyanide managed to worm its way through the heavy guard of the presumable 'suicide proof' Palace of Justice jail, and give Hermann Goering the opportunity to cheat international justice by killing himself with poison some two and one half hours before his scheduled date with the hangman." The once pompous Reichsmarshal, no.2 Nazi, had managed to swallow the small glass container of poison while guards supposedly were keeping their eyes on him.

One of the most unusual things that Don ever bought was a massage machine. We did have a lot of fun with it at first, because none of us had ever seen such a contraption. You plugged the darned thing into a socket to work the five different attachments. They varied in size and softness. There was a small one that tickled, and the great big one that felt as though Gorgeous George, the professional wrestler, was giving you a going-over. Until the novelty wore off, it was a fight to get to the machine, and a waiting line, but our interest faded when the novelty wore off.

Lyn was doing a lot of fascinating things working for The Observer. She covered a lot of fashion shows and society news. One night, she invited us to an Observer party. The party was in honor of an enlisted man who was going home. The party-goers would be a lot of enlisted men and some civilians. Bob, as an officer, felt a little uneasy about going, but he good-naturedly went along.

Lyn was late arriving, as usual. She hadn't told me with whom she had a date and, as it got to be closer and closer to 11:00 o'clock, we became more and more curious. In she came, breathless and looking spiffy, dragging a brigadier general behind her! We were dumfounded, but the more I thought about it, it shouldn't have surprised us at all. The general was very good-looking and very nice and, as Bob was the nearest in rank, they became good friends. The other thing I remember about the party was the Danish pianist because he was so good. He sang the old favorites, "Blue Moon", "Stardust", "My Reverie", "Deep Purple" and we hummed along and danced on air.

You can imagine that there were plenty of jokes circulating around our offices and, as most of us were beginning to speak broken German, a very funny paper was in my in-basket. It was entitled, "EXTRA1 MYSTERY SOLVED" And read:

"Now it can be told! Through an exclusive interview with a captured German field marshal, Heimrich Rausvonhaus Von und Zu Schnitzel, the mystery of the disappearance of Adolf Hitler has been solved.

"The heretofore unpublished statement by General Rausvonhaus and so forth, follows untranslated:

"Ich ben ein locomotiver proceeden mit break-necken speeden. Ein automobilser also ben gecomen mit break-necken speeden. Das locomotiver ben gamaken ein huffen-puffen und stacken-smoken! Das automobilser ben gemaken der grosser motor roaren!

"Ober das graden crossen ben gestanden der Fuhrer-Heil Hitler! Der Fuhrer iss geraisen der handsers mit 'Halten!' und 'stoppen!'

Das locomotiver outgaben mit ein rooten-tootin und dinger-lingen! Der Automobilser outgaben ein grosser honken und braken screechen.

Ich bin gecomen ein exploden mit der grosser crashen mit donder und blitzen! Ach! Der Fuhrer—Heil Hitler! Iss gemincer meaten."

The rate of VD (venereal disease) was pretty high and the officials were doing everything possible to publicize the importance of medical attention. "VD is a plague and, when it seeps into the Army", one notice said, "it has no regard for race or rank, right or wrong." One soldier wrote to "B Bag" (the Letters to the Editor column), "Ridicule, disgrace, and punishment have been the methods used to handle VD cases. VD can be defeated and the diseased should be treated and cured to prevent an epidemic."

A compulsory program was started for the GIs and officers to assemble and see some Germans who had syphilis, to show the horrible effects of the disease. The German men and women were put on a stage in the nude with bags over their heads. After one of these meetings, it was said, a GI rushed out and over to the hospital. He had recognized his girl. I'm not sure how true that anecdote was, but perhaps it was. The boys at 15 Lanstrasse had a poster in their half-bath downstairs. It was Donald Duck and he was saying, "Honest, Doc, I got it from a toilet seat".

Reggie had a Hungarian girl visiting her named Eva. She spoke Hungarian and German and she was pretty and sweet. She had been with Reggie during the war and they were together when the Russians had marched into Berlin. For political reasons, she was afraid to return to Hungary and was living in the Russian Zone. In Hungary, she had been quite wealthy and now she and her aunt were making dresses and had very little. She told us she had wanted to learn English, but it was "verboten" in the Russian Zone and anyone caught teaching it would be sent to prison. We played Ping Pong and kept score in German. I had to stop and figure out each German number and got extremely mixed up

Right after Eva went back to her home, Reggie told me about a friend of hers who could get pretty material for us to have dresses made. We drove up to a magnificent mansion, with a great, big lawn and deck chairs scattered here and there. Around at the side, we entered a room where her friend, Margaret, a woman of about 28, lay in bed reading. She got up and showed us some material that was in the bottom of a large bookcase, which extended the length of the room. She had some perky-looking cotton that had palm trees and beach umbrellas on it. It was cool and summery and enticing and we took some samples of it. When she got out of bed, I saw that she was a heavy woman and her sheer nightgown clung to her body, emphasizing her overweight figure.

When we left, Reggie told me that during the war, Margaret had been a close friend of hers. Margaret had been thin and sickly, and Reggie and other friends of theirs visited her and brought her items that she was unable to get for herself. She told them that if she ever became wealthy, she would share her riches with them. Eventually, she met a Yugoslav and they had cleaned up on the black market, but she promptly forgot about all of her promises. She was still living on the money they made, although the Yugoslav was long gone. We did purchase some dressy material and saw her one other time.

Four Americans disappeared in the Russian Zone in July and the American authorities couldn't find out what had happened to them and were demanding their return. "U.S. Army security authorities have expressed bafflement at their failure to achieve the release of the four Americans, and hinted that it was a matter for the highest authorities to handle", a news column stated. General McNarney and Marshal Vassily Sokolovsky had a long, spirited conversation at one of the meetings. One intelligence officer said it was believed the four were being held in Oranienberg, north of Berlin and site of the Soviet provincial kommandatur.

The missing people were Warrant Officer Samuel Harrison and his wife; Captain Harold Cobin; and Lt. George Wyatt. My family, of course, was frantic and just knew that something like that was going to happen to me.

About three weeks later, they were returned to the U.S. Sector. They had entered the Russian Zone without a pass (which we all knew better than to do) and the Russians had suspected them of espionage. They were merely some over-curious Americans.

I had a nice letter from my grandmother, dated July 8th, with a message for Bob in it, "Tell him I am proud of my two grandsons and will be proud to say I have three of the finest in the land. I like Bob's curly hair and his widow's peak and, most of all, I like him because he shows such good judgment when he selects my darling for his life partner. I shall be glad when you are both home.

"P.S. Stan feels sorry for Bob if he has to depend on your cooking skills.".

Some time in July Harry S. Truman Mess Hall was completed. It was a long, low brick building, right across from OMGUS Headquarters. From then on, the messes in the various clubs were discontinued and we were to eat there. We were disappointed because the smaller messes were more informal. We fondly called this new one: "Harry's Hash House" . . . I ate at the ACA Building while Bob met Margie for lunch at Truman Hall every day. We attended a party where I didn't know very many people and Bob started to introduce me to someone who interrupted and said, "Where is Pat?" We looked at each other with questioning looks on our faces, and then had to laugh. The person had seen Bob and Margie together every day and had assumed that she was me.

For Bob's birthday, which was coming up (August 8th), I had written home for some things for him. He would be needing a whole new wardrobe when he turned civilian. When I called my office at OMGUS to see if I had any mail, the sweetest voice in the world said, "You have four packages"

Some of the things were for me. Mother had sent my black dress, along with some new clothes. The black dress had looked old and tired before, but now it was a sight for my sore eyes. Knowing how I loved wide belts, Mother had sent me a huge, red one. Also, I now had some black shoes. Up to that time, I had been wearing my brown pumps with everything. Needless to say, out of necessity, I hadn't been color-coordinated. There was also a cookbook. Bless their hearts! My family knew that all I could cook was fudge, and they were worried about our eating habits.

Bob had known that there was to be a party (it was his 25th birthday), but he was amazed at the way it unfolded. First of all, it was an old clothes worn backwards party, and people arrived looking pretty strange. There was no end to the exclamations, but I must say it wasn't all that comfortable. Then, Bob opened his presents. There was a subscription to "New Yorker" magazine from Mother and Dad and, he had to stop and read all of the jokes before continuing. There were several ties and he just couldn't get over them. He had to try each one on and there were several envious comments from others. The most popular one with the group was the one my grandmother had sent. It was brown silk, with a gigantic, multi-colored peacock on it. It was as conspicuous as you can get, but after wearing Army ties for several years, this was just what he wanted.

There was a shirt and some socks that Mother sent him, and a tennis cap. It had a tremendously long bill and looked very odd. Bob went around imitating Fearless Fosdick with that cap on and, I think everyone at the party had it on at one time or another. I had gotten him a lamp, the oil painting from my adventure with Reggie, and an electric shaver. He also got a charming galley boat, photo album, cut glass vase, shirt material, handkerchiefs, flowers from the housefraus, and John gave him a dinner gong.

After that, we had a treasure hunt. Reggie had worked all day hiding the notes around the house. Don won the prize. It was a little figurine of two monkeys picking fleas off each other. We had a cake, of course, and sandwiches and wound up sitting around the floor playing games. First, it was Truth or Consequences and we learned that a member of the group had played in a sixth grade Shakespearean play. His one line had been, "Forsooth 'tis not the end, for where is Eglemore the landlord?". He had practiced that line so frequently that the whole class shouted it out when it was time for him to recite his line. We played Pinchie Winchie. One person is not in on what is happening and one other person has charcoal on one finger. We sat in a circle and went around the circle giving a slight tweak to the next person's cheek and saying "Pinchie Winchie". The innocent person, sitting next to the charcoal person, has no idea his or her cheek is getting darker and, as the game goes round and round, looks more and more bewildered as the others can't hold back their laughter. It's a very childish game and the victim was furious.

A most dreadful bottleneck to our wedding plans developed when the head of the Coal Section refused to sign my leave papers unless and until a replacement arrived in the office. August was looming up as the busiest month the Coal Section had ever seen. The coal experts had just made an extensive visit to the American, British and Russian coal mines and there were to be meetings of the Fuel Committee nearly every day for the next month, instead of the usual 3 or 4. Also, the Chief Clerk had gone home on leave and I was the only American girl left in both locations.

Finding a replacement meant scurrying around like a one-armed paper hanger and it began to seem like an impossible task. There were no new shipments of stenographers coming in. The front personnel office felt sorry for me and said they would try very hard to find someone who could be taken from another office. It left us up in the air.

There were more problems. Josette became ill and there was a possibility she would have to go to the hospital. Some of our worries were: getting hotel reservations in Paris and Nice, making transportation arrangements, getting travelers checks, getting cars for the wedding day. We were expecting to get our jeep any day and had to keep checking on that. Bob was busy reading insurance booklets. He had been doing that almost since the day he asked me to marry him. We had lists of lists.

There was a big scandal in OMGUS when Col. Link committed suicide. He was Secretary of the Industry Branch, under which I worked. I knew him only to say hello to. I did know his assistant, Freddie Block, though. They had been mixed up in one of the biggest black market rings yet discovered and owned interest in several German firms.

Another man I knew slightly, Major David Watson, was arrested on charges of conspiracy in connection with the $150,000 Kronberg Castle jewel theft. He was acquitted of the charge of sending several items from the castle to his home in Wisconsin, but accused of sending a handful of gems to Northern Ireland. In his plea to the court, Major Watson's attorney asked for leniency for his client, "who may have been a dupe, but certainly not a regular criminal. Most of you," he continued, "are Regular Army officers. My client is not—but he has served his country voluntarily and served it well. His record has been an exceptional one up to the time when he became mixed up in this affair." He was sentenced to three years imprisonment and dismissal from the Army. I was heartsick for him. The temptation to take for those who had been through the war was universal and, in some cases, understandable. Almost everyone bought a few items with cigarettes and that was sanctioned, as long as they were not the tax-free PX cigarettes.

On August 14th, Mother wrote, "Last night Mr. McMann called us from New Jersey and Dad talked to him. He said if we were half as pleased over this marriage as they were, he would be very glad. He said Bob wanted Goggy and me to have some share in the wedding and had asked him to send us flowers. That was certainly thoughtful of him and we appreciate it immensely. Everything we hear about Bob makes us very proud of him and I am quite sure you will be very, very happy together."

She went on to say that Dick had been to see my family and, in fact, had gone twice. As only Dick could have done, in his eloquent language, he talked Bob up to be a superman and he praised me so my family was fascinated with him and paid strict attention to every detail. Goggy wrote, "He made himself at home right at once. He went to the kitchen with Stan to make sandwiches, then came and sat on my bed and visited. He thinks Bob is tops." The second time he came, Stan and his crowd were ready to go swimming and Dick went along. One of the girls in the group latched onto him and they saw each other a couple of times afterwards.

Mac came for dinner at 15 Lanstrasse and afterwards we went to see his house—the one he was fixing up for his bride. It was on the next corner. There were only 2 houses between it and Bob's. Mac always had grand ideas and we were eager to see what he had come up with. He was having a terrace made and, later, there was to be a pool with colored lights playing on it. In the large yard, he planned to have a volleyball court. Ginny played the piano and to surprise her there was to be a soundproof room with an ivory piano; gold drapes and a soft, sink-in rug. Their initials would be in the big, red tiles on the floor of the bathroom. The front part of the second floor was one, long room. Part of it was a sitting room, and then there were steps leading up to the bed. Silver stars and a moon shone on the ceiling overhead. A large fireplace was partially installed for that cozy feeling. What a romantic guy!

We continued on to see how our house was coming along. It wasn't going to be as elegant, but we loved the way it was beginning to look. A friend of Bob's in the Engineers bunch told him that day that some of them were making a Ping Pong table for him. We measured that third bedroom and there was plenty of space there for a game room. That next day we went to get our wedding rings and they were so pretty! They had been inscribed "Bob 8/25/46" and "Pat 8/25/46

We were on our way to the hospital and I asked him who we were going to visit. It was Mac. We had stopped off at Bob's billet to pick up a bag of apples to take to him and dashed over to the 759th general hospital. Mac's apartment was in the ACA Building. A couple of nights earlier he had been very tired, but wanted to take a sun lamp treatment before retiring. Forty-five minutes later, his friend, Gene Kocherga, banged on his door to invite him to go to a party. Mac had fallen asleep, but the banging awakened him. He got up, dressed, and accompanied his friend. A couple of hours later, he passed out cold.

He looked terrible and was as red as a lobster. His lips were swollen 3 times their normal size and he could hardly talk. We tried to cheer him up, but he asked us not to say anything funny because it hurt him to smile.

The week before the wedding, we began moving things into our new home. We were given a dining room table that opened up to 11 feet. They also gave us some orange rugs for the living room. (Can you imagine orange rugs with rose walls!) Don and Reggie helped us carry items in and then we went for a ride in Don's jeep.

We drove to the Olympic Stadium and the size of it was astonishing. We walked around the oval and then went down underneath the stadium. I wanted a German helmet and Don found me one. I was so pleased until Reggie giggled and said it was an Air Raid Warden's hat.

It wasn't until 4 days before the wedding that my replacement was located. My travel order was signed, but since I was in all-day meetings every day, Bob had to hand-carry my request. My marriage papers had been slow in being implemented, and he had to locate them. That evening Joe, in my office, had a dinner for us at Harnack House. John and Josette were there, as well as Don Wilson, my boss, and Juliette, his new bride. Her little girl, Marie, was there too and she was adorable. Juliette and her first husband had adopted Marie, but it was amazing how much she looked like her new dad. The meal was delicious and it was swell of Joe to do that for us.

Don Wilson told us that he couldn't say how much enjoyment he had gotten out of watching Bob and me the last two months. He said we were so pepped up and enthusiastic and that was the way it should be.

After dinner, we attended a party at Ray O'Neal's house. Mim and Lyn had been cooking it up and had been very secretive about it. I had gleaned, however, that they were planning a bonfire and weenie roast at Lake Wannsee. Heavy rains spoiled that idea; the party was held indoors. There was an orchestra, food, pictures taken of all of us playing in the band (20 of us). There were some crazy presents: teething ring, can opener, K-rations, dinner bell, douche bag, and a rolling pin! That was our "shower" and we had a helluvva good time.

We received our first wedding present. It was 3 doilies from some little girls back in the States. They lived in public housing and I had been their club leader. It was part of the requirement for my degree in sociology and I loved those kids. Their thoughtfulness touched me very much. Mother asked us to pick a silver pattern and she would have service for 12 for us when we returned. We chose Towle's Candlelight. Don Wilson said he would give us the carving set to our silver service (and he brought it to us when we came stateside).

I was beginning to wonder how a bride could possibly look her best on her wedding day. With all the parties, working all day in meetings, packing, moving, getting papers straightened out, trying to find a replacement so I could go on a honeymoon, I was sure I would be a frazzled and wilted-looking bride. I had lost weight and was looking gaunt already.

My white shoes that Mother mailed from the States hadn't arrived and there were only two full days left. My brown pumps and my black pumps would look dreadful with my wedding gown. Lyn got a car for us and, at 9:00 a.m. she, Reggie and I took off for the Russian Sector to a shoemaker who was supposed to be good and also quick. We drove through a lot of back streets, saw a lot of Russian soldiers, and just when I thought we were hopelessly lost, we stopped in front of a small shop, surrounded by high piles of rubble.

Reggie spoke German to the shopkeeper and he nodded his head as she talked. He then took a piece of paper, drew a line around my stockinged foot, and told us to return the next morning and he would have a pair of white shoes for me. He didn't have a sample to show me, but I was desperate and said OK. From there, we went to the dressmaker and tried on our clothes. The dresses were lovely and I began to feel better. It was impossible to believe, however, that I was to be a bride within 48 hours.

Bright and early next morning we entered the shoe shop with anxiety and anticipation and the man proudly held the shoes out to me. What a shock I had! My heart fell. They were white, it was true, but they were clodhoppers! They had ugly, thick heels and there was nothing dainty about them. They were made of white cloth of some kind and were a wedgie style. I didn't show my disappointment because this was it. There was no alternative. I was damned lucky to have white shoes!

CHAPTER TWELVE

It was the day before my wedding! Lyn and I met Bob for lunch, then joined John and Josette at the Standesamt's Office. According to the laws of the land, we had to be married by the Germans. The Standesamt was something like the mayor of a section of Berlin. This wedding was the legal one. The church wedding was not legally necessary, but we wouldn't feel married with just this strange procedure.

We went into the building and then waited for the longest time I have ever waited for anything. Reggie came along also as an interpreter and she and Lyn were to act as our witnesses. The office door finally swung open and we were beckoned into a small room with a large, highly polished table in the center of it. The Standesamt sat on one side of the table; John and Josette, Bob and I sat opposite him; and the two bridesmaids sat at the opposing ends.

The Standesamt began reeling off a lot of Deutsche. He talked and he talked and he talked. Reggie interpreted as he went along. It was something about this being a very serious step in our lives. He would say a long sentence in German and then I would hear "Patritsia Grin Willems" at the end of it. Patritsia Grin Willems! (Patricia Gwynne Williams) That was me!

Unfortunately, Lyn had brought the little terrier pup, Sissy, along. Somewhere in the middle of the ceremony, Sissy broke loose and began meandering down the center of this well-polished table. This brought forth many snickers and Sissy was put on the floor. Then, as the Standesamt was pronouncing us man and wife, Sissy began pulling on John's pant leg. It didn't seem like a wedding.

Reggie would be gone before we got back from our honeymoon, which meant we had to have her going-away party that night, and we held it at 15 Lanstrasse.

We were all tired from the many activities of the week before and we were melancholy because our "Queenie" was leaving. We didn't feel like whooping it up.

Sunday, August 25th, I awakened around 10:00 to find rain pouring in the bedroom window. Something told me it wasn't going to let up either. We had arranged for two horse-drawn carriages to take us from the church to the reception, but would have to ditch that plan. I jumped out of bed. This was THE day!

First on the program was a wedding breakfast at Harnack House and it was arranged for us and given by Margie. When we got there, we learned that a distressing thing had happened the night before. Someone had broken into the flower shop and our flowers had been stolen. At this point, after all that had taken place, we could handle that. There were worse things than walking down the aisle without flowers.

Our apartment was crowded that afternoon. Josette and Reggie came with their clothes and Margie came to help out. The rain continued to pour down. Early in the afternoon, the PX Officer arrived with bunches of chrysanthemums and daisies. They were sort of droopy, but Mim and Margie set about to put them together with big ribbons. Then Minnie, the dressmaker, came to dress me and brought her fiancé with her. For the first time in my life, I was the first one ready. My parachute dress was stunning. It had a short train; and a sweetheart neckline. On either side of the neckline, I wore a pair of paratroop wings, and I wore the pearls that Aunt Rena had sent me. I borrowed a gold bracelet from Lyn and Reggie had sewn a blue ribbon on my undies.

Mim's and Margie's dates came; and then there was Don Wilson, who was going to give me away, and Juliette and Marie. There was standing room only.

It was time to leave for the church and the cars were waiting for us outside. I wasn't a bit nervous until we got there and I saw all of the cars and jeeps outside. It seemed there were hundreds of them. I still don't know how it happened, but there was a bouquet of yellow roses waiting for me at the church and those were the flowers that I carried. I asked Don Wilson to tell me a funny story as we walked down the aisle because I was sure I wouldn't be able to smile. The church was packed. Josette looked like a baby doll. Her dress was white taffeta and suited her perfectly. She looked the way a bride should look on her wedding day.

The wedding ceremony was fairly short. Paul Ruth took movies from the balcony. I had to talk loud when we came to the part of repeating after the minister because Josette didn't know what he was saying and I had to cover for her. It was a double ring ceremony. I was afraid we were going to get the four rings mixed up, but we managed that OK. I couldn't get Bob's ring on his finger and pushed and shoved until he whispered, "Wait until we get outside". He looked so handsome in his uniform with those trooper boots with white laces.

We practically ran out of the church and at last I could smile. The MPs were standing on either side of the walk saluting as we came out. We had wedding photos taken at Harnack House and then stood in a receiving line at the reception. Josette's father had been unable to get to Berlin, but a very nice French major had given her away. What a lot of people were there! My arm ached from all the hand shaking.

The members of my office were attending a special meeting that afternoon so many of them could not come to the wedding, but later began showing up at the reception. Monsieur Tison, the head of the French delegation got up in the middle of the meeting and said, and I quote from the official minutes:

"MR TISON; All members of the Coal Experts Committee wish to express to Miss Williams their regret in not being able to personally extend their greetings to her on the occasion of her marriage. They wish you (Mr. Forester) to do so and give her greetings for herself and her husband.

"MR. FORESTER; I thank the delegation on behalf of Miss Williams for their expression of regret and best wishes for her future. She will be disappointed that we cannot attend her wedding, and I will be glad to convey the expression of this group in writing."

Monsieur Tison gave us a wedding gift of two exquisite Meissen vases and I was astonished at the magnitude of such a generous gift.

There were two wedding cakes and we each cut our cakes at the same time. We had sabers to cut them with and there was plenty of cake for all. Whoever made those cakes was a superlative cook. The taste was fantastic. There were 2 little girls at the reception. One was Marie Wilson, Don Wilson's new daughter, and the other was a little redhead. They brought me some refreshments and stared at me as though I were a princess. There was music and dancing and although the shoes didn't lend themselves to fancy steps, I did a lot of dancing that afternoon. Everyone was having a gay old time.

My former boss, Bill Forqueron, came up to me and handed me a $100 War Bond from the Coal Section. I was so surprised and never dreamed of having such a large War Bond. I was pleased to think that they cared that much about me. We got some lovely gifts that day. When we counted the glasses we had gotten as presents, there were 99 of them.

There was a tiny balcony off one of the rooms and the gals lined up below it and Josette and I prepared to toss our bouquets. We turned our backs to the railing, closed our eyes, and tossed. Reggie caught mine and Mim caught Josette's. It must have been fate because on the following June 1st, both girls, in 2 separate countries, were married.

The party was still going strong when Bob and I made a hurried exit to the car that was waiting for us outside. We told the German driver to go to 9 Herrfurtstrasse where I planned to get my suitcase and a few other things. The driver nodded, "Ja", and continued driving in the wrong direction. We tried in our broken German to tell him to turn around, but he kept going. Looking out the rear window we saw a long procession of jeeps and cars filled with our friends. We just sat back and wondered where they could be taking us.

We ended up at the 822nd MP Headquarters and, as we got out of the car, we were escorted by some young MPs up the steps and inside the front door, where we stood before the Sergeant of the Day. Just about that time, a new ordnance had come out entitled "Public Display of Affection". This ruling held that Americans could show no affection in public, such as holding hands, necking, etc. The Sergeant of the Day proceeded to accuse us of kissing in the church in front of a lot of people and he told the MPs to "take them downstairs".

There was a long, dark hall with some cells all along one side and they were about to throw us in separate cells, but we hung onto each other and both of us were shoved into one cell. Our "friends" stood outside the cell window laughing and jeering and shouting, "Your train leaves tomorrow night? See you tomorrow night," and they all drove off.

In 20 minutes, in came John and Josette. She, too, was still in her wedding dress. We, of course, realized this was some kind of wedding night "gag", but in France they do not play tricks on the wedded couple and Josette's eyes were the size of saucers. She didn't have a clue as to what was going on. She looked at me and said, "Pat, we pretend we sick". We tried to reassure her. Actually, we were getting a kick out of the novelty at first. There was a German sitting on the floor in the corner. He had been arrested for wearing a Russian uniform and he sat there half-smiling, although bewildered. There was a thin bench against the wall with just enough room for the 4 of us to sit on.

We kept expecting to be let out, but as time went on, I began to wonder about the MPs and their sense of humor. Some of them would think nothing of leaving us there all night. We were sure it had been John's boss who had rigged this up. After what seemed like a long time, but was probably forty-five minutes, we heard a key in the lock and we were free. Mim and Lyn had come back and insisted that we be let go. Thank you, Mim and Lyn.

A picture of our wedding appeared in the paper and Lyn wrote the bit underneath, "People who had too much champagne might have thought they were seeing double at this wedding on Sunday, but there really were two brides and two bridegrooms at the double wedding of . . . ." followed by our names. When I sent my request for my travel orders, I asked that they read "Mrs. Patricia McMann". I went on to explain that my name was Miss Patricia Williams, but that I would be married by the time I would use the orders. Ha! My orders came back reading, "Miss Patricia McMann". This wasn't too bad. This would look like I was an unmarried woman, but at least we had the same last name on our papers.

Joe, when he heard about this, drew a cartoon for us. It was a picture of a soldier and his bride in a white dress in a jeep, with a "Just Married" sign on the back and several tin cans tied to the spare tire. A huge MP has stopped the jeep and is saying, "She's yer wife, eh? Can y'prove it?" Then Joe had written "Congratulations T.S.F.C."

The day after our wedding, our train was not leaving until 6:00 p.m. I went to the doctor and had a Plantars Wart removed from the ball of my foot. I can't remember anything being as painful as that needle he stuck in my foot, but it had to be done. There was no after-trauma and it enabled me to enjoy walking and sightseeing on our trip.

CHAPTER THIRTEEN

We rode the Berliner to Frankfurt. The German passenger trains were excellent and this one was fantastic. We had a compartment with a sink in it. There was a fellow in OMGUS named Bob McCann and he and my new husband were often getting each other's mail. He happened to be on our train and dropped in on us and said, "Did you know you actually have my compartment?" Our faces fell. We knew it was too good to be true. "It's OK," he said "because I like yours, so just stay put." There were other acquaintances in the same car that we were in and a couple of the others were able to open up their compartments next to each other to make a room big enough for a party.

In Frankfurt, we walked around USFET Headquarters. Those magnificent buildings had been part of the I.G. Farben industrial complex. We ate lunch overlooking the flowers and pools in the garden. We went to see Kronberg Castle, which looked like a country estate you would expect Mr. Rockefeller to own. It was built during the years 1888-1892 by Kaiserin Friedrich, formerly Princess Royal of Great Britain, and who was also the widow of Emperor Frederick III of Germany. The court architect designed the castle in modern English renaissance style under the personal supervision of the empress. The estate was comprised of 250 acres, with chestnut and cedar trees in abundance. There was a darling donkey in the stable yard and Bob took my picture sitting on it.

We spent a couple of hours at the Red Cross Club. This was one of many clubs that provided recreation for soldiers, and was a wonderful place for a sandwich, a game of Ping Pong or a game of cards. It was right next to the train station and a great many Americans appreciated that particular Red Cross Club while they were waiting in between trains.

We left at 8:30 at night for Paris in a coach that wasn't too sharp. There were 8 of us piled into one compartment and it was a 12-hour ride. Someone said of Paris, "It is a world!" There is no other city like it. We stayed at the Hotel Louvois, an exclusive appearing place, and did some shopping that first day on the famous Champs Elysees. The French had a special system of selling. Items were rationed, but if one did not have a ration ticket, the prices were higher. Usually both prices were listed. I squandered some money on French lingerie and we bought some sunglasses. We felt that we were very "French-looking" in them.

Walking to the Arch de Triomph, we could see what an inspiring structure it is. Always beneath it burns the torch over the Tomb of the Unknown Soldier. The Arch was built by Napoleon in 1806 to commemorate his victories.

The hotel got us some tickets for the Follies Bergere and, of course, we couldn't miss that. There was no censor board in Paris and the girls wore only G-strings. Bob kept asking me if he could look. The stage scenery was exceptional. There was one scene that took place beneath a railroad bridge. A train went across the bridge and the sound and lighting effects were astonishingly realistic. Another scene represented a painting on a wall. There was a group of hunters in red coats sitting around a table drinking a toast of wine. The hunters were real people and the picture was tilted in such a way that it seemed impossible for the men to hold their position. We figured it must have been done with mirrors.

At intermission we paid 25 francs to go downstairs to a "revealing" show. It consisted of 3 girls who wiggled a lot and we felt very naughty to have deliberately spent money to see this.

We called home and spoke to everyone in both families. It was our introduction to our new in-laws. Bob found himself talking to a "Mrs. Tuttle", who he had never heard of, but they chatted like old friends. She was my Aunt Marion's mother (not a blood relative). Then we took a tour of the Palace at Versailles. Louis IV must have lived magnificently here, for there was splendor galore. There was little or no furniture in it because it had all been moved during the war, but the walls were covered with exquisite tapestries and paintings. One room, the Galerie des Glaces, has a place in modern history, for it was there that the Peace Treaty for WWI was signed in 1919.

The Eiffel Tower could be seen from most locations. It loomed 1,000 feet in the air. I was afraid as we went up in the elevator as there was no enclosed shaft and it was like riding up on scaffolding. There were steps all the way up too, and, although there were railings and wire fencing all around, you could look straight down through the steps. Bob, who had at least 20 parachute jumps under his belt, admitted we were pretty high up when we got to the top. The tower was designed by Gustave Eiffel for the Universal Exhibit in 1889. It was used for the transmission of wireless telegrams, and as an observation station during both world wars and it still receives messages from all over the world.

The night we went to the Paris Opera House, "Othello" was playing. The singing was excellent, but we decided it was not one of our favorites. We were amazed at how the people ask for tips, but the payoff came that evening. We were late for the opening and an usher, with a flashlight, showed us to our seats. They were exactly in the center of the row. After we had pushed our way through a sea of legs to get to our seats, who should come right behind us, but the usher asking for a tip. Bob had to fumble in the dark for money as people craned their necks around us to see the stage. At intermission, I was afraid I wasn't going to get out of the ladies room because I didn't have any money with me and the "madame" was very insistent. Bob had to tip the woman in the men's room, who stood around and watched all of the proceedings in there.

The train we rode from Paris was overcrowded. Aisles were piled high with suitcases and small children were sleeping on a dirty floor. We were in First Class in a compartment with a Red Cross worker, two nurses, and a paratrooper. We couldn't make our way to the diner because of the mobs of people we would have to step over in the aisles. We had to wait until the train stopped at a station, get off and run like mad to the diner, and repeat the process back to our car after eating.

We slept head-to-toe on a seat that was two feet wide. Suddenly, in the middle of the night, Bob got up and said, "Pat . . . . no, I better not tell you." I saw him scratching and wormed it out of him that he was being eaten alive by something unseen. Sure enough, there were big, red welts on his arms and legs. The bugs never got to me, but I've always been lucky enough to escape bites when others are itching away. The envious people always tell me I'm not sweet enough. Bob spent a miserable 24 hours on that train ride and was one of the first off the train.

We gasped when we saw the Mediterranean Ocean. It is truly an aqua color and is crystal clear. In back of Nice there are picturesque mountains and vast cliffs and we saw all kinds of palms and cactus. The streets were narrow and the architecture was Spanish with houses in white, yellow and pink. Our hotel, The Ruhl, had a couple of domes on it. We had a room with a balcony overlooking a park. The hotel was reserved for Americans working for the United States Government. We would have all of our meals there and pay only $8.00 per day. It had rained every day since our wedding and, when we saw that hot sun, we dashed to the room and unpacked our suits. But in that short time, a dark cloud appeared and an icy wind came up.

At lunch, we ran into Bea Gwin, a gal Bob was dating at the time he met me. She said she had a one-piece bathing suit and people thought she was quite a novelty. You could tell who the tourists were, she said, because the French girls wore what we would now call bikinis. The skimpy suits hadn't appeared on the scene in the U.S. yet. She told us that the beach in Nice was made up of stone and rocks and the best swimming was at Cannes.

The bikes we rented took us all over Nice, and to a café where some soldiers were teaching French girls to jitterbug and they were catching on fast. We dropped the bikes off and caught a bus to Monte Carlo. The casino there is enormous and looks like a castle out of the Tales of Scherazade. We sat down under awnings at a Parisian-type café and ordered a gin fizz. Looking out over the harbor, it looked like a colorful, creative painting. A highly made-up, bleached blonde woman in her sixties sat at the next table. She smiled at us and, in a friendly fashion, asked if she could join us. It turned out that she made her living showing people through the casino and telling them the points of interest in the town. She was badly crippled and walked with a cane, hanging onto someone's arm.

She took us into the casino and into a back room (we couldn't have gone without her). My mouth was really open! It was the first time I had seen any gambling, with the exception of the time my brother and I charged a penny to play a game we had invented. We had lured the neighborhood kids with the promise that they could make as much as 5 cents if they participated. My father promptly had put an end to that. Suddenly, I was in the most famous gambling joint in the world. It was a casino rule that no one in uniform could gamble, so that let Bob out. A big, bruiser in a tux followed Bob around, with his arms folded in front, to see that the law was not broken. This rule originated in 1911 when a British sailor, who had lost all of his money, threw a bomb from his yacht in an attempt to blow the house to bits.

We had set aside 2,000 francs (about $18) to gamble. We figured that if we never gambled again, it would have been worth it. It took me a couple of hours to lose it at the roulette wheel. At my table, there was a huge man, a rich French manufacturer betting thousands of francs at a throw. Beside him sat a proportionately fat woman with an enormously atrocious hat that bobbed this way and that. There was a 70 year-old woman there too, who had dyed her hair red and used a lot of makeup. She held a poodle in her lap and kept kissing it. We were told that she was the wife of the man who supplied wood to Monte Carlo and they were extremely wealthy. I had never seen so many colorful characters in one place all at once.

Our guide gave us some interesting information about the tiny country of Monaco. The country is surrounded by France on 3 sides and the Mediterranean on the other side. It is divided into 4 parts: the City of Monte Carlo, Monaco Villa, Fontvieille, and La Condamine. There were 40 soldiers and 3 cannons. The soldiers dressed in white uniforms with gold ornaments and looked more like fancy guards. At the time we were there, Louis II was the ruling monarch and had just had his 77th birthday.

We took a trip to Cannes to try out the beach there. The city was very much like Nice, only more modern. It was the chief summer resort and beach life center of France and was developed after WWI. Lunch was in a shop decorated with dark, wooden figures and bright, copper vessels hanging around the room. We had fresh pears! The beach was beautiful and we slept on the hot sand. It was shocking to see the skimpy bathing suits, although we had been warned that they left nothing to the imagination. We rented a paddleboat and went way out, scooting over the waves. We could look down and see the bright green seaweed and the sand, which appeared turquoise out there, and we were amazed that salt water could be so clear.

In the evening we danced at The Plantation, a cute nightclub that played swing music. The place was filled with GIs and girls, who were becoming good at jitterbugging and their skirts were swirling and flaring and exposing a good bit. The GIs loved it. There was a Chinese soldier who jitterbugged with an expressionless face and it was funny to watch him. He never glanced at his girl, just chewed gum and danced. His girl had loads of mascara on and vivid lipstick and couldn't have been more than 15 years old. We moved on to the Candy Club and ran into someone from Economics Division who was having a fling before going back to Michigan. The band was superb and I remember the vocalist singing "Jimmy Crack Corn". People started swarming in around 1:00 a.m. and we stayed because we couldn't tear ourselves away from that music.

I must have eaten something that didn't agree with me, because I awakened at 4:30 with terrible stomach pains, backache, headache, and I was burning up. Bob got up at 8:30 and brought a doctor back with him. I had a temperature of 103. The doc gave me some juice and some pills, but I was miserable all of that day. Poor Bob, who had never taken care of a sick person, was frightened when I became delirious. I kept telling him to get that woman out of the corner of the room and asking him to sell all of my books. He didn't quite know what he had married.

By noon next day, I was completely sound again and raring to go. We took a 5-hour bus ride into the mountains and visited Grasse. Halfway up, we stopped at a colorful shop along the road. It sold pottery and woven baskets, but it was some red plaid material that caught our eyes. We bought some of it to take back and have Minnie make us matching shirts.

It was a lovely drive on narrow roads, winding around on top of cliffs. Oh! How those French men drive! Whew! It was pretty scary. From a distance, we saw ancient villages that were on mountain peaks and were surrounded by stone walls that appeared to be holding up the entire villages. Once, we got to a spot where we could look straight up to what was the highest, steepest mountain yet. There, perched at the peak, was Eagle's Nest, a villa of not more than 20 houses. I couldn't imagine how people got up there, let alone what they would do when they got up there, but that was where Kathleen Norris wrote her books.

In Grasse, we visited Fragonard, a perfumery. There were flower fields (mostly jasmine) and we were shown how they press the flowers, and we saw the huge vats of perfume in the making. The aroma was so strong, that Bob told me from then on, if I wore perfume, it wouldn't even phase him. They told us that the French boys working in the factory were not allowed to eat garlic because their breath might have an effect on the product they were working with. That, we understood, was a great sacrifice for these boys because garlic was a staple in their diets.

They told us that one reason perfume is so expensive is because the bottles are so elaborate. They sold their perfume in small cans and I bought some Christmas Eve, Shalimar, Lavendar, Chanel No.5, and Violette.

Back in Nice, we went to see "Jungle Adventures", an American film with a French soundtrack. We both looked at each other and laughed as we watched the snake open its mouth and speak French.

The front desk told us there was a small village, Juan les Pines, with a beautiful beach that was almost always deserted. We took a bus there, bought some fruit, and found a secluded spot to park our belongings. There were two enormous rocks against the wall at the far end of the beach and we changed into our suits there. We spread out a cloth and our food purchases: large, red tomatoes, sweet green grapes, and then, Bob cut open the melon and we dug into it with our teeth. We finished with some French pastry. We swam and then slept on the sand with the waves breaking a few yards away. When the sun started to go down, we went back to the bus stop to find mobs of people waiting for the bus. Every one that went by had a "Complet" sign on it, so, after an hour of waiting, we hitched a ride with two Frenchmen in a Ford V-8.

Our wedding had been exactly two weeks earlier when we had to say goodbye to Nice. We bought some K-rations to eat on the train and we shared a compartment with a French couple. She was a homely little blonde; wore no makeup; wore a red sweater; ankle socks; shoes with spike heels. He was even homelier, with matted black, greasy hair; glasses; and a dirty blue sweatshirt. They surely were amorous and not the least embarrassed about it. Twenty-four hours later, we were back in Paris.

Our train for home would be leaving the next morning, heading east to Berlin, and we wanted to squeeze as much in as we could in those few hours. Our hotel didn't have the usual extravagances we were becoming used to. How quickly we become spoiled! The light was dim, no hot water, no telephone. We started to gripe, but we sounded so ridiculous, that we stopped in mid-sentence, hugged each other and saw how foolish we were to be so unappreciative of the whole trip. We had all the essentials here. Riding on the Metro to La Place Concorde, it was a glistening sight to see all the lights shining on the buildings. We saw Cleopatra's Needle, the Chamber of Deputies, the Ministry of the Navy, the famous Automobile Club, and, looking far up the Champs Elysees, we could see the Arch all lit up. Paris was "our town"!

We entered the Tuilleries (famous Parisian gardens) and stopped to look at the pond and frightened a tiny frog. Suddenly, we heard a shrill whistle, which meant "Everybody out!" and we just about made it as they closed the gate. After descending the steps down to the Seine, we walked along the river. It was a perfect night for strolling. The moon was full, and was reflected in the water. The arched bridges and the giant trees that lined the river added to the romantic atmosphere. It was the last night of our honeymoon and we were in love!

Crossing a bridge, we came to the Louvre, crossed on the bridge, walked down some narrow, crooked streets; passed a prison; and continued down until we stopped at one of the many small bars and had a glass of beer. French beer tasted flatter and more slippery than our beer, but the French liked it, when they could get it. The bartender gave us this explanation of French drinking habits: They didn't like their drinks iced, nor did they like strong mixtures like cocktails, which they thought ruined your appetite for a meal. They preferred "aperitifs", which were mostly "cooked wines", and they were potent! High society drank the Bordeaux and Burgundies as table wines, to be drunk with food, but "French workmen often like an evening glass of 'blanc' or 'rouge'".

It was 5::00 a.m. when we got on the bus to goto the train station. The American Express man said it would be impossible for us to get on the train because we didn't have tickets. What a terrible thing to have happen so early in the morning! Being half asleep, I didn't much care whether we got on the darned train or not, but Bob was on a new job and he felt he must make an effort to start back home. He saw the train commander and everything cleared up beautifully.

We got on a coach designated "Officers Only", after passing one marked "Female Personnel". When we were comfortably settled in a compartment with several other people, a GI approached Bob, "Sir", he cleared his throat, "you are supposed to ride in the female car." We never did find out why, but it was all right with us because we had a very comfy compartment for four. It had little tables you could pull out. Sandwiches and juice were served and we played cards, wrote postcards, and read "Time" and "Readers Digest".

When we came to Karlsruhe, we saw the terrible devastation as the train traveled through the city. It was a bleak city and, in the dark of night, it was eerie as the moon shone on block after block of ruined buildings. We had dinner in the dungeon-like station. The atmosphere was clammy and we felt as though we were in a prison. We were glad when our train pulled out of Karlsruhe towards Frankfurt and then the last leg of our trip towards Berlin and home.

CHAPTER FOURTEEN

F rau Schellenberg gave us a cheery homecoming as we walked in the front door with our suitcases. We could see that she had filled the house with flowers and plants and there was someone new with her. Her name was Frau Jacobowski and she had been hired to assist Frau Schellenberg in keeping the house spic and span

There were so many things we needed to do that we scarcely knew where to start. The most important task was getting out the many thank you notes. After that, we made a list of people we wanted to entertain in our home. Our first guests were Margie; John and Josette; and Don and Reggie. YES! The nice surprise was that Reggie was still there. Her departure had been postponed a couple of weeks. John and Josette had gone on a fun-filled honeymoon in Switzerland and gave us glowing accounts of all they had seen there.

We received a wedding gift that came as an unanticipated, thrilling surprise that made us speechless. We gazed out the front window and saw some men hefting a rosewood, full concert-size Steinway grand piano. We just gasped at its beauty. The gift was from Lyn. She had given 50 cartons of cigarettes for it (none of them PX cigarettes). I had never been meticulous before, but from then on, when we had company, I was on the lookout for someone to leave a glass on it, or drop an ash on its nice, smooth, shiny surface.

At the end of 1947, when we got back home, the piano arrived safely without a scratch, until the men dropped part of the crate on it and put a dent in it. We had it repaired so that you could never tell where it had been marred. Our problem then was, as we moved 2 or 3 times when Bob was still in college, and when he was starting out on a new job, finding accommodations with a living room large enough for the piano.

After a while, we knew we had to sell it The Steinway people in Washington were not interested in it because of the rosewood case and their fear that it had not been treated with the proper finishes for our climate, When we advertised, the music critic for what was then The Washington Star looked at it and purchased it. We ran into him several years later and asked about it. He said that he collected pianos and had a special building where he kept them. He said that he owned two instruments that he would never get rid of. One was an old harpsichord and the other was our beautiful wedding gift piano.

Early in September we turned in all of our marks and our currency control books. The following day we were issued a new scrip. We had pieces of paper for 5 cents, 10 cents, 25 cents, 50 cents, one dollar, five dollars, and 10 dollars. It didn't make any immediate difference to us, but we were wondering what would happen to the Allied Marks that Russia and France were using. The Russians still had not given us an accounting of how many they had printed and were still "expecting to hear from Moscow any day now."

Russia issued a big protest to the use of scrip by American and British forces and the controversy became loud and bitter at the Allied Control Authority. They said the new money interfered with the German economy and was a violation of a quadripartite agreement that Reichsmarks would be the accepted German currency. It got especially hot when the Americans asked the Kommandatura to make it a crime for Germans to possess scrip.

Special Services put on a couple of dog races and we went with Mim and a friend of hers. Ted had gone home and she was dating a dream of a guy. I had never seen a whippet race and was astonished at how fast they could run. The next race was one for American pets and I just loved it. There were a lot of dachshunds and other small doggies and they were forever getting lost in the tall grass. Some of the little pups would see their masters in the middle of the race and run over to the sidelines with their tails wagging. It was a struggle to urge any of them on over the finish line.

We had just heard from Gus and Olga, who had gone home soon after their wedding. They had a dachshund named Herman, whom they doted on. They had him shipped home, but when they opened the crate, it wasn't Herman at all, but a female dachshund about to have babies. They were heartsick and never found Herman, but they grew to love their new hound and made a good bit of money selling the puppies.

A couple of British officers I knew were going home; decided to throw a going away party for themselves; and invited Joe and his date, and Bob and me to their flat. What a party it turned out to be! One of the officers spent the entire evening in a bedroom with one of the girls. The other got drunk and started harping on how undisciplined the enlisted men were. It made us all disgusted, especially the EMs who were there. Some neighbors banged on the door and complained about all of the noise and a big fight started. Joe was dating a very nice girl named Mara, and she was as shocked as I was over this wild, final fling they called a party. We split while the fighting and arguing was still going on.

John and Josette lived in an apartment house in a section that was not very nice. John was on night duty a lot and Josette was lonesome. There were German families also living in the other 2 apartments, but they were not friendly. Their housefrau was a corker! After parties, she would drink all the unfinished drinks and would sing all of the next day in front of a mirror. She would dance from room to room and it got on Josette's nerves.

They invited us for dinner at 8:00 and we were famished when we arrived. We had a couple of French drinks and, as time passed, began wondering what was holding up dinner. We got hungrier and hungrier and were happy to see Josette going into the kitchen until we heard her exclaim, "Mon Dieu!". The frau had forgotten to turn the oven on under the chicken before she left. At midnight we were just finishing our dinner.

In Moscow, Joseph Stalin made a statement that he saw no danger of war. And Bevin, of Great Britain, agreed with Stalin's approval of the world situation. President Truman, in a speech to West Point cadets, expressed confidence that the world was entering into an era of "permanent peace". He told them, "We are going to need leadership in the future, just as badly as we needed it in this great emergency we have just been through." The President also said, "My definition of leadership is that quality which can make other men do what they do not want to do and like it. That is your duty. That is your job." The atmosphere was becoming less tense at the quadripartite meetings and we began to feel more at east after reading these expressions of world peace.

Bob became a civilian on September 26th. He still had one day of terminal leave left, so on the 25th, we got together with John and Josette to celebrate our first "month-a-versary". We drove to Bagatelle and spent an evening dancing. We hoped all the other months would be as wonderful as this first one. It was hard to believe that a whole month had gone by and that we were old married folks.

His first day at work he had more trouble with his new title than I did with my new name. He kept answering the phone, "Lt. McMann", and he kept saluting the guards. Changing to a civilian actually made very little difference. It meant taking off the officer insignia and replacing it with civilian insignia (my first sewing job! My poor fingers!) The biggest change was in the pay. The amount on his paycheck was twice as much as it had been.

That same day was important in another way. We added a new member to our family, a darling 12 week-old coal black Belgian Shepherd. We named him Trooper and we had a ball chasing him around the house. We realized right away that he was going to be trouble. That first night Bob and I took turns cleaning up after him. He was just so cute though and looked exactly like a little black teddy bear.

Getting Trooper was a victory for me. Bob, at first, thought that getting a dog would be impractical, but, when he saw how much I wanted one, he agreed to get me one for a wedding present. A little dog, he thought, would be just right. All my life my dogs had been small ones and I wanted a big dog. So we "compromised".

After we got him, my Dad wrote, "The family sides with Bob in the argument over the size of the dog. A police dog would be a lot of bother to you and your friends and might be dangerous. It would cost a lot to feed him too. A small dog would serve the same purpose and would be a lot more convenient." I smiled to myself. Too late! Bob had to admit though, "He's as cute as he is irresponsible", and he soon became very fond of him. Trooper learned to shake hands, speak, jump over a stick, and to "platz" (lie down). He was so smart, it was a pleasure to teach him. He loved going along at the golf course and was a great help in finding lost balls.

Lyn and Mim moved out of 9 Herrfurthstrasse into a house and gave a housewarming party. We went and took Trooper with a big, red bow around his neck and he was the life of the party. One fellow there was quite drunk and kept insisting that the dog's name was "Elmer" and that he belonged to him.

We received our first letter from Reggie from Brussels, "I am so homesick to you all and I do miss Don so. How is he doing? Take a little bit care of him, will you. I don't like it here at all and I would give everything I have if only I could come back. It does not look like it right now, but I hope it will change.

"As Don might have told you, I have a job as a governante by a little girl of 4-1/2 years. My aunt got me this job because she was leaving for Suisse and she did not want me to live in a hotel. Also, as you might know from your honeymoon, life in France and Belgium is very expensive."

She had lots of questions and the whole letter showed her thoughts to be in Berlin. We missed her so much too and it didn't seem right to see Don without her.

Some officers we knew received promotions and their invitations were clever. On the cover of one, in big print, were the words 'WE'VE HAD IT'. Then there were two pair of captains' bars with the names: 'RAJSKI' and 'MO' under them; the name 'CHUCK' was beneath a first lieutenant's bar. On the inside page were the words:

We received another original invitation soon after that. The printing on the cover read: "BAR FLIES'

That party was given by Bea (Bob's former girlfriend) and Lola. As we walked in the door, someone met us with a pair of scissors and promptly snipped off the end of Bob's precious peacock tie. The wall over the bar was dotted with bits of lovely ties, but everyone at the party took it in stride and stood around comparing what was left of their ties with each other.

Now that we were married, we were permitted to buy up to $90 per month in groceries at the commissary. It was great fun to go there on Saturdays and pick out what we wanted. Our bill never ran that high as prices were cheap. I remember buying a 4 pound leg of lamb for $1.48. Usually our Saturdays were pretty full and I did a lot of ordering over the phone and the groceries were brought right to the house.

I cooked dinner for Bob 3 times a week. Mother's friend, Amy Lamkin, had given me "The Joy of Cooking" as a wedding gift. I didn't appreciate it so much at the time, but it has remained one of my most treasured possessions. Bob would come home and say, "What page are we on tonight, dear?" Often at noon, Don Wilson and Joe would give me cooking instructions for my meal for that night. I couldn't cook when I was rushed, so if we had dinner guests, Frau Schellenberg (an expert) stayed. to prepare the meal.

We still ate many dinners at Truman Hall. Three meals a day for one person cost only 90 cents. You can always find people who love to gripe about food, but we really got our money's worth. Don used to joke and say, "I wish they would put a little more fruitie in their tutie".

We were given several lamps, but we had no floor lamp and, with no overhead lighting in the living room, needed one there. Bob set off on his bicycle to look for one. He had to ride some distance to a German shop and there he found just what he wanted. It was a tall, slender lamp, made from German airplane aluminum. The lamp was so light, he could lift it easily with one hand. "This was made for us," Bob thought and was quite pleased with himself for finding it so quickly. He paid the man, picked up the lamp, got on his bike and started for home

Halfway home, a German policeman started shouting at him, frantically waving his arms. Bob, not understanding a word, kept right on going. You can imagine the ridiculous picture he made on his bike with this thing that appeared to be a lance. It wasn't until some time later that he realized he had been riding in the street, instead of in the special lane reserved for bicycles.

The new Ping Pong table that his buddies made for us arrived. From then on, every night before retiring, we played a few games. He, of course, was much better than I was, but I played well enough to keep him on his toes and, every once in a while, I slipped over a victory. At least, I'm pretty sure he didn't deliberately let me win. We might never have gotten acquainted had it not been for this sport and we called ourselves "The Ping Pong Champs". Don teased, "Ping Pong Chumps is more like it."

Trooper was growing and getting cuter every day. He was so lively and loved to chase his golf ball around and under furniture. He was so black that, at night, all we could see were his white eyeballs and red tongue in that impish little face. He began to like shaking hands so much that he did it whether you asked him to or not.

One night, when Bob was in an exceptionally good mood, I talked him into letting Trooper sleep in our bedroom. We woke up in the middle of the night with the bed lamp shining directly in our faces. Trooper was pulling on the tassel on the end of the lamp cord, turning the light on and off. He also stepped on Bob's face, which made it the last night he stayed in our room.

Trooper soon learned that he got a light spanking if he made a mess in the house. I noticed that occasionally he would break away from us when playing and go up to the third floor, but he didn't stay long. We never went there and I thought he was just exploring. Out of curiosity, I went to find out what the big draw was, and there I found several small piles on the floor. After that, we made sure we took him outside more often.

I spent Saturday afternoon with Lyn while Bob was in a meeting. Lyn's pup, Sissy, had been very ill and she had left her with a veterinarian for 2 weeks and had taken food to her every day. The poor little thing was as skinny as a matchstick and her hind legs were sore. I felt sure the vet had been eating the food that Lyn had taken to her. We took Sissy home and kept her wrapped in warm blankets. Sissy did recover that time, but she was never the same. Her hind legs were not steady and the poor little thing had a most unhappy attitude towards everyone but Lyn.

CHAPTER FIFTEEN

John and Josette came to our house to have dinner with us. She looked unhappy and said that she hated Berlin. When she and I were alone, she said she hated being alone so much during the day and that John had duty every 4th night. Then she broke down, started to cry and told me that John's ex-frauleine had called him several times and she, Josette, had found some of the girl's belongings in John's jeep. She was planning a trip home to see her father in Paris and she thought John would date the German girl while she was gone.

At first, I had trouble believing these things about John. Josette was hard to understand, due to her heavy accent, and I thought that, surely, I had misunderstood what she was saying. Someone as much in love with Josette as John appeared to be, wouldn't dream of being unfaithful so soon after the wedding. Maybe Josette was overly jealous.

Then, I could see how distraught she was and I knew there were severe problems in their marriage. She then confided in me that she thought she was pregnant. I hardly knew what to say because I had just learned that our friend, John, was a total heel, to put it mildly. All I could do was hug her. John's tour of duty would be over in another month or so and he would be taking her to Florida to meet his mother. I could only hope that getting away from his former lady friend would make things better for them.

Bob left for Stuttgart on October 9th to attend a meeting there and then go on to visit some DP camps (displaced persons). There was one camp in particular where there had been a frightening incident. The United Press reported "Hundreds of Jewish displaced persons, some yelling 'American Gestapo', were forced back into the Foehrenwald DP Camp at bayonet point, after they had surrounded, spat upon, and slapped American military police.

"Six DPs were slightly injured by bayonets. The camp leader 'demanded the American soldiers be turned over to the DPs' . . . The second riot stemmed indirectly from a small riot on Wednesday, when German police shot and killed a DP named Isaac Feldberg."

Major Steers, the Military Government Director of the camp, said, "As far as you could see, there were people coming out of the camp. They surrounded the MPs who were left to guard the camp. The tactical troops jumped from their trucks with bayonets and walked slowly to the crowd. The crowd yelled 'American Gestapo' and 'American SS'. They spat on and slapped the soldiers."

Bob was to be gone four days—our first separation—and I felt lost when I saw the train pull out. Don gave a going-away party for Ruick at 15 Lanstrasse and I went. It was a strange feeling to walk back into that house and it just wasn't a party for me without Bob there. In the middle of the evening, he called and it was wonderful to hear his voice, just as though I hadn't heard it for weeks. Someone said, "He certainly is tied to your apron strings to feel he had to call before he was away a few hours." And everyone hee-hawed.

Paul Ruth, who had taken the movies of our wedding, ended his tour while we were away and left word that the movies were with Ruick. At the party that night I said, "Be sure you leave the movies with us before you exit." To which he replied, "What movies?" Wherever those movies are, someone must be saying, "I wonder who those people getting married are." We never located them.

I fell asleep in a chair and Margie awakened me. She had borrowed someone's jeep and took me home and spent the night at my house.

To keep busy while Bob was gone, I went shopping and took Ingrid, my office friend, with me. I got a baby doll for Angie's 3rd birthday; a shiny, silver cigarette box for my aunt; and some blue satin cloth with gold flamingoes on it to be made into a pillow cover

I invited Ingrid to dinner and, as usual, I enjoyed her company. I felt bad because she was amazed at how much we Americans had. She told me she used one lamp and a radio for 3 hours every night and that was all she was allowed to do. She asked me if she could take a bath because she had no hot water, and she luxuriated in our tub for half an hour.

After she went home, Don and Juliette Wilson and Bill Fourqueron picked me up to attend a party given by the French Industry Branch. Their occasions always started late, so it was after 10 when they picked me up in one of the sedans assigned to Economics Division. As we were nonchalantly driving, some MPs motioned us to the side of the road, looked at the license number in front, and proceded to herd us to headquarters for driving a stolen vehicle. The car had been specifically assigned to Don Wilson and it was definitely not a stolen car, so we were perplexed. It took over an hour with many questions and phone calls and, finally, they got through to the right person at the Motor Pool and we were on our way. Those MPs were right on the ball! Maybe they thought we were spies?

The party was fine, except that I missed my husband. I danced for a while with various people, then tried to find a quiet corner, which was impossible because there were at least 350 people in a few small rooms. I found a Frenchman who had just been married and whose wife was in Paris; so we had something in common; and I talked with a couple of French teenagers; and spent the rest of the time eating and trying to round up some Americans to take me home. It was 4:00 when I went to bed and Bob's train was due in at 9:00. When he walked in the house, I was still asleep. I got up, but was groggy from lack of sleep and not as overjoyed at seeing him as he wanted me to be. Is that the point when you know 'the honeymoon is over'?

His trip to the Zone had been interesting in many ways. He spent most of one day at a place called Bebra, located on the border of the Russian/U.S. Zones. It was used as a refugee and prisoner of war exchange point. While there, he interviewed a trainload of discharged German prisoners from Russia. He had never seen a more miserable looking bunch of men. They had been discharged because they were no longer able to work, due to the loss of a limb, T.B., acute malnutrition, etc.

He watched them being processed—dusted with DDT and examined. One boy especially stood out in his memory. He had been a prisoner for a year and a half; was just 18 years old; and his arms were the size of a broom handle. That case was multiplied by hundreds. The men had no clothing or equipment except the clothes they wore, which were the uniforms they had been captured in, or clothes of those less fortunate who had died while in camp. One prisoner told Bob that 25% of his comrades had died after capture.

On October 18th, we became proud jeep owners. Bob's name had finally made it to the top of the list and he went to pick it up. For $430 we owned a complete pile of junk. It did run though. It was a dilapidated hunk, but we thought it was a chariot! It had 4 wheels and an engine, but little more. It had no top and only a seat for the driver. The windshield had a bullet hole in it and was lying flat on the hood for lack of bolts to hold it onto the frame.

Don loaned us his license plates and we went for a drive that evening (I sat on the floorboard). You would have thought we had just bought a Cadillac convertible. A couple of days later, Don gave us the windshield from his jeep and also his jeep seats. He was having his vehicle remodeled and having a Starr body put on it.

We named ours "Gerry" for "Geronimo". That is a word used by paratroopers when they are getting ready to jump. For the next few evenings, Bob spent his spare time climbing into and under Gerry with all sorts of tools. He tore it apart and adjusted this and adjusted that and had a big time. He told me about the Model T he bought when he was 16 years old. He worked on it and was the envy of his classmates, but his father didn't share his glee with it and made him park it down the street.

There were garages cropping up that did nothing but remodel the jeeps that we were buying. We had a red body put on ours and it shaped up into something quite remarkable. Don was proud of how his finished product looked, but I only rode in it once. The rear had room for one passenger, if that person was small and didn't mind hunching over, bending at the waist.

Bob was better with his German than I was. I was ashamed of my skimpy vocabulary. I told Ingrid that I wanted to take lessons and she read an advertisement in a German paper about a teacher looking for students. Ingrid wrote a letter to Frau Laurent and she came the following Sunday to give Bob and me our first lesson.

We liked her right away. She had been a housekeeper for a man we knew and she spoke English fluently. She had two young children, Reinar and Bettina, and we began sending them candy every time she came. Frau Laurent came every week for 3 or 4 months until we felt we could carry on a conversation, or at least make ourselves understood. Once, she brought me a china collie dog. Reinar wanted her to bring it to me because I had sent him so much candy. That figurine is, and always will be, one of my treasures.

She told us how the Germans had all hoped that the Americans would reach Berlin before the Russians did. It was not to be and the immediate aftermath of their arrival was a time of tremendous fear. She said that a Russian soldier entered her house and had attempted to rape her, but she was able to talk him out of it. She asked him if he had a mother and he told her "You had better leave quickly."

Frau Schellenberg told me an interesting experience she had during the war. She was having a cup of coffee in a coffee house and noted a man staring at her. When he got up to leave, he dropped a card on her table and told her she must call him at that number. It was one of Hitler's henchmen and she dared not disobey. When she called, he said he wanted to talk to her and she must come downtown. The gist of their conversation was that she was 27 years old, very healthy, and attractive, and she would have to have a baby because Hitler was creating a master race. Frau Schellenberg said she would have to think about it. She was unmarried at that time.

She spoke to her parents and to her parents' best friends. They advised her to refuse to do this. She detested the idea of being ordered to have a child and so she did nothing. She did not call him and, miraculously, she never heard from him again. The war was turning sour for Germany and he must have put his efforts elsewhere.

There were still plenty of warm days in October and, with the sun beating down on us, we set out on a Sunday in our new jeep, with our new dog, with Don Ryan, and with our cameras. We drove to the British Sector to the Rundfunken Tower. Rundfunken was the German equivalent of our Radio City, but the buildings were all ruins by then. Brave souls that we were, we decided to climb the tower, which appeared to be 500 feet high. Some of the steps were missing, but we got to within 20 feet of the top I can still see Bob and me climbing on ahead and looking down on Don, who was always a flight behind us. Don would say, "I'll be right with you," while looking scared to death. Trooper got only 20 steps along when he came to a step with the back of it missing. That was it for him. The view of Berlin was grand. We sat for a long time on planks, looking down on the city people and taking photos. It was there that we opened our lunch bag and ate our sandwiches.

Don, Mac, and John came for dinner. It was the largest meal I had attempted to cook. They went to sleep afterwards so I didn't know what to think. We had baked macaroni, a baked carrot dish, veal steaks, asparagus salad and a two-tone gelatin dessert with pineapple. I was pretty proud of my well-rounded, nourishing menu, but was exhausted, so I, too, dozed off along with the others.

We had to wake John up because he got a call that an American civilian had been shot and killed by a Russian in the Russian Sector. He left immediately and came back in a couple of hours. The man (we didn't know him) had been in a taxi in the Russian Sector. The Russians were pretty fussy about who entered their sector and why. They asked this fellow to follow them to the Kommandatura, but he tried to get away from them and got himself killed. If that was actually the way it happened, it was foolish of him not to follow them. His reasons for being there were never divulged and there was probably more to the story than that, but that is all we ever knew.

I took the red plaid material we had bought in France to Minnie to make a skirt for me and a shirt for Bob. She measured very carefully and, with a disappointed look on her face, told me there was only enough material for a skirt for me, although she could manage to make a tie for Bob. We wore our "twin" outfits to Harnack House and people did a double-take when they saw us. I took a good bit of kidding too, about getting hold of the material before Bob did.

A couple of months later, I went back to see Minnie about having another dress made. She didn't know I was coming and she walked in the room wearing—you guessed it—a red plaid shirt. I considered saying something about it, but there wasn't anything I could do about it then, so I bit my tongue. I did measure carefully any material I brought from then on.

October 22nd we learned the results of the Berlin elections. The Socialists won big all over Berlin, even in the Russian Sector. It was a big victory for the Western Powers and we were very pleased. The weather was starting to get quite cold. The people on the streets were bundled up and cold-looking and the stores were like ice boxes. It was not a good feeling to know that we had a nice, warm house to go to and plenty eat when so many people would die that winter because they did not have these things.

We celebrated two months of marriage. Bob called and asked me to meet him after work at the PX. He came in, his face lit up, with a pot of yellow flowers in one hand and rose corsages for Josette and me in the other. Then he insisted on buying me a purse (something I didn't need), but we settled for a pale, blue headscarf. I gave him some bookends.

Josette had just returned from Paris. Margie had gone with her and they stayed at Josette's home. Her mother had been killed by the Germans and her father, an elderly man, was the only one at home. Monsieur Rocourt belonged to the S'il Vous Plait Club. For all members, the club had the service of answering any question they might care to ask. Josette and Margie wracked their brains and made several calls. They found out who had the largest feet in the world, but stumped the experts over the stocking size of King George of England.

Josette was definitely pregnant and did not seem too happy about the prospect of a baby. Her legs were beginning to bother her and she didn't feel well at all. I wondered then if she and John were still as happy as they had been, but chalked it up to her early months of pregnancy.

Sergeant Major Drinkall (we called him "Drinkie") in the British office married a very pretty, very gentle girl named Mary and we attended the wedding. It was a

Church of England wedding and Mary did not wear white but her suit was a soft shade of gray and she wore a hat of flowers. On her shoulder were 4 orchids. There were bags of confetti and the air was thick with bits of colored paper. I was told that the English never have double ring ceremonies. I thought they were missing a great idea. Bob had wanted his ring. He said he wanted to feel as much married as I did.

Drinkie had grown a terrible mustache for the affair. I think he did it to hide his face, because he was extremely nervous. After the wedding, Bob threatened to grow a mustache like that and I told him that if he did, I would get a boyish bob. That put an end to that.

CHAPTER SIXTEEN

Our names had been on the list for the Potsdam Tour for a long time and we were looking forward to it. The city of Potsdam was where the Four Powers met immediately after the war and all of our quadripartite meetings were based on the Potsdam Conference and the agreements that took place there. It was a short distance from Berlin and was in the Russian Zone.

As we got on the Special Services bus, we were handed a list of instructions:

"1. All persons going on the Potsdam Tour with Special Services are forbidden to take any photographs, except when in Sans-Souci Park.

"2. Privately-owned vehicles accompanying the tour must follow the route taken by the bus and must remain with the party after the tour.

"3. Any violations will be reported to the Headquarters Commandant for disciplinary action.

"4. Violations of these rules will cause cancellation of passes for American personnel to Potsdam."

We were warned!

Potsdam, once a beautiful city, was also once the center of German culture. Now it was just a mass of stone and brick ruins, as a result of a 20-minute bombing attack by the RAF. We could not see the marble Palace, where the Potsdam conference had been held, as it was being used as a Russian recreation center. We stopped and visited Frederick the Great's church. Nothing much was left of it but the front of the building and a few radiators hanging in mid-air.

Sans-Souci Park was several kilometers from the center of the city. It was an enormous and magnificent park and, in spite of the instructions allowing us to take photos in the park, the Russian guide who came on board told us it was not allowed. In the park, we visited 3 palaces where Fredericks I, II, and IV had lived, and, standing on a hill, we got a good view of the whole city. At the time of Frederick the Great, Germany was impressed with France and tried to copy French architecture and furnishings, as well as paintings and sculptures and palace names. The King surrounded himself with French leaders, artists, and engineers. Even the official court language was French. It was an interesting and informative excursion into the past.

Helen, my Russian counterpart, used to come into our office to talk to Joe and me. She was a lively, young woman and loved our sense of humor. There wasn't much kidding around in her office.

She told us that soon she would go to Moscow and marry a Russian major who was stationed in Poland. She wasn't the least bit excited about it and her answers to questions were short and unenthusiastic. She did go home, but the wedding was postponed, and she came back to Berlin, bringing gifts for Joe and me. We each received a jeweled Easter egg and she pleaded with us not to tell anyone in her office that she had given us gifts. She was not allowed to fraternize with us and she feared for her family.

On October 30th, we gave a Halloween Going Away party for Margie. A pumpkin or two and some doughnuts we sponged from the Red Cross Club and some candy canes gave the Stateside touch to the festivities. Margie was swamped with presents, ours being a large purse, at her suggestion. She left a couple of days later, with no definite future plans in mind, although she was going to see Dick. We hated to lose her, not knowing if we would ever see her again.

Two minor incidents occurred. One was the disappearance of our bathroom sink. There were two sinks in our "green room" and one of them developed a crack and Bob called the engineers to come and fix it. Instead of fixing it on the spot, they carted it away. Weeks went by and we had no word about our sink. Finally, Bob called the engineers and asked about it. "Sink? We don't have any record of any sink," came the reply. Figure that! The sink never did turn up

The other: I had written my new mother and told her that I would love to see Bob's baby book and one day the package arrived for me. I was in Bob's office when I opened it and his secretary was there too. There were some pictures of a darling, little boy in it and, for the first time, I saw Bob blush. He left the room and she and I ooh'd and aah'd over one snapshot after another of him growing up. All of the photos showed a precious little guy.

Four fellows, who were leaving OMGUS for the States, sent us another unusual invitation to their going away party. It was in the form of a Staff Study, with tabs (enclosures) to make it look as complicated and difficult to understand as most Army studies were. It went as follows:

SUBJECT: Aloha to OMGUS
TO: All our Shipmates in the Port of Berlin
DISCUSSION:
1.   In appreciation for the warmhearted friendship resulting from the very fine business and social associations the undersigned have had in Berlin and particularly in OMGUS, your presence is desired at a week-end party on PIER "75" to assist in launching our ship with a few magnas of champagne and perhaps a schooner or two of beer.

2. The crew on PIER "75" have been privileged to serve on the USS OMGUS under skipper, Lieutenant General Clay, for the periods indicated. (TAB 1). During these many months we have found our deck-washing and hull-scraping made easier and shore leave made more pleasant by the many fine mates, with whom we have traded scuttlebutt, and so it is our desire to say aloha and dankeshoen for the many memories we will cherish in the years to come.

3. At TAB 2 is a sailing chart of our new ship's course.

4. At TAB 3 is your week-end pass to PIER "75" for the period from 1200 hours, 26 October 1946, to 0800 hours, 28 October 1946.

5. ACTION RECOMMENDED;

It is recommended that all our mates in Berlin visit us at PIER "75" during weekend of 26-27 October 1946 that we may bid them farewell and drink a toast to their continued good work in the occupation of Germany.

CONCURRENCES:

Concurrences will be indicated by your presence at PIER "75" during the time specified above. (It is impractical to obtain concurrences prior to the submission of this staff study.)

HENRY F. ROEMELE
Captain

PAUL A. TROWER
Captain

GERALD Q. O'NEAL
1ST Lt

CHARLES R. AULT
1ST Lt.

Tab 3 (the Pass) read:

This is your pass to one of the hottest times ever to be held by any of the mates of the USS OMGUS. Please remember to bring this item with you. Not to get in with, of course, but merely because we're short on napkins and if you should spill your drink, then what would you do without it.

THE CREW

This pass is only good when presented by the person who has it and may not be transferred, eaten, sold, bought, or traded, except under ordinary circumstances. The management reserves the right to get plastered.

I had taken piano lessons all the way through high school. I could read music and had written several songs, even winning a contest once, However, I didn't feel that I played enough for others to enjoy my talent and I started taking piano lessons.

Bob used to sit down and "try" to pick out a few melodies. He got so that he was pretty sharp with a tune called "All of My Life". I could take the dog out for a short walk, wash my hair, put it up in curlers, come back downstairs, and he would just be finishing the same piece he had started on. And how he played Chopin! When I would kid him about it, he would say "You're just nipping a genius in the bud."

So many of our friends were departing, but we made friends with a new couple. An American football league had formed in Germany and Berlin had its own team that played in the Olympic Stadium when in town. The city itself had a logo—a bear that stood upright and looked more like a lion to me. Nevertheless, our team was the Berlin Bears. We started going to the games and the coach and his wife became friends. Mickie and Fred Spiegelberg were as close to a glamorous movie-star looking couple as you could get. She was a brunette with a winning smile; he had blonde, curly hair, and a physique that most men would die for. They were fun people.

Once they came late to a gathering and she quipped, "Didn't mean to be late, but we had to have a quickie." Like Lyn, she was uninhibited. She once told me that they had been in a hotel in Frankfurt when one of the players banged on the door to their room and then barged right in. She was embarrassed because, "you know how you look early in the morning when you first wake up." I knew how I looked, but I couldn't imagine Mickie looking unattractive under any circumstances.

When she was in the hospital, we went to see her. She had just had a miscarriage and the whole team had just been to see her. They came in one at a time and took up the whole visiting time so that we only had a couple of minutes with her. She and Fred wanted children very much. After they went home to Alabama, they had a boy and I cried when I learned that the child had gotten polio and died. This was in the 50's when, as mothers, our biggest fear was that our children would come down with the dreaded disease. That was before Jonas Salk, from my very own University of Pittsburgh (Pitt), developed the Salk Vaccine and alleviated that horrendous disease.

I learned something about Southern cooking from Mickie when they invited us to a New Years Day dinner. We had Hoppin' John, which is stewed tomatoes, rice, black-eyed peas and sausages. She said it was obligatory to serve that on New Years Day and that if you did, it brought you good luck for the coming year.

The first football game we attended with John and Josette. We went to pick them up and, as usual, Josette was slower than molasses and we sat outside in the jeep for half an hour waiting for her. John explained, "She had to fix lunch today." He was sticking up for his darling, but he didn't need to. She took her time, but she always looked breathless and precious.

The stadium was in the British Sector and we were told there would be signs to follow. No signs. Others, who were searching for it too, were: an American Red Cross bus, an Army truck, a jeep full of engineers, and a station wagon, and we formed a procession to scour the area in search of the field. We appeared to be going round in circles, when some British MPs came along and escorted us there. Finally, some smart British MPs!

There was a big crowd, including many Germans. Children were running around picking up cigarette butts and there were two Army bands. Once, when a player was hurt, a German girl shouted, "Ein mann ist kaput." Josette had just learned to keep score and was tickled about it. I missed the hot dogs, but it was a good game. The Bears won 21-7, and they continued to win every game all that season.

Although it was getting colder every day, we still played golf. We always took Trooper with us and the little fellow loved it, although he was always tuckered out afterwards. I could dangle a nylon stocking before his nose, safe in knowing he was too tired to chew it up.

I was saving all of my cigarette butts for Ingrid. She could sell them, or re-roll them for smoking. I would go around emptying ashtrays in several American offices and by the end of every day would have a whole bag full. It made her so happy and she wrote me a nice thank you note and had drawn pretty, blue flowers on the paper.

Lyn and Mim invited us over for a chicken dinner. Lyn had been offered a better job and she was to start it the next day. She was to be with the Public Relations Office of Berlin District and was going to help write the history of the Berlin District. She was going to work for a colonel and would use his diary as a guide. It sounded like an excellent opportunity and that Lyn was just right for the job.

Mim, that night, introduced us to her fiancé, a very good looking Army Sergeant. I didn't think she had gotten over Ted yet, but the two of them were hitting it off rather well. As it turned out, the engagement didn't last and when she went back to the States, she caught up with Ted, they married and traveled all over the world together.

A couple of days later, a picture of Lyn appeared in THE OBSERVER, along with the headline, "LYNDAL LEAVES PAPER'. Reading on, it said, "Unlike the shoemaker whose children go unshod, Miss Lyndal M. Davis, Observer's Society Editor, has been well-known in social circles of OMGUS and Berlin District. Lyn has been a reporter and feature writer for THE OBSERVER since January when she arrived in Berlin.

"Two weeks ago, USFET Circular No. 81, which states that no American civilian employee employed on unit publications are to be paid from War Department funds, was applied to THE OBSERVER staff. During the readjustment to central post funds, the civilian personnel staff had to be cut. The contracts of the other civilian members will terminate this month, and Lyn transferred to the Office of Military government, Berlin Sector, as Deputy Public Relations Officer.

"Lyn, whose home is in Austin, Texas, attended the University of Texas, where she wrote for The Daily Texan for two years as a reporter. She was a public relations officer at the Coast Guard Academy in Washington, D.C. for a year and a half before she came to Berlin.

"One of the most interesting assignments that she had on THE OBSERVER was a field trip into Bavaria from where she brought back the feature stories 'Wanted—Bread for Porcelain' and "Oberammergau". She met the first ship of dependents arriving at Bremerhaven and wrote the story of their arrival in 'Operation Dependency'. She was in on the groundwork at the starting of the Women's Club and has faithfully attended and reported their activities. The summer school for American children and the new experimental club for German youth at 3110th Signal Service Bn. have been duly reported by her.

"Besides news-scooping, Lyn is interested in music. She played the violin with the symphony orchestra of Texas and in Berlin, she had been studying voice. Another pastime has been urging readers to try out the recipes that she has accumulated and printed in THE OBSERVER recently."

There was a colonel in Bob's office who was a dilly. He felt it his personal duty to go around making mountains out of molehills. He arrested a friend of ours for speeding and arrested a fellow in my office for passing a car at 30 mph in a 20 mph zone. His was an office job, but he could arrest people who broke the law because of his rank. He spent his spare time up and down the main roads looking for someone to arrest and it made him feel important.

The Division cars were not supposed to pick up anyone hitchhiking, but they all did it. Rides were hard to get and many Americans depended on a hitched ride to get to work. One morning, Col Abbott, saw the PW and DP Division car pick up an American civilian. He motioned the car to stop and ordered the fellow to get out and swaggered as he did it. Another incident he must have been very proud of was stopping a fellow for singing in the halls of an office building. The fellow, a civilian, spoke respectfully to him, but Col Abbott was not satisfied and had him court-martialed

He spent a great deal of time writing letters of complaint. He wrote a letter to THE OBSERVER telling them to please put their "terms of reference" at the end of each article. The letter wasn't taken very seriously and he called them about the seriousness of it. They thanked him and continued to do as always. They weren't sure what it was he wanted.

We received news on November 6th that Major Laughton Cobb had been on the plane that was missing the day before somewhere between Naples and London. Laughton had lived at 15 Lanstrasse when Bob first moved in and he was as fine a person as any we met in Berlin. He was extremely handsome, a West Pointer, and an Air Force man, with a most likeable personality. It would be impossible to describe him and do him justice.

Laughton had been transferred in March to Weisbaden, where he was in charge of a small airfield. He married the Belgian girl whose family had sheltered him during the war, and they were expecting a baby. On November 5th, he took another officer's run as co-pilot on a plane from Naples to London. Twenty-six planes were searching for the missing plane and it was feared to be lost over the Mediterranean. It was terrible news, but we waited anxiously, hoping that a miracle would turn up.

The plane was never found and the world lost a great citizen. After the first of the year, we received an announcement from his wife of the birth of Anne Laughton Cobb.

CHAPTER SEVENTEEN

After dinner one night, we had some callers. They were Tommy, a soldier Bob knew, and Eleanor, his German wife. The marriage ban had not been lifted and marriage between Americans and Germans was not legal. Tommy and Eleanor were married, however, and living in her apartment.

Two Americans had already been sent home. They left behind two German girls they had married between their discharge and their employment by the War Department through a supposed loophole in the marriage policy. They had been married before peace was declared.

An American chaplain wrote THE OBSERVER protesting the ban on fraulein marriages. He said the ban aided immorality and contributed to the Army's high venereal disease rate and contradicted the efforts of Military Government to democratize Germany. He granted that if it were lifted, some soldiers would be "taken", but said that as long as "some Yanks have two candy bars, they'll be taken for one of them".

In December, an advance copy of Circular 181, the awaited key to the door of heretofore forbidden fraulein marriages, was printed in the paper. It stated that applications must be made at least 3 months before the ceremony takes place. The wedding could not take place, however, prior to one month before the applicant was to leave the theater.

"Only major commanders are allowed to approve marriages to Germans . . . . an application for permission to marry may be approved when the marriage contemplated will not bring discredit to the military service."

But it was a month before this circular came about that Tommy and Eleanor were in our house. The first impression I had of them was that they were a strange couple. They both appeared to be people who had never had many advantages in life and they lacked luster and appeal. The more we talked, though, I came to believe that this was a German marriage that would work out for the best. Eleanor was charming in her own way and Tommy, a small town boy, was sincere in everything he said.

He had been married in the States to a woman who became hateful and mean, drank exceedingly, and ran around with other men. They had two children, and, after six years of marriage, they were divorced. The little boy was adopted by Tommy's best friend, and his parents took the little girl. He came overseas and fought all through the war and when his outfit occupied a village that was now in the Russian Zone, he met Eleanor. Her family had been especially nice to him and he had eaten many delicious meals there. Eleanor said that the Germans in her village loved the Americans because they had come in so peacefully after the Russians left.

Tommy's outfit eventually left for Berlin and one day he decided to go back for her. It must have been quite an experience, as the Russians chased them and stopped them frequently as they were making their way back to Berlin. Eleanor told us some interesting things about Germany before the war. Her father had been a Social Democrat, and therefore they were not privileged to buy many items in the stores. The only reason her father had not been put in a concentration camp was that the Bergemeister had stuck up for him. I can only hope that their marriage went as planned and that they have had a long and happy life together.

My family wrote of the gorgeous fall weather they were having. It was getting colder every day in Berlin and we had frost in the mornings, with occasional snow. There was some terribly thick, dense fog too. It was so bad that sometimes cars could not move in it at all until it cleared.

Josette was in a wreck when her driver slammed into a stalled C&R. She was badly shaken up, but not seriously injured.

In the large cities, the Germans were then getting a ration of two lumps of coal per day. It was depressing to think of it, but it was true. Some of the shops were as cold as it was outside and I could imagine what it must be like to work in such a place and then go home at night to a cold house. I felt bad when I rode home in a warm bus that was only half full, and saw the mobs of people trying to get on a tiny streetcar. They were hardy people, but in Berlin alone there were 60,000 cases of TB.

We were asked to conserve electricity and Mr. Forester wrote to B-Bag, "We of the Coal and Mining Section, Industry Branch, OMGUS, and all of those who are working with us on coal problems, are asking all of us in Allied Military Government to cooperate to the limit to keep unnecessary lights and electrical appliances turned off. Burning lights, and electrical and gas appliances is the same as burning so many pounds of coal. It is quite necessary that we practice what we preach, both officially and personally." Coal was THE critical shortage.

On Armistice Day, Major General Frank A. Keating, then Acting Deputy Military Governor, spoke to the troops at the Berlin Hockey Field and we were there. He said, "Twenty eight years ago this Armistice Day, 4,350,000 American men laid down their arms and returned to their home firm in the belief that the cause for which 126,000 of their comrades gave their lives was secure. Yet a scarce 23 years later 12,000,000 American men were called to again reaffirm to the world that the United States and the other freedom-loving peoples of the world were ready to fight and to die so that the world might live in peace and security . . . .

"This time thousands of American soldiers remained abroad to finish the job; to insure that lasting peace is won and that our sainted missing and dead have not been sacrificed in vain. It is to those who have remained behind, particularly the 8,000 here in Berlin, that I would like to direct this message.

"It is our duty as members of the Army, as citizens, and as participants in the occupation of Germany to assure that every action reflects our determination that never again will any nation be permitted to threaten the peace and security of the world."

Chaplain Marvin E. Utter spoke after the General and at 11:00, a mortar explosion broke the stillness and was followed by a minute of reverent silence. Then, in the morning mist, Taps came from beyond the fringe of trees and the crowd remained motionless as three more bugles at different stations in the OMGUS area, repeated the solemn notes in memory of those who had died in battle.

On a lighter note, there was a Lena the Hyena craze in the ET. Every American in Europe read the comic strip, "'Lil Abner'", in the STARS AND STRIPES and it was just about that time that the poor fellow was to be married to the most gruesome woman on earth. Her picture was never printed in the comic strip, but there was wild speculation everywhere as to just what she looked like.

The Dun' Roamin' Red Cross Club sponsored a Lena the Hyena contest and all Americans were invited to enter drawings or paintings showing just what they thought this hideous woman looked like. An exhibition was held and a collection of more horrible looking creatures had never been seen! Everyone locked their doors and windows that night after viewing these representations! First prize was a call to the States, and second prize was a fountain pen.

Ginny McGilton arrived on November 11th and a couple of days later I went with her and her matron of honor to try on my bridesmaid's dress. Ginny was a cute, little blonde, and I liked her as soon as I met her. She met her matron-of-honor on the ship coming over and they struck up a real friendship.

My dress was a pale pink, with blue flowers appliquéd on it—very beautiful. Ginny's dress was out of this world. The front of it was completely beaded with silver. She had just had her 18th birthday on the ship and a surprise party was planned for her that night at our house. Mac sent over dozens and dozens of flowers and a cake that surprised us all with its elaborate décor.

The McGiltons wedding was November 17th. Josette and I were the bridesmaids and John and Bob were ushers. John came by for Bob and they drove off, Bob taking the house key with him. A short time later, a car came for me and we set out to pick up Josette. We were passing Harnack House when it dawned on me that Josette's and my flowers were on our sun porch on the second floor and Bob had the only key to the house. I panicked, ordered the driver to stop, and I rushed into the lobby, in my long dress, brushing past the Sunday diners. Quickly, I located a phone and tried to get hold of Bob. That didn't work.

Back in the car, I had the driver return to my house, with the idea in mind of breaking a window. What a delightful surprise! In our haste, we had not locked the house! That was something we always double-checked to be sure our house was secure. Now, thanks to our carelessness, Josette and I had flowers!

Ginny was truly a beautiful bride and the whole wedding was elegant. The reception at Harnack House was jammed with people and it was a joyous occasion.

Bob and Don had rounded up six alarm clocks and sneaked off to Mac's apartment to hide them in various spots, set to go off at different times. They also short-sheeted the bed. Alarm clocks were valuable items and I must say Mac gave us a hard time when we tried to get ours back. The one that bugged them the most was the one that had been hidden in the sounding board of the piano. They thought the Russians were marching through Berlin again!

A couple of days after the wedding, the first tragedy in our lives occurred. Trooper had developed distemper and there was no medication available for him. I hadn't had any experience with the disease, and some days he was lively and appeared to be well and we thought from time to time that he was getting better.

Frau Schellenberg put him in the basket on her bicycle and took him to the vet, only to find that the vet was out of town. I planned to take him to another vet that evening. Bob and I had dinner together at the mess hall. He was OMGUS Duty Officer for that entire night and I went to get Lyn and have her spend the night with me. When we walked in the front door, Trooper was lying on a pillow in the hall. He was breathing heavily, but he sat up to greet me. He immediately lay back down and could hardly thump his tail. I was so worried and scared!

I called the Red Cross and they said there would be a vet there from 8:00 to 9:30. We drove there, planning to bring the vet back to the house, but the vet never showed up. A very nice WAAC sergeant offered to take me to another one and we drove all over Berlin. We found a lady vet and brought her back to my house and when we came in, Trooper staggered to meet us in a daze. He could hardly breathe.

She gave him some injections, wrapped a wet towel around his middle and told me what to give him every half hour. The sergeant made coffee for Lyn and me. I gave Trooper some onion juice and wrapped my warm pajamas around him and a half hour later I went to give him some tea. He couldn't open his mouth or his eyes and he was groaning.

I left the room and heard an awful groan and he was dead. A terrible pain shot through me. He was my wonderful, little friend, and I adored him and I had let him die. If only I had done more for him earlier. I didn't see how I could get over it. I called Bob on the phone, but I couldn't speak. Lyn had to take the phone away from me.

Bob came home after his all-night duty. I had slept very little and was very downcast. Trooper should be running in and jumping on my face! The house was strangely quiet and it was hard to comprehend that he wasn't coming back. He was still lying curled up with my pajamas on, under the rug we had put over him to keep him warm. His little ears were up and he looked like he was asleep.

Bob dug a grave out in back and the fireman made a cross, with the words, "Trooper, Nov 19, 1946". Bob, Lyn, Frau Schellenberg and I brought flowers and

Bob said a few words. His grave was beside a cross dedicated to a 20 year-old German boy killed in Russia.

There were special movies at the ACA Building on Wednesdays. Bob met me and we saw one put on by UNRRA about Polish Displaced Persons. The movie was probably doctored to show the best side of UNRRA, but I was pleased to see how well these people were treated. The movie took us through the DP camps and the trip that the DPs made back to Poland. Before the Poles left the camps, they were given a two-month supply of food and cigarettes and, along the way, they were given coffee, milk, and small gifts. When they left the camps, there was a band and a big ceremony.

Pictures of Poland showed the country to be very torn up, but there were many jobs available to help rebuild the country. UNRRA helped the DPs to get back their old jobs, if possible. If not, they did their best to get suitable jobs for them. We saw pictures of a Polish fellow marrying a Yugoslav girl in an UNRRA camp. She automatically became a Polish citizen.

I was taking a class on European governments, which met on Tuesdays and Thursdays. My professor had taught at the University of Dayton. There is a character in every class and, sure enough, we had a petite, dried-up woman, who never seemed to know what was going on. She usually sat and applied her makeup during our discussions and then would add some remarks that had nothing to do with the subject.

We were discussing the inner feelings of the common man concerning Socialism and Democracy as we know it in America while our classmate was meticulously applying lipstick. At the end of the period, the prof said, "Well, I can finish this topic tomorrow."

"Tomorrow?" our friend looked questioningly.

"Don't take me so literally, I meant at the next meeting."

"That's good," a look of relief crossed her face, "I was going to say that I couldn't come tomorrow."

A rather unusual cocktail party was given that Sunday. As we entered the door, we were each given 100 marks to pay for our drinks and our chicken. There was a "barter market" in one corner, where we could use cigarette butts to exchange for toilet paper, girdles and brassieres.

One of the guests stole a bra and got 30 sheets of toilet paper for it. Cigarettes were selling for six marks and some sharp "black marketer" was re-selling them for seven marks. Bob kept us both "broke" by eating a lot of chicken.

November 25th, our third month of marriage, came around. John and Josette were leaving for the States on Thanksgiving Day, which was the 28th. We decided to celebrate the holiday, our anniversary, and their departure the night before Thanksgiving. There were six of us for dinner and I had gotten a 14 pound turkey from the Commissary. I made 2 pumpkin pies, which were sort of soggy, but everyone was polite and didn't notice.

The third couple, Al and Gwen Bartholomew, watched Bob as he attempted his first carving job on the turkey. He mangled the carcass and it was served in jagged pieces, but tasted good. Before they went home that night, Al told Bob that he had been a butcher before he joined the Army. Bob said, "Now you tell me!"

We showed the colored movies we had taken round the city and on our honeymoon. For our first try, we were pleased and thought they were pretty darned good. The scenes along the sea, with the light blue sky, white clouds, dark blue water, yellow sand, and green trees, were easy on the eyes.

We hugged our double wedding buddies, kissed them goodbye and made them promise to write.

Joe sent us a clever anniversary card. "Three months. Will there be another? Come back next month and find out. Good luck!" There was a picture of me, swinging with my right and Bob lying on the ground, saying, "Of course I still love you baby". Ingrid gave me a little, white, fluffy, toy dog, because I had given her so many bags full of butts. Alice gave me a doily, which she made herself. She said she had wanted it for my wedding, but with no electricity at night, she could only work on it on Sundays. I told her it meant a lot to me. The British gave me a medal worn by the Seaforth Highlanders, one of the kiltie regiments.

We had a hard time trying to explain Thanksgiving to the Germans and some of our Allied friends. I couldn't entirely put my heart into the feasting and celebrating, thinking of all the thin, hungry faces around us.

Thanksgiving Day, we went to the big game at Olympic Stadium. The Berlin Bears played the Continental Base Section All Stars from Bad Nauheim and what an exciting game! We had a great time cheering, "Come on Berlin Bears! Beat the Continental Base Section All Stars from Bad Nauheim!" We were winning13-9 up until 2 minutes to go, when the opponents scored, making it 16-13. After seven straight victories, it was quite a disappointment to see the Bears lose, but they were still the top team in the ET. In the evening, we went to the Turkey Trot.

December came along and there was still no snow, although it was hard to believe when one looked at the thermometer. The weather was bitter cold. My mother had made me buy some stadium boots before I left and I was grateful to her every day. They were wool-lined and kept my tootsies warm.

The Daily Bulletin announced, "Conserve electricity. Maximum temperature for office buildings, billets, and instillations (except medical) will not exceed 65 degrees F. Maximum temperatures for medical installations will not exceed 72 degrees F."

The first night in December, we invited Lyn and her date, and Mim and her fiancé for dinner. Mim and the Sergeant arrived right on time at 7:00. We began eating at 8:00 and at 8:30 Lyn and Ed walked in—just one and a half hours late! They had run out of gas on the autobahn. Bob said that Ed wouldn't have run out of gas if he had been out with anyone but Lyn. What a gal! These things just happened to her! I made two tins of baking powder biscuits (my grandmother's recipe) and they were all eaten.

Bob was always complaining that we didn't get enough exercise and said we should get up earlier and walk to work. It would mean rising 45 minutes earlier than our usual time. "Let's see if he really means it," I thought to myself. I jumped out of bed, struggled to get him up and by 8:15, we were ready to start on our way. When we reached the corner, however, a jeep stopped and a voice said, "Would you like a ride?" "Oh, that would be wonderful," says Bob and we jumped inside and rode to work. That was the last time we tried that and there were no more complaints about lack of exercise.

We had a phone call. Another party, this one at 8:00 the following evening. It turned out to be a miserable one for us. I wore the yellow suit I had worn all day at work and the first thing that caught my eye when we entered, was that everyone else was in formal clothing. Nothing had been said about that. Then we saw that the center table was piled high with food. We hadn't been told that it was for dinner. The worst was that it turned out to be a birthday party and we were the only ones who had not brought a gift. How do you rise above that situation!

None of our close friends was there and they seated Bob on the other side of the room. I was uncomfortable about the whole thing and just picked at my food. After we got home, Bob had indigestion, so the whole evening was a total loss.

It was the middle of December when our jeep came back from the garage, finished and in beautiful condition. Gerry was truly a sight of imposing beauty to our eyes and we drove it around showing it off. It had a manifold heater and an automatic windshield wiper, and it was a real jalopy. It added 100% enjoyment to our life by getting us where and when we wanted to go. It had been such a struggle to get a jeep from Motor Pool and now we had no worries.

CHAPTER EIGHTEEN

With Christmas approaching, we got into the merry spirit of it. The Clothing Store and PX were loaded with goodies and we would go there together to find out the perfect gifts for our first Christmas together. Bob would have to stand outside while I shopped for him, then next it would be my turn to stand outside and shiver while he browsed and shopped. All the way home, we would try to guess what the other had bought.

Bob played a mean game of horseshoes and I ordered a set from Sears and Roebuck. The package arrived and I made him carry it. By the time we reached home, he said, "Whew! This box must be full of horseshoes!" I was crushed because I wanted it to be a surprise, but I never said a word. Eventually, when he opened it, I learned that horseshoes had been about the last thing he expected to get and that was why he said that.

I went alone to shop in a small store and was approached by a young girl who held in her hand a Christmas card. On it had been painted the most beautiful angel I had ever seen, and, inside were painted tiny fir trees and pinecones, and in gold letters were the words "Merry Christmas". The work was that of a real artist.

The girl was thin and poor and she looked at me with sad, dark eyes, and she said she would make me as many cards as I liked. Her price was practically nothing and I could not take the cards for such a small fee. I put in a large order and gave her some special things for Christmas. It was sad to think that such talent was crying to be appreciated.

We were thrilled with them when we got all of them. Everyone admired our cards so much that year and we felt so elegant to have our own hand-painted cards.

Ginny and Mac met with an accident and were in the hospital. She had been in Berlin just a month and had been a bride less than that time. A sergeant was taking them home from a party and his jeep skidded completely around and smashed into a streetcar. Mac was knocked clear out of the back seat and was unconscious. Ginny was lying on the seat, groaning, when some Germans took them to a German hospital. From there, they were transferred to the American 279th Hospital. Ginny was just shaken up, but Mac couldn't move his neck or shoulders and was in great pain, although nothing was broken.

We went to see them. Ginny told me about the German hospital—how cold it had been, and how they sewed up a man's hand without an anesthetic because anesthetic was in such short supply. The halls were dark and the rooms were barely lighted. These dreadful conditions sent pangs of compassion in my heart for those people. It was most disturbing to live among such dreadful conditions and suffering, while being safe from those same ordeals. Mac soon improved, but had occasional headaches for some time afterwards.

Our house was beginning to look Christmassy. We bought some wreaths to hang on the door and windows. Frau Schellenberg fixed the house up with branches and tinsel and we thought it quite festive.

There was a big drive on by the dependents to give everything we could for the German children in the TB wards. We gave lots of clothing and a lot of our food rations. Bob, who has a heart as big as all outdoors, wrote home,

"Pat is in the process of trying to divest me of all my clothes. She wants to give practically half of what we own to the relief campaign for the German children stricken with TB. I'm trying to salvage a few pairs of socks and hide them, but she may find them anyway."

Angie was becoming such a fun child to be with. Sometimes she would sit at the dinner table and eat with us and, always, she would want to play as soon as we got home. Her mother read her a story about a wolf who ate little goats. We had to pretend to be "ein wolf" and say, "Ich fresche dich" (I eat you) and then growl. She loved it! Another of her games was running from room to room pretending to be a U-Bahn.

Don had been spending lots of time at our house, always talking about Reggie, and trying to make up his mind about marrying her. He dated other girls, but none of them suited him and, actually, he was lonesome. He was afraid that people at home in Petersburg, Virginia would not accept her. That was foolish thinking, I said. I read letters that his mother had written to Reggie and she was a lovely, caring woman, I could tell. There was no doubt in my mind that there would be no problem with her and I knew Reggie would be welcomed.

He couldn't stand it. He had to go to Brussels to see her. He came back after his "wonderful trip". He and Reggie had talked of marriage and it looked like a June wedding, just before he was to return to his home in Petersburg, Virginia. The timing would be acceptable to the authorities and it would give plenty of time for all of the necessary arrangements.

We thought so much of both of them and hoped everything would go smoothly. Don had 3 years of college ahead of him, but that wasn't a real hindrance. He asked us to help him with the plans. He asked Bob to be his best man and said that Reggie had advised him that I was to be her matron of honor. She wanted the details of her wedding to be as close to my wedding plans as possible.

It was within a few days of Christmas and the weather hovered between 9 and 12 degrees Fahrenheit. Cold and bitter winds coming from Siberia swept the city. Some said it was the coldest winter in 20 years.

I was blue sometimes. Part of it was homesickness and not being with my family for the holidays. I had never spent a Christmas Holiday away from home. Part of it was thinking about so many people who would not have a nice Christmas. How do you totally enjoy yourself when you're surrounded by misery. But there was much holiday excitement and activities and we were busy, busy, busy.

We were able to get a nice tree at the Commissary and we got a nice one for Frau Schellenberg too. At the PX we could get two strings of lights. Bob was like a kid and wanted to put up the tree early, but we waited until the 20th. From that time on, he was busy making decorations with colored paper, cotton, and pipe cleaner.

Ingrid made us a crèche for under the tree and we had mistletoe and candles throughout the house. I made a German village out of paper and cardboard boxes, covered the piano with cotton, and put it there. We stuck the Christmas cards we received in every spare space available and we were ready for Christmas.

The Russians had no Christmas. Actually, their Christmas is January 7th, but since the revolution, it had not been celebrated as a holiday. Helen, my Russian friend, used to like to come into our office and talk about Christmas. We had a manger scene in the corner and she would look at it admiringly and tell us she wished they could celebrate. She sent us each a Christmas card, but asked us not to tell anyone because she was not supposed to do it. It was such a genuine gesture on her part and I loved her for taking that risk.

The German customs were different from ours and we were fascinated as our German friends were describing them to us. We learned that St. Nicolas comes on the night of December 6th and the children must have their shoes well-polished. In them, St. Nicolas leaves small presents to show that Christmas is very near. No one has ever seen him, but he is the right-hand man of Der Weinacht Mann (The Christmas Man) so they figure that he must look like him. Der Weinacht Mann looks suspiciously like our Santa Claus, although somewhat more austere. Christmas Eve at 5 o'clock, people begin to open their gifts and the celebration begins.

. Another lovely custom they have is that four Sundays before Christmas, they put up a wreath, with one candle in it, in the window. Friends come in and they sit down together and sing and tell stories and, before the war, they ate nuts, candy, and hot apples with sugar. Then, three Sundays beforehand, they put two candles in the wreath and the same procedure is followed. Two Sundays before, there are 3 candles; and the Sunday before Christmas, there are 4 candles.

Everything possible was being done to see that Berlin children would have something for the holidays. Every office, the Red Cross, the Woman's Club, every organization, and many private families gave parties. The DP camps had collected thousands of candy bars, toys and clothing. One mechanic whom Bob knew, traveled one hour by U-Bahn and walked one half-hour to our house to get some candy and coffee for his 3 children and his wife. I gave a candy bar to one woman I hardly knew and the next day she sent me a doily. Chocolate meant so much to them, especially at Christmas, and they were very appreciative of the least little thing we did.

December 22nd was the nicest day we had ever spent in the ET. Joe, Bob and I gave a party at our house for 14 German children, ages 2-1/2 to 9. They were the most polite children I had ever seen and were just adorable.

Bob left at noon to pick up Angie and 5 little friends of hers. The smallest one was Gizella (hard "g") and she was darling. Then Bob went to pick up Frau Laurent and her two children. Next, Joe arrived with 6 children that his housefrau had collected for him. They were all so cute and well-behaved and we could speak just enough German to talk to them a little. One little boy had not had any shoes and wasn't going to be able to come, but Joe got him a pair of shiny boots, and he was as proud as punch.

First, they sang many Christmas songs, of which I knew only "Oh Tannenbaum" and "Stille Nacht". We had a dinner for them of meatloaf, mashed potatoes and carrots. For dessert, we had ice cream and one little girl called it "kalter zucker" (cold sugar). Some of them had never tasted ice cream before.

After that, they hunted for cookies, which we had hidden in the living room. Little Gizella fooled us all by finding more than all of the others put together and she wanted to keep going! They thought it was a grand game. We asked them to sing more carols and Bettina said, "Oh, all right, but then let's hunt for more cookies."

Bob was to be Der Weinacht Mann. He went upstairs, got on the bedroom phone extension, and talked to the children, who crowded around the downstairs phone. None of them seemed to notice his accent and broken German.

I went upstairs to help him dress, and it was so funny! He wore his paratrooper boots, red woolen bathrobe, stuffed with a pillow, a red scarf wrapped around his head, and we pasted cotton allover his face. He carried a blue laundry bag, filled with toys, over his shoulder. What a crazy sight he was and he fooled every one of them!

As the children were sitting down in the living room, Bob came to the front window and knocked on it. Angie had been so excited that it frightened her and she began to scream and cry. Der Weinacht Mann stalked into the dining room and 2 little boys rushed up to him and shook his hand, not knowing whether to be frightened or not. As Bob shook hands with each child, they bowed or curtsied, and Bob would say, "Canst du dein gadicht sagen?" (Can you say your poem?). It was so delightful to watch the expressions on their faces, and some of the poems were long. A switch was supposed to go to the child who could not say his poem. Of course, Bob didn't understand the poems, but after each one, he said, "Wonderbar!" Reinar said, "I must have said my poem very well, because Der Weinacht Mann said 'Wonderbar'!"

We had 2 packages for each child. One package contained chocolate and cowboys and Indians (we bought them in a German shop!) I asked one boy if he knew where the Indians lived, and he said they lived in the wild west, but he didn't know where that was. We had wagons and trains for the boys and dolls and cradles for the girls. Reinar said, "I must have been a very good boy to get so much." It brought tears to my eyes. One girl was very shy and hardly spoke at all. She did say that she wanted a doll and her eyes lit up when she saw it, but she didn't smile. Raemuda immediately took her things upstairs and put them with her coat. She couldn't wait to get home and show her family. Wolfgang didn't open his second package because he wanted to wait to open it with his grandmother.

When it was time to go, the children were anxious for another jeep ride. We asked Gizella if she had had a good time and she said, "Nay". We had to laugh because she had been the life of the party and had gotten into the whole spirit of the thing. The whole day was wonderful, gratifying, heartwarming, rewarding, and I wanted to keep them all. Their parents were doing a beautiful job of raising them under dismal circumstances.

Gwen and Bart Bartholomew had us over for dinner and there were 2 tables of bridge. Bart had a gallon bottle of champagne that he had been saving and cherishing, and he brought it out with a flourish. He worked at it and worked at it, but couldn't get the cork to come out. That meant that each man there had to give it a try. They gathered around the bottle in the center of the room, and the women backed off, plugging their ears with their fingers. After 15 minutes, it was Bart's turn again. With a little tug, out came the cork, but instead of a big bang, all we heard was a tiny pop. What a disappointment after all that! We did enjoy sipping it, though, and that night I walked away with first prize, a pair of ear muffs, which were very welcome to have in the blustery, cold weather we were having.

Joe sent us our fourth anniversary card. It was a cartoon picture of me holding one end of a clothesline, and Bob, dressed as Santa, holding the other end. Hanging on the line were four signs: Aug 25, Sept 25, Oct 25, Nov 25, and we were just about to hang up the sign, "Dec 25".

Christmas Eve was a Tuesday and we had a half-day off from work. Lyn, Bob and I had invited over 40 people to our house for an Open House between the hours of 8 and 12. I made the invitations. I cut out of white paper the shape of a beer mug with a handle. Then, in red and green pencil, the wording went:

OPEN HOUSE

8-12

Say, from one mug to another, how's chances

Of youse coming to McMANN'S

PLACE on Christmas Eve?

Free drinks, candlelight, and song, soft

Chairs. Come and light up with: Bob,

Pat and Lyn on

Christmas Eve

Frau Schellenberg offered to return in the evening to help with the party, but we told her to enjoy her Christmas Eve with her family. Little did I realize what I was in for. It was my first time as hostess to a party and I thought it was going to be easy. Ha!

Mid-afternoon, I began baking cookies (chocolate drops and powdered sugar cookies). Bob and I grabbed a snack and at 7 o'clock I was still baking cookies. Bob went after Lyn and I started getting dressed. Andy and Hilda, a British couple, came a half an hour early and I greeted them in bathrobe and curlers.

Bob's job was to make the punch and keep the glasses filled. Lyn and I spent the first 2 hours in the kitchen making sandwiches. Then, with the help of Chris Christensen, we made a big bowl of eggnog. Milk, of course, was out of the question, so we used canned milk. Everyone thought it was delicious and kept coming back for more.

Andy livened things up by asking all the men to try a trick. He placed an orange on one side of the room and a cup on the other side. Then, without using his hands, he sat on the orange, caught it between his legs, got up, walked to the cup and deposited the orange in it. All of the men tried it, and it was such a funny exhibition that we split our sides laughing. The men with skinny legs had more trouble than the stockier fellows.

Bob did most of the door answering, but I took over for a while. I answered a knock and an attractive girl and her date introduced themselves. Her name was Rosemary Murphy. As the party progressed, another Miss Murphy arrived and then, an hour later, a third Miss Murphy appeared. I said, "By any chance do you have a couple of sisters?" "Oh yes," she replied, "they should be here by now." The Murphy sisters turned out to be the daughters of Ambassador Murphy, who had just been appointed as our first Ambassador to Germany.

We gathered at the piano and sang Christmas carols and, around midnight, John Gunn arrived, his head entirely bandaged. As he was leaving for the party, he fell and had to have stitches taken in his head. He said he was determined to come to our party and wouldn't let a few stitches stand in his way. After midnight, there were still several hangers-on, and a few were people we didn't even know and neither did Lyn. Rumors of parties somehow got around. When they were leaving, they all shouted "Merry Christmas" and it was Christmas in Berlin.

We never opened our eyes until 11:00 Christmas morning. We jumped out of bed. Our first thoughts were of our families. I could see my brother, Stan, urging me to hurry up. At least I didn't have to fight with him over who would hand out the presents. I could taste my grandmother's yummy Christmas breakfast and watch my Dad open his annual windup toy, which he would ceremoniously play with for several minutes.

Breakfast was eaten quickly and then we went into the dining room, where our tree was.

It was surrounded by packages from home. There was a box of dog food for Trooper in one box and we had to stop and say a prayer for him. The package had been mailed before they got the news. My family sent Bob a rolling pin and me a dust cloth. Very funny! They also sent me an eggbeater, which Bob took from me when we discovered that it had two gears. He said that when he came home late he would say, "Let's eat in ten minutes. You'd better switch to high gear."

We had just started opening our gifts to each other. I had just opened one with a sweater that had little Swiss dolls for buttons, when there was a knock on the door. It was Don and he had come by with a gift for Bob. It was some kind of steam locomotive and Bob became so engrossed in it that we left our unopened gifts and went into the other room while he played with it. He had great plans for attaching it to the eggbeater and spent 20 minutes trying to get that to work, finally succeeding. Don also brought a present to me from Reggie. It was a black, lace snood with gold sequins on it—very glamorous.

Bob's card to me had these words:

> The thing that makes Christmas so pleasant
> Is sharing it, darling, with YOU
> The way we keep sharing the pleasures
> Of every day—all the year through
> And so, when I wish you at Christmas,
> A long, happy, wonderful life—
> It's something I hope to be sharing
> With the world's most adorable wife!"

It was a dream world I was living in, with a wonderful husband who really and truly loved me It was a Christmas I could never forget.

CHAPTER NINETEEN

A second package from my family arrived a couple of days later. In it was an apron for Bob, "Mama's Little Helper". He was crazy about it and sported it at many of our dinner parties. Also in the package were two gym suits. His was red; mine was blue. We immediately donned them and went for a long drive and Bob wore his a few times later at his ball games. We wrote home, generously thanking the folks. They, however, were puzzled. It wasn't until we got home from overseas that we learned that the "gym suits" were actually pajamas.

The Women's Club put on a benefit horse show. It cost $1.00 per person and the proceeds went to children with TB. We went with Don and Chris Christensen. Rosemary Murphy was in the show and won a prize for horsemanship.

The show ended with a game of Musical Chairs. There were six men who rode bareback on some old nags, and when the music stopped, they had to get off and sit on a chair without letting go of their horses' reins. The crowd roared as the horses refused to cooperate and the men looked silly trying to climb back on again. The benefit was a huge success.

New Years Eve, we met a big gang of people at Harnack House. There were at least 30 people at our table. Lyn loaned me her white formal and Bob gave me two orchids. At my place, there was a little Swedish hat and Bob had a huge, green one that came down way over his ears, making him look preposterous. The men all had wild-looking hats and there were blowers and squeakers, and confetti, and all kinds of decorations.

There were 12 door prizes—bottles of scotch. Chris announced the winners and every time a female came up, he would hand her the bottle and give her a big kiss. He was having quite a time. We got in a conga line that turned out to be more of a crack-the-whip affair. We were whipping around corners and laughing, much to the amusement of the other couples dancing by,

At midnight everyone kissed everyone else. One of the girls said she had kissed everyone and was on her third time around the table. We lasted until 2;30 and left the group still having a whale of a time. Happy NewYear. 1947.

When January 4th rolled around, I stopped to think that just a year ago to the day, I had been all decked out in my fatigues and stepped onto that plane bringing me to Europe. In many ways, the time had simply flown by, but when I thought of all that had happened, in just one year, it seemed much longer. What a fantastic year it had been! General Clay put out a New Year's bulletin that made us all proud and encouraged us to do well in our jobs and in dealing with the problems that lay ahead.

"The New Year brings to Military Government a new phase in its control in Germany, he stated and went on to say that the functions of government were now handed over to the German people and to those who had been elected to become responsible for legislation and administration. Hereafter we would intervene in these matters only if necessary to prevent measures which were inconsistent with our objectives in Germany,

"Some of you who have labored hard and efficiently to produce order in Germany will feel, perhaps, that you have lost some of the authority which you previously exercised. I believe that on sober thought you will understand that the willingness to relinquish authority is the test of our own sincerity of effort to restore democracy to Germany. In looking back over the past year, you have every reason to be proud that through your efforts, German administrations have evolved under democratic procedures which now appear capable of undertaking governmental responsibility.

"Your work to this end during the past years has been in an uncharted field. There have been few precedents founded in experience to serve as a guide. Therefore, in true humility, let us resolve to give our best to the task ahead in a spirit of service with confidence in each other and with tolerance for honest differences of opinion."

Ginny and Mac came for dinner, and, afterwards, we went to the Hockey Club and rented skates. I had to rent a man's size 6 and a half (the smallest they had) and my feet were skating inside the skates. Ginny brought her own and they were too tight. Once around the rink and there was no circulation in her feet. Mac had never skated before and hung on to the railings for dear life. Bob was the only one to get much skating in. Every time he would touch me, I would fall flat on my face.

He started pushing me around on a chair. I had just finished saying "Hey! This could be dangerous", when the chair and I parted company. There were three of us who were black and blue afterwards, but it was fun. We went back to our house and played Ping Pong, a much safer sport.

We went to a couple of operas with them in the Russian Sector. We saw "La Traviata". Violetta was played by Erna Berger and she seemed to improve with every performance we saw her in. There were an astonishing number of curtain calls. They were on the 15th when we left. The next night we saw "Tales of Hoffman". I thought parts of it were excellent, but Bob thought it was a bit long and involved and we were restless by the time it was over. The parts I liked best were the drinking song, the "Barcarole", and the dancing doll.

Don Wilson was getting ready to leave us and go to the Ruhr to work. That meant that Joe and I would be alone at our ACA office and there was very little work left to be done there.

The Germans were having a hard time understanding why they had no coal when there had always been plenty. Many of the mines had been damaged in the war and much of the mining equipment had been broken or destroyed and replacements were not being manufactured yet. Also, transportation was poor, due to destruction of vehicles and roads and, at first, miners were not eating as well as they had been and did not put out as much work as they had before.

We started big incentives to lure the men back to the mines. Miners were given extra heavy food rations, plus a good, hot lunch. They also were allowed to buy certain commodities that weren't displayed for the public. Certain groups of miners and certain individuals were given houses when they exceeded their goals.

The thermometer was registering 5 below zero and there had been no let-up since November. How cruel that it should be this way when people had so little to keep them warm. In Berlin, there were many warming houses. There were 180 just in the U.S. Sector alone. These were vast halls where Germans could go until 8 o'clock in the evenings. They had to leave their coats on, but at least they could get away from the bitter cold. Donations of coffee were being asked for and I drove a jeepload to one of these houses.

Word came from home that Dad had given a speech in Boston. On his way up there, he phoned Bob's parents and talked to Mother Marian (which is what we were calling his aunt now). She told him to be sure to visit them on his return trip.

The way they met was quite strange. When he found out the time of his train departure, he didn't have time to phone them in advance, so he went on to Lincoln Park. He walked out to their house and, by good luck, Mother Marian had just driven in as he got there. She had been on her way to pick up Dad McMann, forgotten something, and returned to get it. Dad then rode with her to the bus stop to greet my father-in-law and gave him quite a surprise. Dad wrote, "We came back to the house and had a fine dinner. I had a couple of hours there and it was a delightful time. They think a lot of their daughter-in-law; and, of course, we feel the same about Bob. They told about Bob's past and all his splendid characteristics, and, likewise, me regarding 'Sissabelle'. It was about a draw."

There was a bizarre predicament that happened in our OMGUS office. We had a German stenographer, Miss Conrad, working for us. She was a sweet and helpful woman in her forties. She was a hard worker and always most agreeable. One day, someone sent a letter (she didn't know who) to the Denazification Board saying that they had often seen Miss Conrad wearing the party badge. Actually, she had never belonged to the Nazi party (the records proved that) and she couldn't imagine who could send such a letter.

She went to the union leader where she had worked during the war. She barely knew him, but she asked him to testify for her. He said, "I've seen you wear the party badge many times." As a result of this, she had to go on trial, and could no longer work for the Americans, until she was proven innocent.

It seemed to be so hopeless and she was terribly upset about it. She didn't know what she could do, because many German firms wouldn't hire anyone who had worked for the Americans. Eventually, it all worked out and she was reinstated in her position in our office. It took several months, however, during which she was bitter and miserably unhappy

I had a letter from Mother that had me very worried. Goggy had to have an operation for gallstones. The X-rays, Mother said, showed something else as well. She went on to tell me that Goggy's general condition was good and that she was cheerful. I was afraid, though that she was trying to paint a good picture.

I didn't hear any more news for two weeks and I was nearly frantic. "Please, dear God," I prayed at night, "Don't let her die. Let her be well so I can be with her again." I placed a call to the States and at midnight, I got to talk to her right in her hospital room. I was fearful and weak when I went into the phone booth, afraid that her voice would be faint. What a pleasant surprise it was to hear her talk and laugh and sound good. "I'm fine, dear. It was just a little problem with my gall bladder. They have removed it and said I came through with flying colors. I'm going home tomorrow."

I burst out crying, I was so relieved. She continued to improve and was soon her usual, efficient self. Way to go!

The phone was ringing and I went to answer it. It was Margie! She had just returned to Berlin. When she left in October, she mentioned that she might come back, but we would have bet our last dollar that we would never see her again.

She had been offered a good job as a Personnel Officer in the Transport Division. In the States, she had called Dick from New York but no one answered, and she never did get to see him. He had given her such a brush-off that we were just as glad that she hadn't seen him, and now she would be back with Chris.

One evening in January Bob came home quite enthusiastic because he had talked to an Hungarian whom, he said, had told him many things about Hungary that he had never known and had never heard anything about. The man, he said, was a young man who had studied in America as an exchange student. He had come to love the States very much and was engaged to an American girl. He had had no intention to return to his country, but in 1939, when he saw what was happening there, he felt that he owed it to his country to return, as they had paid his way to America to learn democracy. His present job was to repatriate some 30,000 Hungarians who were still in Germany. The task was very difficult as most of them were afraid to return at that time because many of them had sided with the Germans. He was telling them that they were of no use to their home country while in Germany and he appealed to their patriotism. They questioned him if they would be put in a concentration camp and he would tell them that they probably would be. But they would then again be free to aid Hungary.

It was a Monday night and we had school the following night. We were studying at the American university program that had recently been organized. I was taking a current events course. Bob said he would gladly give up his class if we could have the man over for dinner.

When he arrived, I liked him the minute I saw him. He was clean looking, very polite, and seemed very pleased that we had thought enough of him to invite him for dinner. His name was Harold Laski, and he was one of the most fascinating people I've ever met and we sat enthralled as he talked on and on into the night. After dinner, we drank, smoked, and listened and I was so fascinated by what he had to say that I hated to see him go when the clock struck one o'clock.

He told of the Hungarian people and how before the war they were a free and easy going people. None of them wanted war, but because a few of their leaders in the government were pro-fascist, they had given up to the ideas of the Nazis. Before they realized it, they were asked to declare war on Russia. Russia was extremely surprised, as was the Hungarian Ambassador in Moscow. These two countries had absolutely nothing against each other, he said. But, the Hungarian boys went out to fight with but one gun for every two men. They were fighting side by side with Germans, yet were treated like swine.

He told us that the Hungarians had never been anti-Jewish, but when the Germans came, they rounded up all of the Jews in Budapest, roped them in and shot them down with machine guns. Finally, Hungary signed a treaty with Russia, but the Germans declared it void and marched into Budapest to occupy it.

He told of the downfall of their currency (the pengo). It was caused by speculation. Gold was the only thing that meant anything. One time his wife had sold some jewelry and by the time she had reached home, she discovered that the money was worth just one half of what it had been. When the pengo went out, 33 trillion equaled one dollar. The florin became the new currency. There was an open black market in Hungary and you could buy anything for a price.

We said goodnight to him and he said he was leaving Berlin in the morning. A few months later, there was an article in the paper that he had disappeared and noone had heard from him again. He had attended a meting in Vienna, had gotten into a car afterwards and that was the last he had been seen. He was involved in so much intrigue, we were sure foul play had bee n involved and it made us sad to think this bright, young man, helping so many people, and so proud of his country, had met such an end.

Then, another news article appeared, "Hungarian Cops Uncover Plot". They had found 40 American Army uniforms which, they said, were to be used by Storm Troopers to create the impression that a plot to overthrow the republic was supported by the Western Powers. The wife of the lawyer in whose flat the uniforms had been found told police that her husband had purchased them in France as a business deal.

The timing was close to that of our friend's disappearance, and yet it is hard to imagine what his involvement in discovering this plot could have been. We shall never know, but we were sad to think he had probably been killed.

A new information program, stressing the importance of human understanding between the German people and the American soldier, began late in January. Replacements arriving in the ET would study the occupation mission in Germany under the revised program, and troops in the field would be discussing the new subjects as part of their weekly troop information hour.

Re-education of German youth, Germany's self-government, the soldier's attitude toward DPs, and the GIs behavior in public, as well as in private life, would be among the topics.

At the same time, as a result of hundreds of letters written by German youths who wanted to correspond with American counterparts, arrangements were made to encourage such correspondence. The plan would be helpful in letting these young people understand how democracy works and would create a better understanding between the young people of the two countries.

One of my Christmas gifts had been some aromatic sachet, which I put in the drawer with my clothes. I also put some with Bob's things. I was shocked awake the next morning, "What do you mean, putting bath salts in with my shorts?" "What?" I blinked, not understanding what he meant. Bath salts? When I explained that they definitely were not bath salts, but sachet, he had never heard the word.

We started taking a poll to find out how many men knew what sachet was. We got some pretty crazy answers, "fancy name for perfume", "sweet smelling deodorant", "strong, nice smelling soap to catch a guy with", etc.

Bill Fourqueron, for whom I worked in the beginning, got married on our 5th month anniversary and we went to the wedding. Peggy, his bride, wore a short, white dress, with silver trim, and she looked smashing.

Bill had known her in Washington and she and her 12 year-old son had just arrived in Berlin. I never thought I would see Bill looking scared, but, sure enough, he was trembling. The French and British came, and even a couple of the Russians; and Simone the French girl, caught the bouquet.

We took pictures of our office force and there was dancing. The French, polite as always, kept offering me French cigarettes. Rather than refuse the awful-tasting things, I would accept, then wander off and get rid of them. They were twice as strong as Camels and left an indescribably unpleasant taste in your mouth.

It was exactly one year ago that I met Bob and then began dating him. Was it really that long ago that Lyn had her birthday party?!

I heard from Reggie, "Imagine how surprised I was to learn that you know the big news because Don had said to me that he wanted to wait a while before telling anybody. Otherwise, Patsie dear, I would have written it to you as the first to know. I'm very happy that you know and it is wonderful to know that you are as happy about it as I am."

Reggie had a new job. She was working for the Netherlands Chamber of Commerce. We were alarmed when she wrote, "I must take it easy for a while for my heart. It is not bad, you know, but just a little bit and when I take it easy for 3 or 4 months, it will be passed and all right. I'm not worried about it any more." But we were worried. Reggie had been through so much, we hoped and prayed the strain had not been too much for her.

That same day, we got a letter from John. "Dear Bob and Pat (our better half)". It went on to say that their trip across was rather uneventful, except that Josette had an insatiable desire for bananas, which were impossible to get in the middle of the Atlantic Ocean.

"Josette was able to see the Capitol with all the lights on and was very impressed. We thought about the 'Pittsburgh Kid' while passing through Pennsylvania.

"Josette was very excited about the folks and they got along swell. Josette is crazy about Florida and her new parents—everything except the heat and I don't blame her since it hasn't dropped below 85 degrees yet this winter. It's a little too hot and dry, but preferable to Berlin for me.

"I'm in pre-med at Stetson. It is rather difficult to buckle down and study, but that will work out soon. We are having to live with the folks at present, but hope to get a place of our own this next summer. Our expenses are not very much, even with getting things ready for the baby. Josette feels fine and wants a boy. In fact, if it's a girl, I don't know what we'll do."

That was the first and last letter from John. Through friends, we learned that they had twins—a boy and a girl. They named them John and Josette. It didn't work out for them, though, in spite of his glowing comments. They moved to California when the twins were very small and, when Josette was pregnant again, John deserted her. She had a miscarriage and was helped a lot by Ginny McGilton, who was then back in California (with Mac, of course). Josette had a rough time, with two babies, no husband and still a bit of a language problem. She went on to become a successful realtor, and later re-married. We got in touch with each other some time after that and we have kept up our friendship. Perky little Josette got a much better husband in Andre Lagardere. They have a daughter and now live near Seattle.

There was a fun-filled party at the McGiltons some time in February. The 3 German fellows we often had as a band group were there. We liked this group because they played such good jazz and they were very popular at American parties. It was so funny to hear them sing "Open Ze Door, Richard" in their German accents.

The party broke up around 3 and Ginny and Mac went to bed, but the orchestra remained. At 4, the housefrau awakened Mac and said that the 3 fellows couldn't get their car started. Mac went out in his pajamas, half-asleep, and told them he would pull them.

He got in his jeep and they started out. All of a sudden, he heard a crash, got out and saw that they had tied the cable to his gas tank. The spout, bumper, and backlight lay on the ground. For once, Mac told us, he was too angry to say anything, but just turned around and went back into his house.

Some more trials were going on with grisly and gruesome details coming to light. At the trial of the staff of Ravensbruck concentration camp, Martej Hellenger, a German dentist, admitted that it was his duty to wait in the crematorium while executions were carried out, so he could extract the victims' gold teeth.

He was the last of sixteen members to go into the witness box, and told how, as the women's bodies were brought into the crematorium, he carried out his work.

"It was easy," he declared. He said that he thought the executions were legal and he was just doing a job.

The first Nazi women criminals were executed when Dr. Hilde Wernicke, and nurse, Helene Wieczorek, were guillotined at the Lehrter Strasse Jail. They were a doctor and head nurse at the Oberwalde insane asylum in Saxony, where they murdered over 600 patients during 1943 and 1944. The doctor had selected the victims while the head nurse had given the injections. They were sentenced to death by a German court on March 25, 1946.

The Grooper had headlined them as "Condemned Women" who felt "No Remorse". The Grooper reporter interviewed them and found their "bitte-danke" politeness a mask, wholly irreconcilable with the character which had brought about their condemnation. Complaining that they had been done a "great injustice", they proceeded to relate how they had slaughtered humans out of pity—and because they were so ordered.

Describing the humane practice of putting mentally ill patients in the asylum out of their misery, Dr. Wernicke smilingly related that her superior, who was not a doctor, but a staunch party member, had suggested some lethal injection as the most practical method. Asked by the reporter how she, as a doctor, could approve of this, she answered, "I was only doing my duty. We were told The Fuhrer had ordered it and we could not dispute his will. The patients were hopeless and incurable. There was nothing better we could do for them."

The doctor had no comment when reminded that another physician in the same situation had resigned his position rather than carry out a similar order. The nurse who administered the injections, and who was also "under orders" admitted she did so for fear of losing her job. Patients who did not respond to the 6-hour "cure", were subjected to further treatments. Very few families were said to have complained when they read the death certificate copy stating the patient had died of pneumonia or a heart attack.

It was inconceivable to me that so much evil could have existed in a country supposedly as civilized as Germany. I felt so gloomy and downhearted that human beings could do these horrible things to other human beings. The total lack of compassion was such an eye opener and shook my faith in the wonderful world I had always lived in.

Coal continued to be about the biggest problem Germany was facing. Lt General Lucius Clay, the Military Governor, announced a drive to recruit 50,000 German workers from the U.S. Zone for the British Zone Ruhr coal mines. The coal shortage was mainly a problem of manpower, he said, and efforts were also being made to obtain additional manpower from Italy.

The United States was exporting 20,000 tons of coal a year to Germany and yet the annual deficit was 32,000,000 tons. New pits would have to be opened, new equipment installed, and many long-range problems solved before the ultimate goal of 400,000 tons daily could be achieved.

Already, the mines were recruiting 1,000 workers a week, a few of them by compulsory direction, but most of them voluntarily. This was the first large-scale transfer of Germans from one zone of Germany to another and was being coordinated with the housing program in the British Zone.

CHAPTER TWENTY

Everyone who had been on a Swiss tour raved about it. In February, we left on a 2-week tour. The night we left, Ginny and Mac invited us over for dinner and promised to take us to the station. When it was time to leave, we climbed into their jeep, val-pack, musette bags, and magazines. Ginny stepped on the starter. No sound. Bob, Mac and I pushed a good part of the way to the station, but we made it, just in the nick of time. Bob was coming down with a horrible cold and I had doped him up pretty well with a variety of home remedies.

The train out of Frankfurt left before our arrival time so we spent a day and night there. In Karlsruhe, we filled out our customs papers, paid for our tour, and received our Swiss money. The trip cost us each $47.50 for 7 days and that included travel, room and board. $4.00 more paid for cable trips, ski lessons, and skiing and skating equipment.

At the Swiss border, the train stopped for several minutes in the countryside, and there we saw a sight that will always remain vivid in our memories. Not far from the train, was a sheep herder. He was dressed in a long, black cape, an enormous hat, and he carried a wooden staff. His pipe hung from his mouth and reached to where his belt might have been, then curved up and out. The sheep herder looked old, and the pipe looked like it had survived many generations. At a signal from his master, the dog, a small black and white collie, ran pell mell in a large circle, surrounding a small group of sheep that were scattered about. The dog's circle became smaller and smaller until the sheep were packed so tightly, one would have thought it impossible for them to breathe.

The train's passengers were held spellbound during this performance, and when the old fellow took off his hat and bowed nearly to the ground, he was showered with candy, cigarettes, and money. He repeated his show several times before the train moved on and we were enchanted each time. This man met all of the trains coming across the border and was, most likely, wealthy.

The scenery was becoming more quaint. The little towns huddled together and everything looked fresh and clean. When we arrived in Basel, it was starting to get dark. We expected, from what we were told, that the customs examination was very stiff, but all the inspectors did, was open our suitcases and then close them.

We stayed overnight in Basel at the Hotel Hofer and ate dinner with our tour guide, Jean. The dinner was served on a big tray over a candle. Jean gave us a lot of information about Switzerland that we had not previously known. The Swiss population was 4.2 million with Zurich being the largest city and Basel (pronounced 'Ball') was second. Nearly everyone spoke German and French; many also spoke Italian; and some spoke English and Romansh.

After dinner we went for a walk. My throat was beginning to get sore and I was coming down with Bob's cold. I suggested a streetcar ride and we got on a No. 3. Bob asked, "Was costet dese?" We were asked how far we were going and, of course, we didn't know. There was a different price for different distances. The driver scratched his head, then told us a number, we paid, and he closed the door. The people were so polite. It was nice to have the men let me on the streetcar first, and for people to move over so I could sit down. We rode a long time and got off, only to discover we were outside the city limits. Not to worry. A lovely lady walked us to a spot where we could catch a bus. This was something we learned about the Swiss. If you needed directions, they would walk out of their way to take you where you wanted to go.

On our way to Davos, we rode in a real Swiss train with wooden benches, so that our fannies were nicely striped by the end of the ride. The electric trains traveled amazingly fast through the mountains. The Swiss towns were so cute, with narrow roads and houses with huge roofs in every color of the rainbow—yellow, blue, pink, and even purple.

We passed through Zurich and followed Lake Zurich, which is a huge body of water right at the base of steep mountains. There is practically no shore and the lake is deep along the edge and there were many loons on the water. Soon we began climbing and there was lots of snow and then we were forever scooting through tunnels. I had never seen such gorgeous scenery. No picture could ever do it justice. The mountains reminded me of a fairy tale and pictures I had seen as a child of woodland forests.

It was getting dark as we came into Davos. It was a rather small village, partly on a hill, with mountains rising all about it. The first thing that we saw was a horse-drawn, brightly-painted sleigh with a black fur blanket in it. The horse had a red plume on his head and bells that jangled when he moved. What a perfect welcome! Obviously, we had to ride in it!

We stayed at the Palace Hotel, a very large and lovely building, with a roaring fire in the lobby fireplace. Our room was fairly small, but had a large sun porch leading from it. The temperature in the room would freeze water into ice (almost) and I had to wear a coat.

When we arrived there, I felt very strongly the need of a bath, but all the baths were locked. There was one on every floor and I tried every one, with no luck. I asked the chambermaid about the bath situation and discovered that she carried the key to the baths and would run the water for me for two and a half francs (60 cents). The water was so hot, I couldn't get in the tub at first and, when I did and sat down, the water was way up to my neck. It felt wonderfully soothing and relaxing.

It was nearly 9 o'clock when we went down to the dining room and found a table full of hungry people waiting for us. They couldn't be served until we were all present. And what a dinner we had! The menu included Brussel sprouts, cooked with chestnuts; barley broth; cheese soufflé, lamb, apple with cranberries, potato patties, brandied peach with whipped cream and meringue; green nuts; and wafers.

My throat was hurting more and more, but after dinner we played Ping Pong and chess. Bob, jokingly, kept insisting that I was always springing new rules on him.

We learned that there was no extra charge for breakfast in bed, so we went for it. Such luxury! After breakfast, we went to the Sports Shop and got our equipment—skies, boots, and poles. I bought a red ski cap that I was most proud of. It matched my red slacks that Bob had given me for Christmas.

Bob had skied a lot and was very good, but I had never worn a pair of skis in my life and I was an anxious beginner. We walked down the hill through the town, across a little valley, and over to the ski school. When we reached the place, we stood and gazed in wonderment at the little Swiss town settled in the snow and at the surrounding, magnificent, white mountains. The hill was dotted with hotels, and all of them had sun porches for each room. TB patients came here from many countries. The atmosphere was perfect for recovery from this disease. Our favorite building was a little church, with dark wooden eaves, and a pointed steeple. It looked like a church you would see painted on a Christmas card.

I joined a beginners' ski class and learned to go downhill, bending my knees, and then to go down while practically stooping. I learned to go uphill with the side step and the herringbone. I soon graduated to a steeper hill and went down sideways.

Earlier, I had laughed at Bob and told him he would freeze with the light clothing he was wearing. I soon learned that it was I who was over-dressed. The sun was out and I was astonished at how warm it was. My hands, without gloves, were perspiring.

After lunch, we did some shopping. We bought 2 Davos ashtrays to add to our collection; a clock that played "Dixie" for an alarm. We bought Angie a dish with a giraffe on the bottom of it. I was then exhausted and my throat was bothering me, so I took a nap and Bob went out scouting around.

He came back with a cute little carved wooden figure on a cork. It was a fat, little bear sitting on top of a barrel. He smiled as he showed me a cigarette box and, when he opened it, two carved figures popped up and kissed each other. Then he said, "Our trip is a success!" and he produced a musical toilet roll that played "Rose Marie" and "Beautiful Blue Danube". Our goal had been to find one of these and so we were triumphant.

In the afternoon, we took a red bus to ride up the cable to the Parsenn. The Parsenn is an extensive mountainous region north of Davos. It is the finest ski country in Europe, possibly in the whole world. The ride we took to the Weissfluhjoch was straight up! It took 22 minutes to reach the top and what a ride! I must admit, I had my fingers crossed the whole way to the top. Most of the people we rode with had their skis with them and skied down. They averaged 40 mph going down.

At the top, we could scarcely see the village below, but could see over the tops of the other mountains and it was breathtaking. We discovered that we were at 8,738 feet altitude and the skiers had a choice of two dozen runs in every direction, being from 3 to 11 miles in length.

By bedtime, my throat felt as though it had been scraped by a knife. All night long, I tossed and turned and talked in my sleep. By morning, I felt like I had been through the mill. It just about killed me to miss an entire day of skiing, but I stayed in bed all day. I loved skiing already and had visions of being able to jump through the air by the time we left, but here I was in bed. Bob went out skiing and skating with the other members of the tour.

The next night was a repeat performance by me of the night before and I really scared Bob with my idiotic talk in my sleep. He went out early in the morning and brought back a doctor. He diagnosed, "very inflamed throat", but said it was nothing serious. I was dying for a banana split, but he said that Swiss icecream was different from ours, and it might give me an abcess. Darn it! This was the first cold I had all winter, and I spent my last day in Davos in bed feeling miserable.

On the train to Zurich, we met a student, a freshman at the University of Zurich. John was friendly, and polite, and offered to spend the afternoon with us to show us the best places to shop. We were overcome with his generosity in giving us so much of his time. John took us to a large department store and I nearly went wild. Imagine going into the first, large, stocked department store you had encountered in over a year!

I bought some pink satin-backed crepe for an evening gown; black and white plaid for a dress; all kinds of buttons; and an eye-catching, purple angora sweater set. Bob got brown tweed for a sports jacket, a brown overcoat (which he wore for years and years), and some socks made in the USA.

There was some kind of strange holiday going on in that part of the country. It was called Fasching, which was, and is, a pre-Lenten period of uninhibited revelry celebrated in Germany, Austria and parts of Switzerland. It apparently lasted for days and people were going through the streets at night in bizarre costumes and everyone was throwing confetti. There was plenty of music and celebrating going on. I was still under the weather and too ill to feel like participating. Others in our group did, however, and the next morning, when we met at the train station, some of them still looked groggy.

We sat across from two colonels' wives, who were returning from the Swiss-Rome tour. At first, they were talkative and seemed to be pretty nice, but it wasn't long before they began to grate on our nerves. They began by telling about the lieutenant in Karlsruhe, who was in charge of their tour. He told them they could not go along, as the tour was already filled to capacity. They "just told that lieutenant a thing or two, and he finally said we could go." They were simply positive that he was telling people they couldn't go and then taking extra money from them when he added them to the tour. They had taken his name and were going to report the "little smart aleck".

Their next complaint was about how rude the GI's and officers on the trains had been. At some of the stations, no one had helped them with their luggage. If some of those boys had been their sons, they would have slapped their faces.

One of the women said, "Did I ever tell you, dear, about the time during the war, when I was out in Oregon and my husband called from Switzerland? I was furious, simply furious. I waited 5 days for the call to come through, and then he reversed the charges! What did I care if he was in Switzerland."

"Yes, dear, and you probably missed a good cocktail party," replied her friend.

"The food in Rome was simply marvelous. Why can't the Germans cook like that?" "They're just too stupid!" was another exchange.

"Mrs. Unhappy" had brought home lots of material for herself, and paintings, and treasures. For her husband, she bought a shirt. "But I just didn't know what to get Junior. He's 12 now and so hard to find anything for. I think he'll like the rosary, even though he's not Catholic." (I could imagine how thrilled Junior would be.)

"Oh, how I hate to get back to the old grind!" "Oh yes! That old Commissary!"

At Karlsruhe, the old bags were delighted to see their husbands, "Oh good! We'll have someone to carry our luggage."

I felt sorry for the men they had married. Thank heavens all dependents were not like these two grumblers, but I could see why dependents had gotten a bad reputation. We had dinner that night with a couple who had been on the Swiss-Rome tour. They said it had been grand, all except for 2 colonels' wives, who had tried to run the show.

We left Switzerland with a warm feeling for the Swiss people. There was beauty such as we had never seen and we were much impressed with everything we had seen and done.

CHAPTER TWENTY-ONE

When we returned from Switzerland, I was alarmed by what my mother had to say. Goggy was very, very sick and was recovering slowly from her gall bladder operation. Her heart had stopped beating on the operating table and they had a terrible time trying to revive her. She had my picture beside her bed the whole time she was in the hospital. I wished I could have been there in person beside her bed, instead of a picture.

On Monday, March 10th, Military government surprised us by announcing suddenly that all scrip was to be turned in before 1400 hours. It was done to squelch the counterfeit ring they believed had its origin in Naples. The counterfeit money was found in Paris, and some of it was in Germany. The new scrip was the same, except for the colors. It was now in pink and blue.

This was also the beginning of a 40-hour work week. Previously, we had worked on Saturday mornings, making 44 hours at work. Now, half of us would take Saturday mornings off one week, and the next week would take Wednesday afternoons off, and continue in that pattern.

We were already making plans for our return to the States in the coming fall. Bob had a year and a half of college to finish, and had written to the University of Southern California and had forwarded his transcripts. We were anxiously waiting to hear whether he had been accepted for the spring of 1948. A lot of our plans hinged on that acceptance. Mac had already been accepted there for the fall of '48. Ginny and I thought it would be loads of fun to be college wives together, and most of our conversations centered on this subject and possible preparations to be together.

While Ginny was away on a trip to Czechoslovakia, Mac and Chris came for dinner and afterwards we took a jeep ride into the Russian Sector. We put the jeep in four-wheel drive and went roaring over snow and ice, through the woods, going around and avoiding trees as we went. It would have been impossible to do what we did with an ordinary car. We came to an old, German hotel, high on a cliff, where you could look out at the lake. Inside, they had separate rooms, just large enough for a table and a sofa for two, with very soft, silk pillows; obviously a spot where lovers could meet, draw a curtain, and have a quiet, romantic time together. We stopped at the bar for a glass of beer and warmed ourselves for a while.

I was offered a good job in another office at OMGUS Headquarters. There wasn't much for me to do anymore down at the ACA Building, so I was anxious to take this new one. The chief of my section, however, refused to release me until he could get a replacement for me. The personnel office said it would be two months before they could send someone. It began to look like I would not be able to take the position.

The March winds were blowing very strong. A heavy windstorm knocked over 20 buildings in one day. Bremerhaven was having some heavy floods, perhaps the worst in its history. The last of the 4 bridges leading into that city collapsed and hundreds of people were stranded away from their homes overnight. The Elbe River in Berlin was ice-clogged and they used dynamite to break up the ice in order to save the supply bridge going into the city.

The first day of spring finally came and we went to Harry's Hash House without our coats. After lunch, we went to the Berlin Zoo. There were a few mangy animals that had survived the war, but much of the zoo was closed. It had once been the pride of Europe, but I was overcome with the fact that one of the terrible consequences of war was that many of these unfortunate animals had starved to death.

There was a man there who tried to sell us a dog. He was a nine-month old German Shepherd, very thin and hungry looking. He was a black and tan and had a rather frightening appearance. I really wanted a younger puppy, but something about this dog made me sorry for him and he had a certain appeal about him. I begged Bob to let me buy him and he didn't offer much resistance.

We put him in the back of the jeep and, on the ride back to OMGUS, I expected him to pounce on my neck any minute. I stopped off at my office and he immediately made friends with everyone there. Then, when we brought him home, he just about scared Frau Schellenberg and Frau Jacobowski out of their wits.

I took him upstairs and put him in the bedroom. I thought I had closed the door, but, as I descended, he was right at my heels. I led him back to the bedroom, this time making sure I had closed the door tightly. As I descended, he was right at my heels again. Puzzled, we went back and I watched as he put his big paw on the door handle, and pulled down on it to open the door. This was only the first of many amazing things I was to learn about the dog.

Bob really wasn't happy about the new addition, and he let me know it. The dog was just too big. We had our first fight over Blitz (meaning "lightning"), but Blitz won. He was so intelligent that our friends soon almost expected him to answer the phone when they called.

We soon learned, though, that it was difficult to keep him in the house. When we would leave, we would lock the doors, but he could open all of the downstairs windows. They were the type that opened outward by pressing a lever.

The basement had a window that not only was high up, but also had a catch on it that I found difficult to figure out. One particular day, a gang of us planned to go on a jeep ride. We put Blitz in the basement, thinking that it would solve our problem of keeping him at home. But by the time the jeep reached the corner, Blitz was racing beside us (he was very fast). He had jumped against a box, knocking it over so he could climb up to the window, and the catch was a cinch for him to figure out. Blitz was the best protection we could have against theft. He was so big that just to look at him was enough to frighten away a burglar. Bob was still in school two nights a week and I was no longer afraid to be at home alone.

It was such a pleasure to teach Blitz anything. In the first week we had him, he learned to "sit", "platz" (lie down), shake hands, speak, and he wouldn't touch his food all night unless I told him it was OK.

He liked me the best and didn't mind Bob as well as he did me. If Bob called him, he would wag his tail and look up at me to see what I wanted him to do. When we got home, he always made little excited barking noises and talked to us. Bob didn't like him at first, but when people admired him, Bob would beam and explain that "Blitz' father was a champion". He had such a kind, intelligent face that everyone liked him. Bob's boss wanted to buy him from us and one colonel said to me, "That is a real dog. He is what a German Shepherd should look like."

Later, Ginny and Mac got a police dog, a silver color, and named him Alf. Alf and Blitz became buddies, and it was fun to watch them play together, they were both so big and clumsy. The first time we took Blitz to meet Alf (about 4 miles from our house), they had a great time. Meanwhile, he learned where the OMGUS parking lot was and got into the habit of going there just before 5 o'clock and waiting for us beside the jeep. One night, we worked a little late and, when we came out, there was no dog waiting. He wasn't at home either and, by the time we had finished eating dinner, we were really getting worried. The phone rang and Ginny asked, "Are you looking for your dog?" He had arrived at their house about 5:30 and had come to play with Alf.

His most amazing feat happened later in the summer on a Saturday. We met Don for lunch at Truman Hall and left Blitz in the jeep. He had learned to open the jeep doors and windows (we had sliding windows). Escape artist that he was, we had locks put on the windows.

As we approached the jeep, Blitz was sitting beside it, wagging his tail. He was bleeding at the mouth, so we rushed up to him to see what had happened. Blitz had broken the right window and then, in order not to cut his body when he jumped through the window, he had picked out, with his teeth, all the remaining jagged pieces of glass from the edges of the window frame. There they lay, inside on the front seat. We were so intrigued by his intelligence, that we just couldn't be angry about the broken window.

One Sunday, we got up early and met Ginny and Mac, took both jeeps (theirs was a super duper job) and drove through Grunewald Forest, in and out of the mud.

We drove to the Bismarck Tower overlooking Wannsee. The view from the tower was panoramic and we busily took pictures. The guys took a movie of Ginny and me in a mock race and, at the end of our "competition", we got out of our vehicles, strode over to each other with silly grins on our faces, looked at the cameras and shook hands.

We took the dogs down to the shore of the lake and walked along. We began throwing sticks out into the lake and Alf would go out and bring them back. Blitz didn't like the water and waited until Alf brought the stick back and playfully took it away from him; Alf went for another stick and Blitz would wait patiently on shore then take it from his pal. Ginny and Mac sort of smirked about Blitz being afraid of the water, but we thought it was rather clever of him to let the other dog do the work. We were like parents being proud of our kids.

Blitz did something that earned him the respect and gratitude of Frau Schellenberg. Angie wandered away from our yard and was headed out into the boulevard at the head of our cul-de-sac. True to his name, like a streak of lightning, Blitz dashed out into the road, grabbed her little dress by his teeth and pulled her back onto the sidewalk, while her frantic mother came running out of the house. He had become attached to the child and we were never afraid for her after that when he was around. He was her protector.

It was particularly sad for me when I had to agree with Bob that since we would be living in an apartment when we returned home, we could not bring the dog with us. Bob's boss was ecstatic, however, as he had always wanted us to give Blitz to him. He lived several miles from our house and we had never taken Blitz there before, but, after we were gone, Blitz came back to our house. Frau Schellenberg and Frau Jacobowski were still there and later wrote to me that they had given him to the Berlin Police Department, where he developed a reputation for his ability to assist in capturing thieves. Bob's boss had given the OK because he realized he could not keep Blitz in his house.

My thoughts were always about my grandmother and how she was getting along and I called home and was pleased to hear her sounding chipper. It was such a relief to learn that she had made a remarkable recovery after her temporary setback. I could relax with the knowledge that she would be there when I returned home. She asked about the dog; Dad was getting ready to go golfing; Mother wanted to know about my piano lessons; and Stan sounded sleepy (it was 8 a.m. there). It was Dad's birthday, so I had another special reason for calling and this year I remembered to wish him a happy birthday. Mothers are such wonderful people. The very next letter I got from mine, she was worried because she thought I had sounded as though I had a cold.

On March 25th, I changed jobs. I went to work as secretary to Oren McJunkins, who was Chief of Reparations. I missed the people from my old office, but I was glad to be using my shorthand again. I wrote to my shorthand professor at Pitt and he read my letter to the class and explained to them how his class had helped me get my job.

The Little Theater Group in Berlin was very active and put on some wonderful plays. Chris and Helen went with us to see "Born Yesterday" and we were impressed with the performance. Chris and Margie had not picked up on their relationship when she came back, and he continued to date Helen Murr She was very much in love with him.

After the show, Bob and Chris discussed the possibilities for their softball team for spring so Helen and I decided that we ought to have a girls' team. Shortly after that, Helen called a luncheon meeting of girls who would be interested in playing. I was in bed with another cold and had to miss the meeting, but I was determined to play on the team.

April came to the European Theater. Bob still had no word from the University of Southern California. Dad applied for Bob at George Washington University in Washington, D.C., where my brother was going. Stan wrote us concerning the university situation: "I'm afraid you people are not aware of the crowded conditions in the universities over here. Enrollments have increased anywhere from fifty to three hundred percent and I would suggest that you write to several colleges and universities in the near future and secure entrance papers. Seriously, even at George Washington some of the vets who were discharged last summer have not been able to get in yet. Probably by next fall, the situation will be eased somewhat, but it's hard to tell. To show you how crowded the schools are here, when I went to GW before, there were about 5,000 students. Now the enrollment has jumped to 14,000." We began to bite our nails a bit.

We wanted to share a house with Ginny and Mac in California and Stan's letter gave us cause for concern. Then we read an article in The Saturday Evening Post entitled "Stay East, Young Man". So many returning veterans wanted to live in California that housing was impossible to get. Some kids were living in chicken coops.

Meanwhile, Bob had taken on some additional duties in his Division and was due for a raise soon. Not only was he doing the work of the Asst. Executive of the Division, but that of the Secretary as well. His new work consisted of going to 5 or 6 quadripartite meetings a month and preparing the agendas for the division meetings, then writing up the minutes after the meetings. He was working hard and long hours and was enjoying his job immensely.

We made a purchase we were very proud of. We went to the Barter Mart and got a lovely German radio/record player combination. The cabinet was a rich mahogany, and the radio tone was high quality. The bass tones were deep and mellow. The dial face was interesting because it had on it the names of practically every large city in Europe—Warsaw, Vienna, Frankfurt, Paris, and even Moscow. The record player could only play one record at a time, but we had it changed to a 10-record automatic player. This appealing piece of furniture made an interesting conversation piece when we returned Stateside.

In early April, Don returned from Belgium after visiting Reggie. While he was there, he left his car (he had gotten a 1941 Pontiac) in an all-night garage. The morning he went to get his car, he learned that it had been stolen at gunpoint during the night. The owner of the garage had given the police a description of the man and by the next day, he was caught and the car returned. The man was an American soldier who had been AWOL since the Battle of the Bulge.

This time Don was more serious about Regina, and excited about a June wedding.

Friday, April 4th there was an unusual and exciting evening event. We went to Olympic Stadium where the Allied Boxing Matches were being held. They began on Monday of that week and were to end on Saturday night. The countries represented were: Holland, Belgium, France, Czechoslovakia, and the United States. The U.S. was represented by 2 Hawaiians and 5 Negroes. It was startling to hear people cheering in several different languages. The Frenchmen in front of us kept calling out, "attaque" and: "continue".

As a whole, the Czechs were very stocky fellows, with thick necks and bushy hair. They were sluggers. The Frenchmen were swarthy, with oily hair; the Dutch were blonde, tall and pinched looking; and the Belgian fighters were fair, with dark hair, and were clean-cut looking. I liked to see them win because each one had a teddy bear for a mascot, which they hugged and made formal bows to all 4 sides of the ring. The Czechs had the funniest technique of all. They wiggled their shoulders in the strangest way and crouched very low.

The U.S. won 5 of the 7 fights that night. We had a terrific fighter named Jefferson. At that time, he had 14 straight knockouts to his credit. He got the most applause of any boxer.

I walked into my office one day to find a German girl crying her eyes out because she couldn't get a ration card to buy herself a pair of shoes to wear to work. The shoes she had on were full of holes. I went to the QM store and bought her a pair—rules or no rules. I did it because I felt guilty for complaining because I had to wear rayon stockings. My family often sent me clothing to give to people in need and I was able to give the girl a good, warm sweater and some pretty unmentionables.

Easter came. It was my second Easter in the ET. Bob gave me a leather picture frame, made in Spain and it later surrounded the first professional picture taken of us together.

We invited Ginny and Mac, Don and Chris for Easter dinner. When they arrived, my meal was cooking away on the stove. I went to check on the progress when, lo and behold, the stove stopped functioning. It was the first big dinner I had planned for some time and everyone had come with a big appetite. The food just wasn't fit to eat in its partially-cooked state.

I gasped in horror when I realized we had no food for dinner, and then a bright idea occurred to me. The "dinner" was converted to a "breakfast". Our toaster and our coffee pot worked. Everyone went nonchalantly along with the new arrangement and there was plenty to eat.

It rained cats and dogs, but we had a memorable afternoon playing rummy, Ping Pong, and just lounging. At 6:00, we took all of the partially-cooked food to Ginny and Mac's and finished ocoking it there. It was kind of a screwball Easter, but fun!

The following day was Army Day and a holiday. We had breakfast with the Macs, saw the parade, and then went jeep riding again. We stumbled upon an old Prussian church on a hill overlooking the lake. An ancient caretaker took us into the cellar and showed us the caskets of Prince Karl of Prussia and his wife; and Prince Wilhelm and his wife. The Russians had opened the caskets and we could see the skeletons in their uniforms. Their hair was still in perfect condition, although the remains were over 60 years old.

CHAPTER TWENTY-TWO

We used to laugh so about our jeeps. When McGilton's jeep was up and running, ours was "kaput" and vice versa. After Army Day, however, we had to put both of them in the garage at the same time. We were having differential trouble (whatever that is) and the Macs had a problem with their gas tank. They were losing gas at a rapid rate.

Bob finally received his acceptance at USC and we were plenty excited and happy. At last, we could begin making definite plans. We wanted to share a house with the Macs and had such fun talking about it together. Chris' father was a contractor in Los Angeles and there was a good possibility that he might be able to locate a house for us to rent.

I had been corresponding with a former piano teacher of mine, who lived in Pittsburgh. She grew up in Germany and I called her Tante Leni. When I was a young girl, she was a friend of my mother's and she practically lived at our house. She had been a good friend to me as well as a teacher. She was very beautiful and I can remember many nights when she would go out on a date and, when she left our house, dressed to perfection, I would wish that I could be just like her. She played the piano extremely well and played often in concerts. I used to tease her because she always had a case of nerves before her concerts and she kept a bottle of something called "Nervine" handy.

Tante Leni's parents were now living in the Russian Zone of Germany. They were getting on in years, were not well, and she was very worried about them. Packages were not permitted to be sent to the Russian Zone, so she asked me if I could help her get some packages to her family. I wrote that I would do everything possible to help them

Time went by and then a letter came from her that made me eager to help: "I had really thought, Patricia, that I wouldn't have to take you up on that offer to help me with my packages. Since January 15, we are allowed to send 10 lb. packages into the Russian Zone. My sister now writes that they receive notification and will have to go to Berlin to get them. She is glad to do that, but what will my parents do. I don't know. I have already sent 13 packages to my parents, but they don't seem to get them. My sister and her family have lost everything and need linens badly. I would

155

also like to send her lots of my old clothes. She will have to go to Berlin anyhow and I cannot have the packages insured and they cannot weigh over 10 pounds. Do you mind, Patricia, if I sent her large packages to your address. Her son, Rudi, is often in Berlin and he could come to your house to get them. I have told him to look you up. I told him to learn English so he could speak with you. It would be grand if you would meet some of my folks. I am afraid, though, that their minds are probably very filled with their calamity and they might not be very cheerful company. I hate to ask you so many favors and I do hope, Patricia, that some day, I will be able to repay you. But if it has to be, would you mind too much?"

Then, one Friday afternoon, I was taking dictation when two old German women came to see me. They had to wait quite a while until I was through and then I went out in the hall to talk to them. Tante Leni had mailed some packages to a post office in Berlin. The women said that the parents were too old to travel to Berlin and they had come to get the articles for them. The packages weighed 80 pounds and these women wanted me to help them move the packages from the post office to the bus depot. Unfortunately, it was impossible for me to leave the office at that time and, anyhow, our jeep was in the shop. Transportation was difficult to line up, but I told the women to come back the next day at noon when I got off work and I would try my best to get a car.

On Saturday, I was lucky enough to be able to get a taxi, and I waited an hour, but the ladies never came back. I felt badly to think that these elderly women had come all the way to Berlin for the packages of items we took so for granted. I knew they hadn't had much to eat on their trip and I wanted to give them a good lunch. I just hoped they had gotten someone to help them.

With the coming of nice weather, we had the fireman take down the bomb shelter in the back yard. We put grass seed in it place. We found a birdbath in the basement and set it in the center of the yard and planted petunias around it. The yard looked fresh and inviting. This year, the owners decided not to have a garden. I sent to the States for some seeds and did some planting myself: carrots, squash, green beans, and parsley. Bob built a fireplace out in back with some bricks that had been used in the air raid shelter and we put in our horseshoe court at the very back.

Softball practice began in April and we were a busy little family. The only trouble was that our teams practiced on different nights, which meant that we devoted nearly every week-night to softball. Bob's team looked very promising. He played 3rd base, Don played left field, and Chris was the catcher.

I wound up as shortstop for the civilian girls' team; Margie was catcher; Helen Murr played first base. Fred Grewing was our coach, and he really gave us gals a workout. There was only one other girls' team in Berlin, the WAACS, and we were eager for our first game.

A new bowling alley opened up and we managed to go there, and to play golf, and even some tennis. We were sure getting our exercise. Margie had paired back with Chris and Helen Murr was out. She was desolate. I felt sorry for her because she had become a good friend and I tried to console her. She was known for her hats. Everywhere she went, she had a phenomenal hat on—and was always looking very chic. Chris and Margie, though, had been our friends for a longer time, and we were back to doing activities with them. We got in some pretty hot bridge games. They would last into the wee hours.

One morning, Joe visited me in my new office and brought me a little, wooden box and said that Paula Melzian had sent it to me from the ACA Building. Mrs. Meltzian was the German woman who had the angelic little curly-headed blonde boy, Johann. I had been so impressed with him one time when she brought him into the office. He had taken my hand and bowed deeply and the little fellow couldn't have been more than three years old, if that advanced in years. Nevertheless, I was surprised to receive this darling little box from her and I looked questioningly at Joe, who shrugged his shoulders and walked off down the hall. I opened the box and found a rather long letter inside.:

"Dear Pat: First, I must apologize for not having said thank you earlier, you will understand if I tell you later why. It is indeed awfully kind of you still to remember us, though you are no longer here in the ACA Building. You were, by the way, the only one to remember our kiddies. My little Johann was much delighted with his 'Easter egg'. He has grown a great deal since you last saw him, he talks a good deal already and has some, if only nebulous, ideas of the 'Osterhasse' (Easter-hare) and "Weihnachtsmann" (Father Christmas) and through your kindness he was not disappointed at Easter.

"Will you allow me to give you that little wooden box? I hope you'll like it. It is really nothing valuable, but it may prove useful for you. I hear you have been ill lately, but as you are back to your job, it was nothing serious, I presume.

"Now I must tell you what has troubled me so much, that I nearly forgot to thank you. Some days after Easter, I was robbed of all my ration cards for Johann and me for the remaining 3 weeks of April. It was stolen out of my handbag in the overcrowded train by a pickpocket. I was and still am terribly distressed, as I lost in this way anything in the way of food, soap, coal, etc. My ration card for potatoes, which is our staple food, was for 7 weeks, to the end of May. The authorities have no possibility to compensate the loss by a single ounce. All I received was an advance of one-weeks ration which will bring me through 3 weeks and which will be reduced for next month. Potatoes, they did not give me a single ounce. I would not mind so much if it only concerned me, I would manage somehow, though it is really very hard to do one's duty (and I have a full lot of them with job, household and kid) on an empty stomach, for 3 weeks.

"What worries me so much is that I must let my child starve. My friends all live in Berlin on the same starvation rations as I. None of them can help me effectually, none of them has something to spare. My colleagues are very sweet and do their best, it is really touching to see how they try to help me. But it is obvious they can give nothing but trifles compared with the amount I have lost.

"There is that Care Committee, who have at their disposal for the benefit of anonymous addressees a certain amount of the incoming care parcels. Those are destined for families in particular need, who don't receive any gifts from abroad. I wonder whether you could be kind enough to try to get me such a 'Bonus Parcel', it is the ration of one person for 4 weeks. That would take me and my kid nicely through these awful 3 weeks, as he does not eat as much as an adult. And even if it would take some time until I receive it, it would help me very much, as I am compelled to take all sorts of loans (bread, potatoes, fat, sugar, etc.) which I must return later. That is the worst and my trouble is by no means over after these 3 weeks. I shall have to pay off my food debts for 1 or 2 months. We are all on the verge of starvation, as you may know, at least those who have no friends and connections abroad, a loss like mine is a disaster, no less than that.

"I would never have asked for such a favor, you may remember me that I never begged for anything. And I never would have done it if not this catastrophe had befallen me and my child, him particularly, as I would never ask anything for myself. But it is heartrending to be unable to give your baby what it needs, to be compelled to let him starve. I would never have asked you if I would not know your kindness to children, you seem to have really a heart for these little ones. Perhaps, if it is not too much trouble for you, and you will try to get us, Johann and me, more of the Bonus Parcels, it may prove useful if I give you the particulars concerning me:

"Paula Melzian, Berlin-Charlottenburg 4, Sybelstrasse 29, widow, no pension or income besides what I earn at TSFC. 1 boy, 2-years old. I never received a parcel from abroad and never shall. I never as yet received any assistance from outside and never until today applied for it, trying to manage myself under the ordinary today's conditions of life.

"I am sorry, you will forgive me, I hope, that I trouble you with my worries. There is amongst you so much goodwill to help the needy, that I dare to ask you this time in my distress. I would not do it, if it were not really the only hope. There is no hope from the German side, even if they want to, which they do, they can't help. Yours truly, Paula Melzian."

I had to re-read the letter to make sure that this tragic story was not just a bad dream and, then, before I put the paper down, I was on the phone. It took several phone calls, but I located the correct office. They took Mrs. Melzian's name and address and said they would put her on their waiting list. This was at least a help, but it did not sound like an immediate answer.

I called Mrs. Melzian on the phone and asked her directions to her apartment. When she had given them to me, I told her that I would bring some groceries that night. I told her that it might be rather late when we arrived, but that we would definitely be there.

I left the office a little early that afternoon and went to the Commissary. I enjoyed shopping there more that time than I had before or since. I bought potatoes, fresh vegetables, meat, cereals, canned fruits, dried beans, macaroni, apples, sugar, flour, cheese, bread, crackers, etc. My bill came to $27.67 and it was a rather heavy load.

That night, Bob and I had dinner at home and it was 9:00 before we started out on our journey to visit Mrs. Melzian and little Johann. We went down some mighty dark streets and batted over and through a lot of rubble. Her directions were excellent, however, and we found ourselves on Sybelstrasse without too much difficulty. She lived in a bombed-out apartment building amid other bombed-out dwellings. We went up some steps, under a gate, through a dark courtyard, and Bob lit a match to find number 29. Through the door and up some rickety steps we went and knocked at the first door we came to on the second floor. We knocked several times and were just about to give up when the door came open and there stood Mrs. Melzian in her nightie, holding a candle in her hand.

She could hardly believe her eyes when she saw us bringing in all of the groceries. The look on her face was something never to be forgotten. She begged to be forgiven for having gone to bed, but she had given up hope that we would come. She got little Johann out of bed and he gave me a great big hug and looked at me with solemn eyes. For those of us who have never known sheer desperation, it is shocking to see and gratifying to know that we can help

Don announced that he and Reggie had definitely decided on a June wedding and now we could go ahead with plans. She could come to Berlin, but would only be able to stay in Berlin for a couple of weeks. I could scarcely contain my excitement. They were both such nice people and I wanted to do everything I could to help.

The first really hot Sunday of the year, we took advantage of it by gathering at Ginny and Mac's. It was a gorgeous day! Don and Chris and Margie were there and 3 other couples. We started out by playing volleyball and what a rough game we had! After several games in the hot sun, we were bushed. My ankle, after being stepped on several times, was bandaged, and Ginny's face was red and swollen. We next played horseshoes and Bob and I wound up as the doubles champs. I had made potato salad and Ginny had gotten some franks and rolls and we were a hungry bunch.

While we were eating, who should ride up on a motorcycle, but Gene Kocherga. Gene was an American civilian, but had originally come from Russia and his parents had been Russian nobility. He was dressed in a ragged, old jacket, and a funny looking German hat, with little charms dangling from it. He had a big grin, as usual, as he pulled into the yard. We were not allowed to own or ride motorcycles, but Gene had an answer for every situation. If the Germans stopped him, he pretended to be Russian (he spoke Russian fluently); if the Russians stopped him, he was an American; and if the Americans stopped him, he pretended to be German. He had a perfect out for any event.

Two weeks after the German women came to my office, a young fellow came to my house to see me. He was Tante Leni's nephew, Rudi, a clean-cut boy, and we talked for quite a while. He was studying medicine at the University of Berlin and wanted to become a veterinarian. He looked at Blitz, said he had raised German Shepherds and that Blitz was as fine a dog as he had seen.

I had written Tante Leni that I would be glad to receive packages at my address for her family, but I had not received any as yet. The nephew had a car, so could come and pick them up at my house. He gave me his address and phone number and I gave him ours. I offered him a cigarette and he was delighted with it. He said he hadn't had one for several months. I told him I would call him when any packages arrived and had several opportunities later on to do just that. It meant so much to that family and made me feel good that I could at least do that much for them.

Don got me aside and showed me the astoundingly pretty ring he had gotten for Reggie. It sparkled in the sunlight and I knew she would love it. He was excited because she would be arriving at the end of May. I was so happy to hear that. I was even happier when I learned that Don had also made an application at USC, and the prospects of having the Ryans out there with us and the Macs made it all the more fun to plan.

Reggie wrote to me, "Dear Patsie, I just got a letter from Don with the application for marriage. I have to fill it out. Oh boy! Am I excited! I believe you can imagine it. So exciting that I don't know what to do. I'm telling you I can hardly wait to get on that train. That means, if everything goes right, and I'm keeping my fingers crossed for it then we can have one of our long talks, Patsie. There will be a lot to tell, don't you think so."

Our eighth month-a-versary came around and we were on cloud nine. Every month seemed better and every day I felt I was luckier. I wrote my family, "I think that you must know by now that I could never have found anyone anywhere half as nice." I could hardly wait for them to meet him.

The social life in Berlin was pretty fast and active. There were so many things to do and see and so many opportunities to take advantage of and we wanted to do as much as we could. My family asked me if we ever did any work and I wrote and told them that we certainly did! "Guess you'd be bored if I wrote 'I worked an hour overtime last night and am working late tonight too!" I actually was kept very busy on my new job. Bob was even busier. He was holding 2 jobs in his office and often he worked until 9 o'clock.

Bob went to the Soviet Headquarters in Potsdam on a mission. Much to his surprise he rode right through Potsdam, with its huge, red flags and pictures of Stalin and Molotov, and right through the gate of the headquarters. He walked right into the office of a Russian major general without being stopped or challenged. Those fellows could give you a bad time if they wanted to. He had expected the headquarters of all Soviet-controlled Germany to be heavily guarded, but there was no one to stop him and question him.

Two of the German newspapers about this time wrote interesting articles explaining how Germany was in the situation it was in. These were interesting because they seemed to indicate that, after all, it was their own fault.

From the Frankfurter Neue Presse on April 22nd, "It seems necessary to clarify what has taken place in Germany in the sphere of nutrition. Fifteen years ago a half-pound of butter cost 89 pfennigs, ten oranges 50 pfennigs, ribs and cabbage in a good restaurant 70 pfennigs. In spite of that, there were many people in Germany who said things must change. It cannot go on like this in our Fatherland. We were in an abyss. We must impose a rigid militaristic discipline on our young people. Only then would they become good citizens. We must have the Ukraine, that is more important than butter. An important part of the German population voted for these people and by 1 September 1939 we had made so much progress that cannon finally took the place of butter. The second world war had broken out and the first ration period came in."

The Darmstaedter Echo had this to say about the reason Germany was in such bad shape: It scorned the people who said, "There is no bread and fat in Germany. The English and Americans probably want us to starve."

It went on to say, "It is senseless to emphasize to those hypocrites and slanderers again and again that Germany has no bread and no fat, and no clothing because for twelve years we produced guns instead of butter, because we destroyed and robbed our neighbors, because we led a totalitarian war against the whole world and also against our own country; because pilferage of our remaining stores was permitted before the surrender."

CHAPTER
TWENTY-THREE

Dad was asked to write a paragraph concerning reparations for the Collier's Encyclopedia and asked me to send him some information on the subject. I did so, but it was a little late and, meanwhile, he had written it and sent it on to me for approval. I found a big error in it, corrected it, and returned it to him before the date he was to submit it.

He had gotten the information that "In 1946, the United States, in ending deliveries to Russia, took the position that, until the overall Potsdam principle of economic unification of Germany should be put into effect, the reparation plan could not be further executed, since the four zones could not exist separately if such dismantling of German industry should take place."

This, of course, was not true. We were very busy dismantling plants and shipping them to Russia. This was one of the biggest tasks of the Reparations office in Germany at this time. We had four dismantling teams that visited in the four zones to inspect plants and the Reparations Committee made up the lists of plants that were to be dismantled and decided which countries they should go to.

I sent the following information to Dad: "We are still and never have stopped making deliveries and allocations to Russia and the reparations plan has never ceased. There are three plant categories: 1. Advance delivery plants. These were chosen by Eisenhower and his opposites to be repatriated first. There are 24 of these plants in the U.S. Zone, of which 22 are mostly completed. 2. War plants. 3. Current Production plants.

"In 1946, the U.S. took the position that, since there was no free flow of economic goods among the zones, that nothing from current production would be allocated until there was economic unity. Some of these current production plants had already been allocated and we followed through with these.

"Now we are still dismantling and shipping out Advance Delivery Plants and War Plants. We are still allocating War Plants. A directive is now out that all War Plants will be allocated and shipped or liquidated before June 1948.

"Twenty-five percent of our allocations go to Russia and seventy-five percent go to the Western Nations (18 of them). The seventy-five percent that are allocated to the Western nations are put up to the Inter-Allied Reparation Agency in Brussels.

The member nations bid for the plants and the Assembly sub-allocates them to one or more recipient nations."

It really tickled my Dad that I had been able to help him on his technical assignment. He is the author of several books on politics and world events and I was so proud that I could add details to his writing.

I sent him a shirt for his birthday and he wrote back, "I played golf with a colonel the other day. He mentioned his daughter in China and another one somewhere else. So I told him, 'Heck, that's nothing. I just got this shirt yesterday from my daughter in Berlin.' He admitted that it was a pretty good-looking shirt."

Our friends, the Finch's returned home and we were anxious to have a report from them about how they found things there. "It's good to be back in the good ole U.S.A., but with every trip to the grocery store, we long for Berlin and Commissary prices.

"Kenton (their son) got quite a lot of publicity. He was the first American born of Occupation Forces to return. Photographers and newspaper men met the plane here and we have some clippings and pictures, etc. for his scrapbook."

Back in October, a ruling had come out that only one member of a family could receive the 25 percent extra overseas pay. In our family, it meant that Bob would receive the overseas differential, but I would not. I was sorry to lose it, but didn't have too much to gripe about. There were many who felt differently, however, and several people tried to fight the ruling. In April, these people won out and it was good news for me. It meant that I would be receiving $50 more each month, plus $350 of retroactive pay. That was going to be a big help for us in the future when Bob would be back in school.

Nylons, again, were as scarce as hen's teeth. I took turns wearing a pair with runs in them, and next day a pair of rayon ones. Mother sent me a very precious package containing a pair of nylons and the very next day, they were selling them in the QM store. What a rat race! We were each only allowed one pair, but now I had 2 pair with no runs. I treated them like gold.

My first tooth pulling experience was in the ET. I still swear those Army dentists didn't know how to fill teeth. Everyone got the same treatment. I was scared to death before I went to have the tooth pulled and, of course, Bob's friends enjoyed telling me how much it hurt and that I would have to go to bed afterwards. The needle hurt for a split second and after that, I didn't feel a thing. When the novacaine wore off, I took 2 aspirins and was never bothered by it at all. I went around showing the blank spot to everyone. I told Bob that when I got my false tooth, I was going to take it out at nights and put it in a glass of water beside the bed.

VE Day was a holiday. Ten of us went to Lake Wannsee. I made potato salad and we had a gourmet picnic. We went to the Allied Control Authority (ACA) Cottage. I had never seen it before and not many people knew about it. What an adorable place it was! It had a kitchenette, living room with modern furniture, and a big terrace close to the lake. We played volleyball and cards and were there from noon to midnight. I got sick on the potato salad and, of course, got razzed because I had made it (no one else got sick). I swore I'd never eat the stuff again

An amusing incident happened on May 7th. Bob and I, as usual, went to work together at OMGUS. Bob was in his civilian uniform, but I wasn't wearing mine and had forgotten my ID card. I borrowed his card, flashed it at the guard, and got in OK. Bob, being in uniform, didn't need his card. Three hours later, I got a phone call from him, "The next time you forget your ID Card, you've had it!" He and another fellow had to make a quick trip to the ACA Building, where they always check your card. Bob suddenly realized he didn't have his with him, but the other fellow happened to have his 7 year-old daughter's card with him and loaned it to Bob. This particular guard was meticulously scrutinizing all cards and was amazed when he looked at Bob, then back at the card and saw a picture of a 7 year-old girl! That was life in Berlin for you!

That same afternoon, he went to British Headquarters to obtain a paper. The man at the desk told him that the messenger would bring him his paper as soon as he made his "T" rounds. Bob said, "I beg your pardon?" The man explained that the messenger took tea to every office every day at 3:30.

We began plans for a trip to drive our jeep through Bavaria and, possibly, Austria during the first part of July. We had no idea that old Gerry could get us that far, but Bob started right away getting it in condition for a long motor trip and thought we could give it a try. The Army had gas stations and repair points along the autobahns, so we decided we couldn't get into any trouble that we couldn't get out of. There were several advantages to driving; mainly, it would be cheaper. Prior to May 1st, Americans were permitted to ride the German trains anywhere in Germany for nothing, but after that date, we had to pay fares. Our second reason for driving was that we could be our own bosses and go where we wished. We hoped to see the Bavarian Alps, Black Forest, Heidelberg Castle and Hitler's Crow's Nest at Berchtesgaden.

Bob felt pretty sure he could get permission to drive directly through the Russian Zone into the American Zone. The normal route was to take the autobahn west to Kassel and then start south. This autobahn, although it went through the Russian Zone, belonged to us. Later, it was shut off during the Berlin Blockade. At any rate, we had to drive 100 miles out of the way, when we took this route.

Bob and I were crazy about little Angie. She was the sweetest, dearest little thing. Angie had a real mother instinct and her favorite pastime was playing with her doll, Grettel. Grettel, however, was becoming quite bedraggled and I wrote mother and asked her if she could get a Dydee Doll for Angie.

When the package arrived, I took the doll to the mess hall and everyone wanted to hold it and took turns playing Mama and Papa with it. When I gave it to Angie, her eyes lit up like a Christmas tree. The first day, she fed it over 20 times and each time, she would hang the little diaper out on the line. She told me she wanted to take it to church to give it a name. Angie thought about it a long time before she named her baby and finally she named it "Chris" after the American girl next door.

Chris, a sweet, plump child, and Angie were becoming fast friends. Angie was often invited over there for lunch and the 2 of them were so cute together. Chris went to nursery school for half a day and every morning Angie would look for School Bus No. 5 that came to get Chris.

Don and Reggie set the date. It would take place on June 1st, 2 days after Reggie's 25th birthday. I was thrilled at the prospect of being Matron of Honor, but I said that matrons were supposed to be old and decrepit. Bob said, "You little stinker, you look like anything but the matronly type." He and Chris and Margie would round out the wedding party. Margie and I would wear the brides-maids dresses that were worn at my wedding.

Since Reggie would arrive such a short time before the wedding, I did all of the planning that would normally go to the bride. I ordered and addressed the invitations, wrote up the announcement for the paper, and gave it to Lyn to have published; got a picture of Reggie for the paper. I also made plans for the wedding breakfast to be at our house. I ordered the flowers for the wedding. They were to be white roses for Reggie and yellow roses for Margie and me; gardenia corsages for the breakfast, and an orchid corsage for going away. Don was planning on a week in Bavaria for a honeymoon. Don and Reggie's wedding invitations read:

The honor of your presence is requested
At the marriage of
Maria Regina van der Vloet
To
Donald Hillsden Ryan

Sunday, the first of June,
Nineteen hundred and forty seven
At four o'clock
The American Church of Berlin
(Ernst Moritz Arndt Church)
Onkel Tom Strasse and Wilski Strasse
Berlin

And the enclosed card went as follows:

Mr. And Mrs. Donald H. Ryan

Reception immediately
Following ceremony   31 Auf dem Grat
R.S.V.P.

The invitations and reception cards were on the same lousy paper that ours had been on, but Don and Reggie thought they were beautiful.

Chris had a badminton court set up in his back yard and got equipment from Special Services and we spent many evenings playing some energetic games of badminton. One night we played until 10:45, just to show you how late it got dark. We vacillated among badminton at Chris', volleyball at the Macs; and horseshoes and Ping Pong at our house.

Bob came home spent after he had been in a meeting from 10 am to 4:30 p.m. The last 3 hours they had been discussing just one point. The Soviet member, at a previous meeting, had made a statement, which was recorded in the minutes. He wanted to have it deleted, but to the Americans, it was very important to have it remain in the minutes and Bob refused to have it deleted. That poor Russian surely wished he could have swallowed his words, because it was obvious he was in big trouble over his remark. It was just so typical of our meetings, though. hours and hours were spent just trying to reach an agreement on one word. We had an especially hard time on wording since many of their words have different meanings to us. Translation is a difficult thing. You can translate the words, but not necessarily the meaning of those words.

Our girls' softball team was getting to be hot. We practiced a lot and our coach put us through our paces. The only trouble was that we hadn't played a game yet. Twice we were rained out, but finally the big day came when we were to play our first game with the WAACS. They had been practicing too and were chomping at the bit. When they arrived on the field, we were alarmed to see how many of them there were, but they were swell girls and good sports and the game started off pretty well.

Bob, along with other husbands and boyfriends were cheering from the sidelines. Someone set up a stand with ice-cold cokes, so it was a big event.

It was heartbreaking to lose our first game. Final score: 15 to 9. We were hyped up, though, and eager for revenge.

Poor Don was having his troubles. Everything was all set for the June 1st wedding, and we got the invitations out in the mail. Then, on Sunday, one week before the wedding, he got a call from Reggie. The cable from Berlin giving her clearance to come, had not arrived in the Brussels office and, since Monday was a holiday, the proper officials would not get the cable until Tuesday. Then, when the cable arrived in Brussels and they got around to taking action, she would need 8 days to get a train reservation. That definitely would make her late for her own wedding.

We spent all day Sunday on the telephone, trying to find someone who might be flying to Brussels and back during the week, or someone planning to drive to and from Brussels. By evening, I learned of a new Pan American route from Brussels to Frankfurt, which cost only $22. Don could easily get transportation for Reggie from Frankfort, so we breathed a little easier. It meant that Reggie could get to Berlin on Wednesday but it still wouldn't give much time as her wedding dress was being made in Berlin.

Reggie did arrive on Wednesday and she looked wonderful. We had so much catching up to do. Margie and I went with her to the dressmaker and were assured that her dress would be ready on time. From there, we went to a hairdresser and were pretty pleased with our new hairdos. We each bought chignons and we couldn't wait for the boys to see us. They didn't have much to say at first, but, by the end of the evening, they had to admit that our coiffures were pretty sharp.

We had a wedding rehearsal and Reggie was sorry that Chaplain Weaver was no longer there. The new chaplain did things differently. Reggie wanted her wedding to be just like mine and was disappointed when the chaplain told her how it should be done.

Saturday they were married by the Standersamt and that night was a big stag party for Don. The girls had dinner with me and spent the night at my house. We stayed up late, doing our nails and talking about getting together in the States and wondering what was going on at the stag party. We had good reason to wonder. All week the fellows had been talking about the girls who were coming to dance at the party. We managed to get some sleeping powder and made Frau Schneider promise to put it in the punch if dancing girls showed up. We giggled all night thinking we had put one over on the boys. We had visions of Don yawning at his wedding when saying "I do". Fortunately for the boys, there were no dancing girls and the sleeping powder wasn't necessary.

CHAPTER TWENTY-FOUR

We had 14 people for the wedding breakfast and the table looked so pretty with the corsages on it. Frau Schellenberg and Frau Jacobowski went all-out to make everything nice. We had champagne and all the trimmings. After breakfast, we went out on the lawn and took pictures of the group. It was a lovely, sunny day (quite different from our wedding day) and the afternoon promised to be a scorcher.

The boys left for Don's house and we girls got dressed for the wedding. It was to be at 4 o'clock. Reggie surely made a beautiful bride and Lyn's dress, the one she had worn at my wedding, fit me perfectly. The flowers weren't exactly what we had ordered. Reggie carried yellow and pale pink roses. We had red roses and peonies. The wedding went off beautifully. Don looked serious and couldn't smile and it was the third time that Bob and I had walked out of that church in a wedding party.

The reception was held on Chris' lawn. There were lots of people and lots of lovely gifts. We gave them a wooden guest book with their names carved on the cover. It was inlaid with many fine pieces of wood and read, "Guest Book for the Ryan Family". I spent the afternoon arranging the gifts and carrying the book around to get people to sign in it. The cake was delicious and there was a balcony seemingly just made for Reggie to throw her bouquet from. The girl who caught it was Hank Rommele's date!

The McGiltons had just gotten back from their leave the day before the wedding. We went to their house for a nice, cool supper after the reception. We assumed that Chris had taken care of a trick to play on the Ryans, but we couldn't locate Chris and we agreed that it would be a shame for them to get away without something happening to them.

The wind was let out of our sails when who should walk in the door but Mr. And Mrs. Don Ryan. They had gone to Don's house where Reggie had fixed him some supper. Don was laughing because, already, Reggie had burned the toast! They had gone for a drive, saw our jeep parked in front of McGilton's house and decided to come and join the party. We chatted for a while and they left.

We didn't know where they were staying, but Mac made a call to the Gossler Hotel. Mac said that he was an Inspector for the CIC (Central Intelligence Corps) and was trying to track down a Mr. Don Ryan. He found out that Don and Reggie had come in and left their luggage, and gone out. We sat around wracking our brains trying to figure out where to go from there.

Mac could get some pretty fiendish ideas. 'He called the hotel again and we listened to his end of a remarkable conversation. Ginny, Bob and I sat back in the corner of the room, doubled up with laughter as he talked. A German desk clerk answered the phone. Mac said that he was the Inspector again and his checkpoint had just phoned in that Mr. Ryan's car was headed for the hotel. He said that he had been tracking Mr. Ryan all over Europe and that Mr. Ryan had just gotten married to a Belgian girl and was going to try to leave town as soon as possible. He asked the desk clerk to keep Mr. Ryan from his room until his men could get there. Mr. Ryan had a gun in his room and the Inspector's men were ready to close in on him. He said by no means to let Mr. Ryan in his room because he didn't want any shooting. He sounded so authoritative that we nearly split our sides. After he hung up, we could hardly wait for Don and Reggie to get back from Bavaria to find out what happened.

It was a let-down when they came back and said that they had had no trouble at all in getting to their room.

Bob's softball team was winning all of its games, and it promised to be a bang-up season for the boys. In The Observer, there appeared an article commending the team, "The current league leader, the Harnack House team, is a smooth-running, closely-knit ball club . . . . composed of ex-servicemen ranging in rank from colonel to Pfc . . . . it is a cross section of what used to be Army, Navy, and Air Force. It is said of the team, that there are no standout players as all work equally well in their respective positions; and for a team that leads the league, this speaks rather highly of each player.

"Chris has been the team's catcher . . . often spoken of as the best third baseman in the league, Bob McMann contributes his share to the winning form of the team."

Ginny McGilton got me aside and told me she thought she was pregnant. I thought it was wonderful and urged her to see a doctor immediately. I was very indignant when I learned that the doctor didn't want to see her for a few weeks, and I was sure she should immediately start on a green vegetable and milk diet.

Two of our friends had had miscarriages and there had been so many in Berlin that we all wanted Ginny to take very good care of herself. The Berlin streets were too bumpy and full of shell holes, and Army vehicles are not the easiest to ride in. These factors probably accounted for the large percentage of mishaps.

One end-of-June Sunday, our gang got together for a nice breakfast and Chris took us sailing. Margie wasn't feeling well that day. She had pains in her side and she spent most of the afternoon curled up in the cabin of the boat.

This wasn't like our Margie. We suspected appendicitis, but she felt certain the pains would go away. By evening, we returned to shore and gathered at the McGiltons for a Sunday night supper. When the dishes had been cleared away, we began to play cards. Bob and I were playing bridge with Chris and Margie, and it became more and more apparent that she was in distress. We kept urging her to go to the hospital and, finally, she agreed to go after we finished the rubber. Chris took her home so she could put a few things together in a bag and off they went to the good old 279th. It wasn't long before she was on the operating table, minus her appendix.

We visited her the next day and she looked pretty good considering what she had been through. She was having trouble getting any information about the operation from the doctor.

After we left the hospital, we went to the movies with Ginny and Mac and then decided to go to Harnack House for a hot fudge sundae. Ginny drove us and she drove pretty fast over the cut-up roads. We got to Harnack house OK and were savoring our sundaes, when Ginny turned a deathly green. She was a pretty sick little girl. Mac tucked her in the jeep and they took off for the 279th.

When we got up the next morning, the first thing we thought about was Margie and Ginny together in the hospital and we sped over there. They were in the same room, comparing notes. There was no official explanation for Ginny's distress, but she was feeling better. She hated milk, but when we left, Mac was trying unsuccessfully to get her to drink some milk for the sake of the baby.

We played our second ball game with the WAACS and this time we won 16-7, so we were tied; one game apiece.

I ran into Don Wilson as I was entering and he was leaving Truman Hall. He was working in Essen and I hadn't seen him for some time. What a grand guy! He really spoiled me for working for anyone else. He said he had good jobs for both Bob and me if we wanted to remain in Europe a little longer. I told him thanks, but we were beginning to be anxious to get home. He reminded me that I was to let him know my silver pattern when I got home because he and Juliette would track us down and give us the carving set.

After years of suppression, German women's groups again began meeting together, gradually developing powers of discussion and a sense of responsibility for activities in their country. Representatives of women's organizations from all over Germany met in June to acquaint each other with activities in progress, pool their experiences and ideas, and discuss the part that women could and should play in the reconstruction of Germany.

On the topic of "Peace and Understanding", the physicist Freda Wuesthoff spoke about understanding the absolute necessity of avoiding any future war and gave a description of atomic energy and the atomic bomb. The immense popularity of her talk showed how thirsty the women were for precise knowledge about atomic energy and their reactions indicated that widespread information might be the best preventive of war.

Katrina von Kardorff of Berlin spoke. She was a former member of the Reichstag and her husband was for many years its vice-president. Hers was a plea for the unification of Germany, for economic recovery and an appeal to women that the fault for the past was with men, and that the women had let themselves be ruled too long.

One whole day was devoted to youth problems. One speaker, Frau Heidrich, emphasized the necessity of excluding all fear from parent-teacher child relationships. She described the three R's as taught at her German school as Reverence, Rectitude, and Responsibility, and praised American schools for their development in children of a sensibility for the feelings of others, self-help, and absolute honesty. She said it would be impossible to imagine a school in Germany where children did not copy their work from each other. Some in the audience, however, insisted that this was no longer true.

There were those who saw the salvation of Germany in a religious revival; and there were programs concerning civic responsibility. All in all, the women came away more knowledgeable and felt ready to go back and build on the future.

We had been having trouble with people breaking into our jeep. One of the windows had a broken lock on it and it was easy to force open. Sometimes, a burglar would give up because he couldn't figure how to unlock the door. One night I lost a white sweater and some nylons. Another time, someone took most of our groceries. Then, the very next night, someone stole Bob's uniform and all of his keys were in it. We immediately had the locks on our house changed.

Bob took the jeep to the garage and had them install a burglar alarm in it. The alarm was hooked up to the windows, doors, and even to the spare tire on the rear. The bell was lodged in the inside well where a spare tire could be fitted. It was huge, and when it went off, it sounded like a school bell. A couple of times, the alarm went off at Bob's ball games and we would see a bunch of kids running away. It wouldn't stop by itself, and we had to go and get to it to turn it off. We never had anything stolen out of it again.

We had a real treat when the Commissary announced that it had milk for sale—real cow's milk in a bottle. We tore down there and bought several bottles. They also had fresh ears of corn and we bought several of them. We gave some of the milk to Frau Schellenburg for Angie and then we had a milk and corn party.

Frau Jacobowski was a trip. She wasn't particularly bright, but, oh, how she wanted to please us. When we came down the stairs in the mornings, she would be standing there with a cloth in her hands. Every morning, she would have a big grin on her face and say to Bob, "Shoe putzin, herr lieutenant" and seesaw the cloth back and forth.

We took her for a ride in our jeep once. Blitz, whom she adored, was riding along too. I don't know what he had eaten, but he let out a powerful odor, and we slid open the windows to let it waft out. When we got back to our house, Frau Jacobowski said, "Dahnke fer de schoen fahrt" (Thank you for the lovely ride), but under the circumstances, it sounded a little bit like she was thanking us for something else.

CHAPTER
TWENTY-FIVE

In mid-July, we left for our trip through Bavaria. Blitz was very ill with distemper, and we hated to leave him, but Frau Schellenburg said she would take special care of him. I had become terribly fond of him and couldn't bear the thought that the same thing might happen to him that had happened to Trooper. but I knew how much our two German housekeepers thought of him and I knew he was in good hands.

Bob had been unable to get permission to take the direct route south through the Russian Zone, so we had to take the long way around. Because of the condition of Gerry, the Jeep, we never drove over 40 mph. Gerry tended to heat up if we drove any faster. We put the front passenger seat down flat and covered it with a soft blanket so we could lie down and stretch out full-length when the other person was driving. It made for a comfortable ride. There was scarcely another car on the autobahn and we stopped at noon and had our picnic lunch under a beautiful roadside tree.

Almost every bridge was bombed-out and some of the detours were lengthy. On the second day, we got to Heidelberg and we tried to find the University of Heidelberg. It was a disappointment because all we could locate were 2 old square buildings. The other classrooms were so scattered that we couldn't find them.

Heidelberg itself was a quaint city that probably looked the way it had a hundred years earlier. The highlight, of course, was the Heidelberg Castle. It was a thrilling sight and it was immense. It had been built in1308 and many German kings had lived there. It had been blown up by the French and one tower was split in half and one half had sunk into the moat. Once inside the gate, there was a large cobblestone courtyard; a tree under which was a watering trough; a huge well and a big fountain. There was a servants' building and an English-style palace for the king.

We entered the wine cellar and saw the largest wine barrel in the world. It held 50,000 gallons of wine and had been filled only 3 times in the 17th century. There was a fabulous view of the city and I could almost see the knights riding into the courtyard, and hear the clatter of horses' hooves on the cobblestones.

At the hotel where we stayed in Stuttgart, there was a Displaced Person in uniform guarding the vehicles in the parking lot. Stuttgart was block after block of immense marble buildings in ruins. It made you feel so insignificant and weak to think of the millions of dollars that man pays to make such a large city into mere rubble, only to be built again. The city reeked of misery and tragedy.

When we came out of the hotel in the morning, the DP shook his head and said, "What a crazy jeep!" The alarm had gone off at 2 a.m. and no one knew how to turn it off. People were shouting out of the windows to "turn that thing off", but it continued on for 2 hours until it wore itself out. All the while we slept peacefully, undisturbed. We checked our rear tire and, sure enough, it had been loosened and the would-be thief had quickly disappeared into the night.

That afternoon we pulled into the Rasthaus on Lake Chiemsee. This was where we would be staying and relaxing for 8 days. Chiemsee is often called "The Bavarian Sea" and the Rasthaus was the kind of resort just made for a dream vacation. This hotel complex was reserved strictly for Americans. Aside from swimming, boating, Ping Pong, bridge games, movies and wonderful food, there were beautiful drives to take and interesting side trips.

The scenery on the drive through the mountains was gorgeous and we stopped and had lunch at Berchtesgarden and, there, although I thought I had eaten everything, we had cold beer soup with whipped cream and raisins. It was awful. We also had potato salad with pineapple, which was something I thought I might make at home when we got back. Not bad.

After lunch, we set out for Hitler's Eagles Nest, something we had heard much of and were terribly curious. We had been told that Hitler could see Salzburg, Austria from up there, but no one below had ever caught a glimpse of his hideaway. We drove straight up for 4 miles and came to huge, bomb-destroyed barracks beyond which was the entrance to Hitler's private drive.

The winding road from there was the steepest, narrowest, winding road you can imagine and we could look straight down into the valley. Halfway up, we hit clouds and could only see 10 feet ahead of us. Near the top, we parked and rode an elevator right into the house, which is exactly on the peak of the mountain. The house is of stone and not as large as I had expected it would be. We didn't see the bedroom, but there was a large dining room and living room, with a red marble fireplace that had been donated by Mussolini. There was a small room with a wide glass window, where Adolf and Eva took their after-dinner coffee. Who would have ever thought I would be standing here!

When we got back to our car, we discovered that we were trapped there by some huge boulders which had fallen onto the road. It was some time before they were removed and we could leave. Near the barracks, we saw the bombed homes of Goering and Bormann and we picked up a piece of carved wood from Goering's furniture.

"Back at the ranch", they were rounding up people for a boat trip to an island where King Ludwig II had built one of his many palaces and we joined the group. The palace was copied after the Palace at Versailles and it seemed that Luddy had quite a crush on Louis XIV. His picture was in every room and all of his ideas were copied after Louie's plans. Louis received visitors in his bedroom; likewise did Ludwig. Their initials were the same, so Ludwig used the same signature of crossed "L's".

He had a collection of the most extraordinary clocks. The prize was an immense cuckoo clock, but instead of a cuckoo, out popped Louis XIV every hour on the hour. He didn't like to have to wait for his food at the table, so a table already set with the food, came up through the floor on an elevator arrangement. We saw his huge bathing pool and all his furniture and draperies were gold in color.

Ludwig became very depressed and it was said that he drowned himself. He was such a peculiar duck that it was obvious why they called him "Mad King Ludwig".

Our side trip to Salzburg, Austria was very worthwhile. While we were there, a baroness showed us around. She was very charming, very eccentric, and wore a wig that didn't quite fit. She showed Mozart's birthplace to us and then she explained that in the 11th century, the Archbishop lived in Salzburg, but he raised the taxes on salt and it made the villagers very angry. He then moved to a castle, which he had built overlooking the town. We climbed up there to take a look at it.

There was a huge pile of cannon balls and there were gigantic hooks on the ceilings where they hung tubs of water in case of fire. We climbed into the tower and entered the room where they had tortured political prisoners. There was a hole where you could look down into all of the cells. We saw the stretching racks and the stocks. Then we crossed to the torture room for witches. They tied them to a stove to make them tell their secrets. It all made me shudder.

On the way back down the hill, we saw doors and windows built right into the side of the mountain. We opened a door and went inside and it was a church that had been built in the 4th century.

After lunch, we went to another Archbishop's palace and that old boy must have really been mad! It was the grounds that were so amazing. The garden was full of all kinds of crazy things. One place had 2 stone turtles spitting water into each other's mouths. Along the path, there were tiny moving figures run by waterpower. One was a man making pottery; one was churning butter; another was a torture scene.

There was a large banquet table where, as soon as his guests were seated, the Archbishop would signal to have the water squirted up through a hole in each seat, lifting the guests right up in the air.

Continuing on, we saw a little stone house and inside, on a mound, was a royal crown. As you watched it, a stream of water raised and lowered it before your eyes. Suddenly, the whole ceiling was sprinkling water and squirting down on you as you ran out the door and down the path. What a jokester!

At the front door of his palace, there was a very large, devilish face whose tongue came out and touched its nose and the eyes rolled all the way around. The most unusual thing inside was a room that had walls at angles and gave you the impression that the room was about to collapse. I'll bet that old Archbishop could tell some really good jokes.

Gerry held up beautifully for the entire trip with one exception. A bearing burned out when we reached Munich and we were held over there for an extra day. We didn't mind at all because we got to explore that famous city.

The people in the cities were so thin and there was so much sickness, but we noticed in the country, they looked healthy like farmers do anywhere in the world.

When we got home, Blitz was much better, but he was sneezing a lot. He soon recovered completely and we played our game of tag with him every night in the back yard. It was going to break my heart to leave him as he had become such a pal to us. He was so friendly with people and the only time I heard him growl was at the German Shepherd across the street.

Don and Reggie were gone and Chris left suddenly and the departure of Margie, Mac and Ginny was imminent. We had a farewell party the night before they left. It was a progressive dinner party, starting at Margie's billet, then our house for the main course, and ending at the Macs. We were stuffed by the time we were through.

The three of them came to our house for dinner the next night, after which we drove them to the train station. It was so hard to say goodbye. We felt deserted and lonely. All of our regular group was now gone and we had 3 or maybe even 4 months to feel left behind.

It wasn't as though we weren't active socially. There were 1 or 2 farewell parties a week now that people's tours and contracts were up. We had lots of dinner invitations and bridge games in people's homes. The French had a big shindig celebrating something or other; and there was one couple who kept wanting us to play a game of Hearts with them.

That particular couple kept daily track of how many more days until he was discharged from the Army.

I was planning to stop working on August 20th so I would have plenty of time to get ready for our date of departure. Bob's contract ended on September 15th and, since he had 15 days of leave left, we planned on one final trip before we set out for home in October. Bob was definitely accepted now at both USC and GW University, but our chances of getting a decent place to live in California seemed minimal and I was losing interest in that plan. Bob preferred it, but not at the expense of living in a dump. We told my folks to go ahead and put in our application for an apartment where they lived in Fairlington, Arlington, Virginia.

I was pleased and surprised to hear the prices of apartments in the Washington area. We had set a top price of $60 a month as a goal and found we could get a one-bedroom apartment there for that price. Mother offered us a spot in her home, but we preferred our own little space, near them if possible. I asked her to look for an apartment that accepted dogs. I still had a slight bit of hope that I could keep my one-in-a million dog.

Then, we were almost speechless when we heard from Chris that his father had gotten a house that we could rent. What to do? We mulled it over and thought it best if we stayed in the East where all of our family members lived. We hated to tell Chris, since he had gone to that trouble, but it was our future and we had to tell him that we had changed our minds

A CID man called me. He said they were investigating a case about the house across the street where several things were missing. He wanted to know all about Frau Schellenberg. I spoke very highly of her and told him to forget her, if he was even considering that she was the culprit. I decided to go across the street to find out what had happened. A man lived there by himself. While he lived there, he had had one hausfrau and three different firemen. He accused one of the firemen of stealing. The maid wasn't in the house much of the time. One of her duties was to see that no one entered the billet during the day and so he felt she was responsible for anything that was amiss.

It peeved me that Frau Schellenberg should be brought into this. We had never missed a thing and she was at our house every minute of every day guarding our things. They didn't bother her again after that

Some of the top U.S. Tennis players were making a tour of the European Command playing exhibition matches. They were coming to Berlin to play before U.S. military and civilian personnel. The matches were to be held on a weekday but Mr. McJunkins said that our office could not attend,. as he was to leave for Frankfurt in a few days and much work needed to be done to prepare for his coming meeting. Bob had gotten tickets and I wanted very much to go, but was resigned to hearing about it from him.

The day before the matches, Mr McJunkins called us into his office and said that somebody higher up had called him a 'sonovabitch' and as he didn't want to be called a 'sunovabitch', he would give us the afternoon off.

We were certainly fortunate to be able to see some famous people play topnotch tennis. They were: Don Budge; Bobby Riggs; Pauline Betz; and Sarah Cooke. They played both singles and mixed doubles. It was a lovely, clear, warm afternoon, but the thing that I remember the most, was Don Budge's bright red hair.

On Bob's birthday (his 26th), Frau Schellenberg baked him a birthday cake and when she showed it to me, she burst out crying. It looked fine to me, but the bottom wasn't so nice. She wanted to make another one, but I assured her that Bob would be pleased with it. Some of the German women didn't seem to know how to make cakes like ours—nice, soft, fluffy ones. Theirs were always hard, and this one was no exception. It was as hard as a rock and we just couldn't eat it.

She had given him some flowers and she had put her heart into making the cake and we didn't want to hurt her feelings, so we decided that every night we would cut 2 pieces and break them up and throw them away until the whole thing was gone. She wasn't just our hausfrau, she had become our friend.

We went to the Stardust Ball, and to Tattoo, which was a monumental show, outdoors in the Olympic Stadium, and put on by the British. The next night we went to a cocktail party, followed by a Coal Section party celebrating the birthdays of Bob and two other people. There just wasn't any end to fun activities and events and we knew that life back home would be much slower-going.

I became the one loyal fan to Bob's ball team. At each game, I wore 9 watches; kept 9 cigarette lighters; and several packs of cigarettes for safekeeping. The boys, ages 4-14, who hung around and watched the games, were always practicing on the sidelines. They picked up the slang and swear words they heard the fellows use. The little guys were so thin, barefoot, and scratched-up looking, it would break your heart. I nearly cried one day. I took a Ladies Home Journal magazine to the field and the kids all wanted to look at the pictures. What do you think they looked at? It wasn't pictures of boats or cars, but pictures of food. They went into rapture over pictures of hot dogs and casseroles and kept saying, "That's mine", "No it isn't, it's mine". One little boy pointed to a cigarette ad and said, "That's mine"!

Bob hit another home run before the big tournament. His team was leading the league and was the only civilian team in Berlin. The only trouble was that no civilian team could go to play in the ET championships, so the 2nd best team would be chosen to leave Berlin for the finals.

I stayed home one day and Frau Jacobowski spent the day bringing me cokes and ashtrays. I felt so spoiled! She was so worried and sad that we were leaving. In fact, she cried and begged us to take her with us. She couldn't read or write and had a fairly low IQ and had no interest except scrubbing and cleaning, which she loved to do. She was no slacker.

She cleaned the inside of our jeep once. The spotless windows gleamed and shone, but when she got out of the vehicle, she was unaware that she had left a big, dark footprint on one of the seats.

She asked Bob if there were any other good Americans besides ourselves and he assured her that there were some. When she realized she couldn't come with us, she became determined not to work for anyone but Americans.

Frau Schellenberg was very intelligent. She was certainly capable of doing better things than housekeeping, but with this job, she could come and go as she pleased and she was able to keep Angie with her as well as provide more food for her. She and I had long and interesting talks.

She came to me and asked me to help her. She and her husband owned a very nice house, which was occupied by an American family. They, along with Angie, shared a two-room apartment with another family. The owner of this apartment had been away since the end of the war and now wanted his apartment back. She knew several people who knew him and said that he had been an SS man, and that, at the end of the war, he managed to get papers describing him as a member of the regular infantry. The French secret police had searched the apartment before the Schellenbergs moved in, and found a paper showing that Bormann had given him a large sum of money to buy a house outside of Berlin. The Americans, however, never investigated this man.

A German hearing was held and Frau Schellenberg went to it. It was decided that the man could have his apartment back. There was an American man who must sign the final papers after these hearings, but he was so busy that he didn't have time to investigate these problems or to see the Germans who protested.

It took me two days to find this American man and I was worried and afraid that he would not be interested and would refuse to do anything about it. He was very interested, however, and said he would investigate immediately. He was hopeful that the German man might even be able to give a clue as to how to find Bormann. Also, he said that the man would have to have a physical, as all SS men were marked under the arm so it would be fairly easy to prove. They must have proved it, because he was not allowed to go back to his apartment. Frau Schellenberg was so grateful that she brought dishes from home that we could use when ours were packed.

I spent an entire morning with her listening to her experiences during the war. She said that most of the Germans would like a Socialist government, but she and her husband did not belong to a political party because, if the Americans left, it would be bad for them if it was found out that they belonged to the Socialist party. We talked about Russia and how the tactics they used were the same as the Gestapo and SS methods. And she said that if the Americans left them to the Russians, it would be terrible and she would leave, even if it meant walking to the Western Zones.

Then she told me about the first three weeks that the Russians were in Berlin before the Americans came; how she watched through the windows and, if they came anywhere near, she would rush out the other way. One day a man came to her and her husband and cried for help. A Russian had come into his store and pointed a gun at him and at his two, old parents. He gave the man just so much time to get him a watch, or he would shoot the two old parents.

Another time, she was in a store and heard a woman pleading with the storekeeper for some medicine that the man did not have. Frau Schellenberg said she had some of that medicine and went and brought it to her. She did this because the woman said that her 9 year-old daughter had been raped and had been bleeding for three weeks.

There was big excitement in the offices and clubs and the talk centered around the rescue at sea of 69 persons on a trans-Atlantic flight from New York to Shannon airport in Ireland. The craft, The Bermuda Sky Queen, a huge Boeing flying boat, was forced down between Newfoundland and Ireland and landed in the ocean three miles from the U.S. Coast guard weather ship, Bibb.

There was a tremendous storm. Rough seas hampered rescue efforts for seven hours as the plane was riding huge swells amid a 38-knot gale. We gathered around radios and listened breathlessly to the reports as the rescue progressed.

The pilot radioed "Flying boat now breaking up". Then came a message from the Bibb to the Coast Guard, "Darkness approaching. Plane leaking. Passeners mostly prostrated by seasickness. Winds of gale force. Rough seas. Three persons removed unharmed with small life raft.

"Continuing operations with boat and raft. Second successful boat and raft operation brings total saved thus far to five men, two women, two little boys and one baby. Baby appeared to have stood ordeal better than rest."

The Sky Queen had taxied the three miles to the Bibb after its forced landing, while two other trans-Atlantic planes, attracted by the SOS flew overhead. The plane, operated by American International Airways, was carrying Americans and Britons, many of them emigrating to new homes in the U.S. and Canada. There were at least eight children aboard.

The British Press Association said that this was the largest number of passengers ever taken on a trans-Atlantic flight. You can bet we breathed a sigh of relief when we heard the pilot of the Trans-Canada Airlines say in a telephone interview at Prestwick, Scotland, "all is well".

The headlines in the October 8, 1947 Stars and Stripes issue read: ARMY BREAD RATION IN EC CUT 25%" It went on to outline the cuts that would take place. The changes were to affect every mess, snack bar and dependent. Brig. General Thomas F. Bresnahan, Commander of the Bremerhaven Port, stated, "Save a slice of bread a day. If each member of the Command follows this slogan, it is estimated that a total of 15,000 pounds will be saved daily . . . Wastage, when so many people are hungry, when what you throw away might save a life, is virtually criminal."

There followed a list of 9 items that would be cut short, including one day a week that was to be meatless. This was certainly no real hardship on us and did, I believe, save lives.

CHAPTER TWENTY-SIX

W e had a letter from Reggie. Poor dear, after traveling all the way across the ocean, and then to Petersburg, Virginia, she was rushed to the hospital for an appendectomy.

We called her and Don and I asked her how she liked America and she said it was fine and she liked Don's family, but she hated the bread. Europeans like heavy breads and, at that time, the stores were full of Wonder Bread and other soft white breads and hadn't caught on to the many wonderful breads we have here today.

We began packing for our departure. The Army sent in packers, so it was mostly a matter of supervising, but the organizing was frustrating. I was mostly concerned about how our piano would make it on its long journey. It was going to be two or three months after we got home that our furniture would arrive. I saw that it was packed very well and felt it had a reasonably good chance of arriving safely. There was a woman who was excited about buying our jeep. We hated to give it up, but its better days were gone and there was no reason to bring it home with us.

Bob had a lot of leave time, so we planned a 3-week trip right after his last day of work, which was to be September 15th. The American Express office made all of the travel and hotel arrangements and the plan was to go to Brussels, Amsterdam, London, and Luxembourg. We would not be part of a tour group, so we would be totally on our own. Mr. Forbes from Bob's office was taking the same train, so he came by with an office car to take us to the station.

As we stopped at the edge of the Russian Zone, all of the Germans were pulled off the train to stand on the platform until they were checked by the Russians. This took 3 hours. Mr. Forbes was quite annoyed. He didn't mind the "Huns" going through this procedure, but he didn't want it to inconvenience him. He wondered why we couldn't be allowed to go and wait in a nice club until all this was over with. This very attitude galled me and was why we were despised by so many Germans. Some of these "Huns" were old women and children with their worldly goods strapped to their backs. We had no idea what they were escaping from or what hope they had for wherever it was they were headed.

There was a British girl in our car, who had some gin and a lot of sandwiches. We thought there would be a diner and there was not (this was not like our special

Berliner), but she kindly offered us some of her refreshments and we gobbled down the sandwiches and appreciated the gin.

Our coach was not checked by anyone and a few Germans managed to sneak into the car. The British were as anti-"Hun" as Mr. Forbes, and they had a smashing good time making a lot of nasty cracks. The conversation lost its humor for me and I went to sleep.

When I woke up, the British girl was gone and an English couple, Mr. And Mrs. Dear sat across from me. She was studying French and had a book with the French on one side and the English translation on the other. Mr. Dear read the stories aloud and kept us amused for some time. One was:

"I think I shall have to pull that tooth"

"Oh, but I want to keep it."

"Alas, you have but 8 teeth left."

"Yes, but I want to keep the bicuspid."

Another story:

"Jean, draw the curtains."

"Shall I fetch you your gown and night cap?"

"No, just my stockings and pantaloons."

The Dears were also staying at the Hotel Atlanta and we caught a taxicab together, or, at least we tried to. The porter who carried our bags demanded 10 francs. Mr. Dear gave him 3 francs. The old boy called a cop, who made us get out because there were too many in the taxi. Welcome to Brussels!

We took a bus tour of the city and some of the places we visited or saw were: the Royal Museum, which used to be the home of Kings of Spain; Eglise de Larken, where Kings Leopold I and II are buried; Summer Palace; National Shooting Gallery, which was used as a place of torture by the Germans; Groenendael Race Track; Village of Waterloo, home of Victor Hugo and where he wrote "Les Miserables"; and Village of Mont St. Jean, where the Battle of Waterloo was actually fought. We stopped there at a round building where there was a panorama of the famous battle, and where we had some delicious tea and raisin bread.

In a small lace shop, we saw an 83-year old woman, sitting there making lace who had learned to make lace at age 7. There were a dozen large spools, which she moved so rapidly that it was impossible to discover just how and what she was doing, but the finished product was exquisite. I thought she was amazing and hoped I would be that productive when I reached my eighties.

We saw the Palace of Justice, one of the largest buildings in Europe and, some years later, very famous trials would be held. Everywhere we went, there had been a Tomb to the Unknown Soldier. Belgium was no different and we visited it. I couldn't help but wonder how many mothers around the world were still wondering what had happened to their sons.

I was surprised and disappointed in the Manneken Pis. It was just a tiny statue on the side of a building; a little boy peeing into a fountain. It seemed strange that this small statue could be so famous. He has many costumes that he wears on different holidays. One is an American MP uniform and he has uniforms of many armies. One story was that a government official lost his little boy. When he found him, he was in the position the statue is in. The man was so happy to have found him that he had this likeness made.

We went across the street from the hotel to Maxima Café, where they had a good, American jazz band. There were several girls there and every 20 minutes, one of them would get up and dance. Each girl sat at a table, but they kept moving to other tables. They were homely and didn't have much talent and they weren't having much luck snaring anybody.

There was a big strike going on. The people were striking because prices were so high. As we stood in one of the squares, an airplane dropped pamphlets asking people not to buy anything except at controlled prices.

We boarded the Amsterdam train and were off to Holland, a new chapter and new adventure. On the train was a young American couple. She was a designer and he was going to study in Geneva. She was telling me about the new styles in America and I didn't like the sound of them. Dresses were much longer, going 4 inches below the knee. Since all of my skirts were knee length, it would make them all out of style. What poor timing—to come home with a wardrobe of beautiful exclusive clothes and be old-fashioned already.

We also met a very nice Dutch fellow, who told us a lot about the German occupation of Holland. The Dutch people, he said, got a half a loaf of bread and some sugar beets per week and no meat at all. Train-loads of Dutch food kept going to Germany. Things got so bad, that people started eating tulip bulbs. They would ride on their bikes without tires to the country to get potatoes. If the bikes had tires, the Germans took them away. For every German killed, he said, hundreds of Dutch people were rounded up and many were killed.

We stayed at the Amstel Hotel ($8.50 per night). I must say that American Express did very well for us so far. The hotel was extravagantly luxurious. The city is truly a city of canals; a photogenic city; so picturesque and clean! We looked out our hotel window at the Amstel River.

I thought it was the funniest, strangest language. I got a kick out of it, for instance, the word for "telephone" is "telefoon". Some of the words are like German words, and yet, it reminded me of Old English.

Our hour and a half boat ride through the canals took us by the old trading companies and merchant houses. Boats, boats, boats everywhere. Venice has nothing on Amsterdam, that's for sure. We wanted to see the famous diamond factories. When we asked the Chinese waiter where they were, he said, "I don' lo. Better ask a policely".

We did find the Aascher Diamond Factory. The girl who showed us around was an expert gum-chewer. Somehow, she seemed out of place amid such extravagance. We saw how they cut the stones. Most diamonds have to be sawed before they can be shaped and there were hundreds of little machines sawing through stones. It takes a whole day to saw through one. The saws are small, round, copper plates. Because diamonds are so hard, they can only be cut with other diamonds. The copper plate is porous and they mix diamond dust with olive oil to put on the saws. The guide said, "I'm sorry that we no longer give diamonds away as souvenirs, but we can give you a saw that cuts diamonds."

We went into the room where they were shaping and polishing the stones. One hundred workers sat at benches with their machines and they were each using a half cut diamond to shape a rough diamond. By the time the rough diamond is half ready, the other one being used is ready for the process of forming the facets; 58 facets to a stone. What a fascinating show this was!

They tried to charge us twice as much as we actually owed when we checked out of the hotel. Fortunately, we caught the error and a big argument ensued. We asked for the manager and, after carefully studying the bill, he had to admit that we were right. I don't know if it was an honest mistake, or if the clerk thought he could put one over on us.

We boarded a boat on the Zuyder Zee and went to the old-world island of Marken. I had thought we might see one or two Dutch costumes, but this was just like a picture out of National Geographic. The women wore bright blouses and colorful aprons and caps that fit close to their heads. The men wore red vests, pantaloons, and blouses with brass buttons. Everyone wore wooden shoes.

The children were adorable; all of them were blonde and had beautiful hair. But the women had the most god-awful hairdos! Their heads were shaved in the back, and their hair, which was quite long, hung down at the sides. The younger women braided theirs on top of their heads. They wore absolutely no makeup and were as homely as sin.

We were permitted to go into one of the small houses. There were copper kettles hanging everywhere, and a table, but no other furniture in the main room. The bed was built into the wall and looked very short. Bob couldn't believe that it was large enough, but measured it and it was. The children slept on a rack above the bed, and there was a cupboard underneath where older children could sleep. There was an attic for overflow and a tiny room on the side was piled high with boxes, where they kept their clothes. The lady of the house said she was from a family of 14, but had only 5 children herself.

Children wore dresses and long hair until age 7. At that age, a boy wore pants, and, at 9, he had his hair cut and was then a real boy. A girl wore a colored cap until she was 18 and then could wear a white cap and became "eligible". When they got married, the boy had to carve the wedding shoes.

There were only 7 families on the island, and each family had 1 wedding dress that was worn each time a girl in that family married.

We went into the Dutch kitchen and put on Dutch costumes and took pictures. Bob looked so strange in his wide pantaloons, as though dressed for a Halloween party. We clomped down the sidewalk in our wooden shoes and I must say, it felt awfully awkward.

From there, we went to the island of Vollendam. The costumes there were quite different. The women wore full, black skirts, black and white striped blouses, and black, peaked hats. As we were sitting, having coffee and cake, we started talking with another couple. They were Venezuelans and had traveled all over the world. She was dark and very pretty. He was a representative of the Alfa Rubber Company. They had three children, who were in school in New York and showed us pictures of them—all of them most attractive like their mother. They had rented a limousine, a long, black Cadillac and we rode back to Amsterdam with them.

We caught a train to The Hague and gawked at the Peace Palace while there, after which we took a boat-train to The Hook. Then we boarded a big ship and were on our way to England. We had a tiny cabin to ourselves, but it was 3 decks down; at sea level; and right next to the engines. They were loud and the noise was frightening and I scarcely slept a wink. The steward knocked on our door at 5:30 am with some delicious, strong, hot tea and before long, we docked.

When we reached London, we took a taxi and told the driver "King's Court Hotel, please". We had become so used to high-class lodgings, that we were sure he would know where it was. Instead, in a strong cockney accent, he said, "King's Court? King's Court? Never 'eard of it. Must be a gloreefied boarding 'ouse". And you know what? He was right.

It was quite a dingy place and was in the process of repair work. The damage had been done by German bombs. There was none of the elegance we had seen at all our other hotels, but we were comfortable and everyone was so polite!

The atmosphere was that of a boarding house and we sat around and discussed many things at the table. We found that all clothing was rationed. Food was scarce and the meals were scanty. They weren't like the sumptuous meals we had eaten in Brussels, for instance, but there was enough, and I certainly couldn't complain.

The tour we took of the area was fascinating and our guide was an "astonishingly amusing bloke"! He told us about the Sunday morning market, which was always jam-packed because you could buy "coupon-free" there. It used to be called "Petticoat Lane" because you could lose your petticoat at one end and buy it back at the other. It was so crowded that pickpockets could make a lucrative living.

I learned why the policemen are called "bobbies". Sir Robert Peale originated the current police system, so they were called "bobbies" or "pealies". They didn't carry guns, but they were very well-trained in how to handle tough criminals. I had my picture taken with some "cute" bobbies.

At Eton, we saw a lot of lively boys running all over the place in tails with Eton jackets and top hats; which they were supposed to wear all of the time. King George III had been quite a friend to the boys at this school, and, when he died, the boys all wore these costumes and they became standard attire from then on. The school, at the time we visited there, was booked up until 1960.

Among the important people who attended Eton were: Anthony Eden; Shelly; Gray; the King of Siam; and many of England's prime ministers. There were lots of traditions, among them being punishment by switching; we saw the switching block. When a boy was punished, it was charged on his bill, but he got to keep the switch. I wonder how many of them wanted to keep this item of torture, but I suppose it was a badge of honor.

The boys were required to play sports and they were either "wet bobs" or "dry bobs". The "wet bobs" were those who participated in water sports. The scholarship boys were called "King's Scholars" and they wore black robes over their suits.

Windsor Castle was tremendously large and grand. It was built originally by William The Conqueror and added to over time. In the Chapel, the banners of the current knights hung above the stalls where each particular knight sat. When he died, his banner was taken down, but a copper plate with his emblem remained forever in the stall. All of the monarchs since George III are buried in this chapel with the exception of Queen Victoria. Her husband, Prince Albert, could not be buried there. This really bothered her and so she had a mausoleum built not far from the castle and they could be together for all time. When the monarch is in residence, his flag flies at the castle entrance; it is taken down and a British flag flies when he is not there.

We drove through the fields where the Battle of Runnymeade was fought. It was dotted with picnickers on that day. We saw the island where the Magna Carta was signed; and our last stop was at Hampton Court Palace, which was a gift to Woolsey from Henry VIII. Plaques of the Roman emperors were on the walls. Henry must have been much in love with Ann Boleyn at the time, because her initials and roses and love knots can be seen everywhere. William and Mary lived here when they were joint sovereigns. The hedges of the lawn formed a "W" or an "M".

Another day we saw the home of Ramsey McDonald, the first prime minister. We saw "The Olde Curiosity Shoppe", of which it is said Charles Dickens wrote his famous book. We saw long queues of people waiting for busses and at entrances to buildings. Some of them sat on stools as they waited. We learned that if you must stand in line for a long, long time, you can rent a stool, leave it there, and come back to where you left off.

St. Paul's Church was so large that I felt certain it had to be the largest church in the world. It has an immense dome over it and inside is a monument to the Duke of Wellington and also one to Lord Cornwallis. The guide told us that, after he lost to the Americans, he went to India, where he became a huge success.

We saw the Mansion House, where the Lord Mayor lives; Lloyds of London; and we crossed the London Bridge over the Thames. Coming back across, we used the Tower Bridge and, staring us in the face, was London Tower. William The Conqueror built it in 1078 as a fortress, and also as a royal residence. Those who are accused of treason are brought to this tower during the time of their trials. Rudolph Hess was here for a while. The guard at the entrance wore a funny, old red uniform, which was the former uniform of the king's bodyguards. We passed by the Bloody Tower, where Sir Walter Raleigh was held years ago. He was in love with a Lady in Queen Elizabeth's Court. Elizabeth, being quite jealous, had him put in prison. The Lady, however, sneaked into the tower, and they were married in the chapel there. It was here that he wrote his history of the world and, after 14 years of imprisonment, he was executed.

The Thames River used to come up as far as the tower and prisoners arrived in boats. The entrance was called "Traitors' Gate".

We saw part of the original Roman Wall, which was built in 100 A.D. Inside the wall is the White Tower, which was then an armory, and we saw all types of armor and weaponry. The crown jewels were usually kept here, but had been temporarily removed while they were working on an elaborate alarm system, which would go off when anyone came too close to the jewels.

We saw the theater where Shakespeare gave his first performance; the new Waterloo Bridge, Savoy Hotel; and Cleopatra's Needle. (We had seen one like it in Paris and one in Potsdam.) I was interested in the bridge because, during the war I had seen a very romantic movie with Vivien Leigh and Robert Taylor playing the leads and it was called "Waterloo Bridge". It was a love story about a soldier and his sweetheart during the bombing of London and has always been one of my all-time favorite movies.

Andy, who had gotten out of the service and was living just outside London, called us and we met him at Paddington Station. We rode in their marvelous underground system and Andy told us that during the war, they had cots on the platforms that you could rent for a shilling (20 cents) for the night

He took us to the famous Wax Museum. First, we went in the Hall of Mirrors and I laughed so hard that I had pains in my side. The wax figures were so well done that I could scarcely believe they were not real. They had nearly every imaginable famous person: war heroes; generals; American presidents; authors, movie stars; and all of the British kings. I thought of my history teacher in high school, who had made historical events so interesting, and I was thankful that I had the background on most of these people and could appreciate what I was seeing. The Chamber of Horrors was gruesome. They used to give 5 pounds ($20) to anyone who would spend the night there!!

I was thrilled to see Scotland Yard, a large gray gabled house; and then on to No. 10 Downing Street, where all of the prime ministers have lived. The street was very short, and the house was dark and plain, but Andy said it was elegant inside. The Parliament buildings were fantastically beautiful, with their narrow, graceful spires and intricate designs. I stood and admired Big Ben, that famous clock I had heard so much about. We had dinner at the Picadilly Hotel and drinks at the Cumberland and we said goodbye to Andy and begged him to visit us when we got home.

The highlight of the visit to London was feeding the pigeons in Trafalgar Square. It seemed such a romantic thing to do that we bought several bags of bread bits and birdseed before we moved on.